Sexual Ideology in the
Works of Alan Moore

Sexual Ideology in the Works of Alan Moore

Critical Essays on the Graphic Novels

Edited by TODD A. COMER *and* JOSEPH MICHAEL SOMMERS

Afterword by Annalisa Di Liddo

McFarland & Company, Inc., Publishers
Jefferson, North Carolina, and London

LIBRARY OF CONGRESS CATALOGUING-IN-PUBLICATION DATA

Sexual ideology in the works of Alan Moore : critical essays
    on the graphic novels / edited by Todd A. Comer and
    Joseph Michael Sommers.
         p.   cm.
    Includes bibliographical references and index.

    ISBN 978-0-7864-6453-1
    softcover : acid free paper ∞

    1. Moore, Alan, 1953– —Criticisim and interpretation.
    I. Comer, Todd A., 1972– editor of compilation. II. Sommers,
    Joseph Michael, 1976– editor of compilation.
    PN6737.M66Z87 2012
    741.5'942—dc23   2011053466

BRITISH LIBRARY CATALOGUING DATA ARE AVAILABLE

© 2012 Todd A. Comer and Joseph Michael Sommers.
All rights reserved

*No part of this book may be reproduced or transmitted in any form
or by any means, electronic or mechanical, including photocopying
or recording, or by any information storage and retrieval system,
without permission in writing from the publisher.*

Front cover image: Hugo Weaving in *V for Vendetta*, 2005 (Warner
Bros./Photofest); front cover design by TG Design

Manufactured in the United States of America

McFarland & Company, Inc., Publishers
  Box 611, Jefferson, North Carolina 28640
    www.mcfarlandpub.com

Table of Contents

Preface and Acknowledgments   1
Introduction: The Polarizing of Alan Moore's Sexual Politics
    TODD A. COMER *and* JOSEPH MICHAEL SOMMERS   5

Part I: The "Low Form": Moore and the Complex Relationships of the Comic Book Superhero

1. Libidinal Ecologies: Eroticism and Environmentalism in *Swamp Thing*
    BRIAN JOHNSON   16

2. Green Love, Red Sex: The Conflation of the Flora and the Flesh in *Swamp Thing*
    MATTHEW CANDELARIA   28

3. When "One Bad Day" Becomes One *Dark Knight*: Love, Madness, and Obsession in the Adaptation of *The Killing Joke* into Christopher Nolan's *The Dark Knight*
    JOSEPH MICHAEL SOMMERS   40

4. "Don't laugh, Daddy, we're in love": Mockery, Fulfillment, and Subversion of Popular Romance Conventions in *The Ballad of Halo Jones*
    KATE FLYNN   52

5. The Love of Nationalism, Internationalism and Sacred Space in *Watchmen*
    KARL MARTIN   65

Part II: The Vicious Cabaret of Love, Sexual Desire ... and Torture

6. Theorizing Sexual Domination in *From Hell* and *Lost Girls*: Jack the Ripper versus Wonderlands of Desire
    ZOË BRIGLEY-THOMPSON   76

7. "Do you understand how I have loved you?" Terrible Loves and Divine Visions in *From Hell*
   MERVI MIETTINEN 88

8. Body Politics: Unearthing an Embodied Ethics in *V for Vendetta*
   TODD A. COMER 100

9. The Poles of Wantonness: Male Asexuality in Alan Moore's Film Adaptations
   EVAN TORNER 111

10. Reflections on the Looking Glass: Adaptation as Sex and Psychosis in *Lost Girls*
    NICO DICECCO 124

Part III: Victorian Sexualities and the *Écriture Féminine*: Women Writing and the Women of Writing

11. "Avast, Land-Lubbers!" Reading *Lost Girls* as a Post-Sadeian Text
    K. A. LAITY 138

12. The Undying Fire: Erotic Love as Divine Grace in *Promethea*
    CHRISTINE HOFF KRAEMER 150

13. "It came out of nothing except our love": Queer Desire and Transcendental Love in *Promethea*
    PAUL PETROVIC 163

14. Self-Conscious Sexuality in *Promethea*
    ORION USSNER KIDDER 177

15. I Remain Your Own: Epistolamory in "The New Adventures of Fanny Hill"
    LLOYD ISAAC VAYO 189

Afterword: Disgust with the Revolution
  ANNALISA DI LIDDO 201

Selected Bibliography 207

About the Contributors 217

Index 219

Preface and Acknowledgments

While the genesis for the collection that you are now holding likely differs between the two editors — for Todd, this book follows from his interest in postmodernism and his extensive teaching of Alan Moore; for Joe, it was likely the culmination of a boyhood dream to get paid to read and discuss comics, something, essentially, he would otherwise do for free. It goes without saying that, at some point, one initial question spurred us on: Where is the collection discussing one of the greatest comic book and graphic novel writers of all time, Alan Moore? That question provoked others: Where are the seasoned minds, in print, debating the issues and questions that are otherwise ghettoized in internet website talkbacks, or in the pub after a movie, or, most likely, in a comic book store with a non-academic whose vast storeroom of knowledge outpaces the collected lot of us presented here on our finest day? Could we write it, and, perhaps more importantly, would someone buy it?

Yes, dear fanboy and fangirl, novice or aficionado, this collection is as much for you as it is for us in the academy. Please be kind in your eviscerations of us when we forget something that you are very, very passionate about.

Because that is what this collection of essays concerns: passion! Passion for a wild man who writes, lives, and loves his passions on the page and, increasingly, on the silver screen, despite his strong desire against any such translation. Truly, Alan Moore has become a model for the modern age regardless of whether he writes about the social propriety of a Victorian past or the lascivious sex dens of a far-distant future. Since *Time*'s Lev Grossman and Richard Lacayo ranked *Watchmen* as one of the top 100 books of the twentieth century — a *comic book* alongside Faulkner's *The Sound and the Fury* and Orwell's *1984* — his importance to the medium of comics, let alone contemporary culture, has been unchallenged. Couched alongside writers such as Frank Miller (*Batman: The Dark Knight Returns, Sin City, 300*), Neil Gaiman (*The Sandman, Death: The High Cost of Living, Stardust*) and Art Spiegelman (*Maus, In the Shadow of No Towers, Raw*), Moore is simply the benchmark for readers of popular fiction, writers, and illustrators of sequential art (comics and graphic novels), and scholars interested in postmodern aesthetics, politics, paganism, spiritual mysticism, anarchy, and ... possibly madness. Throughout all of his work, Moore has revitalized, and occasionally demonized, comics through his critique and reorientation of the superhero genre in such books as *Watchmen, Batman: The Killing Joke, Swamp Thing, Supreme,* and *Superman: Whatever Happened to the Man of Tomorrow?* In the midst of all of the above, he also achieved crossover success when a lackluster movie industry, anxious to locate new material, began plundering the world of comics. Ironically, for many comic writers, to really achieve success is to have one's work adapted for the silver screen. Moore has achieved such "success." Even if it appalls him.

Moore has achieved the literary, not to mention popular, success of an artist worthy of scholarly discussion. And, thus, it is our great honor to present to you a humble clutch of scholars spanning the globe who share an interest in the magus who was born Allan Oswald Moore.

The essays contained within this volume radiate from his (and Melinda Gebbie's) infamous, self-labeled "pornography," *Lost Girls*. That book reconceptualizes young female protagonists from Victorian childhood classics (*The Wonderful Wizard of Oz, Peter Pan,* and *Alice's Adventures in Wonderland*), describing the childhood traumas (veiled so delicately in their original stories) and imagining what such sexually traumatized characters might be like in the modern world. *Lost Girls* has been challenged and, in some cases, banned outright for visuals and a storyline involving sexual intercourse between youthful adolescents; from our perspective, *Lost Girls* has become a sort of Rosetta Stone for understanding Moore's career. The essays in this collection interrogate the political, social, cultural, and sexual ideologies that emerge from *Lost Girls* and demonstrate how these ideologies, while always in flux, have been part and parcel of the larger corpus of Moore's work. Our book investigates this work and shows how Moore connects and comments upon our global culture: a discordant space united by threads of sexual revolution and geopolitical uncertainty. The essays presented offer multiple interpretations of his writing to an audience who has often been left shocked by his bravado, if not brash disinterest in their reaction to his work.

No work such as ours exists in a vacuum (even if serious scholarship on Moore remains a high commodity) and we would be remiss if we did not acknowledge some of the predecessors who blazed a path for this volume. At the forefront of that pack is Annalisa Di Liddo, a gracious contributor to our book, and her brilliant monograph *Alan Moore: Comics and Performance, Fiction as Scalpel* (2009). Di Liddo includes an entire chapter on Moore's *Lost Girls* in which she addresses its critical reception and provides a strong critique of the novel as well. Likewise, most recently, Gary Spencer Milidge brought forth *Alan Moore: Storyteller* (2011), perhaps the first real treatment of Moore's biography besides the author's own autobiographical statements in *The Mindscape of Alan Moore* (2003) with director DeZ Vylenz. There are, of course, pieces of scholarship that deal with individual Moore works such as William Irwin's collection *Watchmen and Philosophy: A Rorschach Test* and James Keller's similar study *V for Vendetta as Cultural Pastiche: A Critical Study of the Graphic Novel and Film* (2008). All are admirable in their own ways and, for the serious study of a man still very much in the prime of his career, worthwhile reads.

There are several people to whom we are both indebted. We express *joint* and immediate appreciation to Cynthia Miller, Annalisa Di Liddo, and Matthew J. Smith (without whose tutelage we might never have understood our task at hand).

Two universities, in particular, played a prominent role in our work: Defiance College and Central Michigan University, and, particularly, the College of Humanities and Social and Behavioral Sciences at Central, whose exceedingly generous (and frequent) monetary contributions enabled us to complete this project in good speed and with a comfortable cushion (not to mention paid labor!). Likewise, the State of Michigan Library system provided us with unprecedented access to texts and research that otherwise would have been difficult to say the least.

And, finally, to our gracious, patient (please note that "patience" occurs frequently in our thanks), occasionally frustrating but otherwise brilliant collection of writers in this book, without whom there would be no book, thank you.

Individually, we would also like to acknowledge a few people.

Todd A. Comer: This book has had a long gestation period. I was fortunate enough to present my research on Moore at the 2008 Canadian Disability Studies Association conference and as part of the 2010 Film and History conference panels on "Love and Sex in the Films and Graphic Novels of Alan Moore." Both conferences were marvelous, but I especially enjoyed meeting and learning from all of the Moore scholars at Film and History. Thank you.

My greatest thanks goes to Dawn Comer, my wife, who patiently endured my personal vendetta against/with/for Alan Moore. Even if she tired of my early mornings, late nights, and my obsessive monologuing, she was, well, generally nice about it. I also want to extend my thanks to Chris Hansen, editor of an excellent critical anthology on *Doctor Who*, who planted the seed that became this collection; Mary Catherine Harper and Amy Drees, colleagues, who (willingly) read or discussed my work; and Collette Knight, circulation coordinator of the Defiance College Pilgrim Library, who endured innumerable interlibrary requests for obscure and arcane tomes, and survived. Thank you.

Joseph Michael Sommers: I'd like to thank first the people who forced me to profess to something in the first place. To my friends and mentors Giselle Anatol, Kathryn Conrad, Frank Farmer, and, particularly, the man who taught me to follow my damn fool dreams and ridiculous ideas, Michael Cadden, I owe you all a debt that simply can never be repaid, but consider this as a couple bucks towards the balance. Similarly, to the students of Central Michigan University, you who have been a gracious sounding board to my thoughts and generously donated your time (one in particular, Justin Wigard, who helped Todd and me complete our editing process on this book) to talk with an old man such as myself about funny books like he was a peer, thank you. To the former chair of my department, Marcy Taylor, and the dean of my college, Pamela Gates, I express my deepest gratitude for every dollar invested in my work and for the continued and never-ending support for my research. *Déme la libertad o déme la muerte.* And you both gave me the freedom I sought. (Thankfully. The alternative seemed a little grim.)

Finally, there are two little women to whom I dedicate this work: my beautiful, and patient, wife, Sulynn, and the brightest light in my life, my daughter Maggie (who will not be allowed to read this book until she is at least 18). While I am proud of the work Todd and I have accomplished here, the greatest thing I have ever done was to become the proud husband and father to these ladies. Without your love and support, I'm fairly certain nothing I do would be as worthwhile, and, with your love and support, I know that I am simply the most blessed man alive. I love you.

* * *

We'd also like to thank Alan (if, for nothing else) for existing and continuing to exist. Besides bringing the lot of us together to talk and write and argue about you and your work, you have generally made this world a much more interesting place. We're not sure what *exactly* the hallmark of great literary achievement is, but we do know that you are a part of it. And, for that and so much more, we are incredibly grateful.

Introduction
The Polarizing of Alan Moore's Sexual Politics
Todd A. Comer *and* Joseph Michael Sommers

"*Sexually progressive cultures gave us literature, philosophy, civilisation and the rest, while sexually restrictive cultures gave us the Dark Ages, and the Holocaust.*"—Alan Moore

Today, in the same year that Arthur C. Clarke once imagined that Earthlings would make first contact with a race of non-corporeal, terraforming aliens by traveling (note: returning!) to Jupiter and be invited to explore the lengths of the universe,[1] we, actual human beings, seem to have come up somewhat short of such lofty aspirations. But how could Clarke have realized back in 1982 that we would have achieved such distractions as *Jersey Shore*, the social media explosion, and internet porn? We must not forget pornography. How could we? It has seemingly been around since the monoliths first taught our Paleloithic ancestors how to work with tools, and, after warming our hands by the newly-discovered fire, we began to festoon our caves with fish, bison, and tasteful nudes. Fast-forward 32,000 years and we have refined our process slightly. Now, we use social media to tweet snark at 140 characters a post both to each other and into the void when we are not exchanging pornography or purchasing episodes of *Jersey Shore* on iTunes. Somewhere beneath ten miles of ice on Europa, a betentacled group of proto-life forms might, at this very moment, be making their first advances toward tentacle porn.[2]

Which brings us to the subject of our examination. When one peruses Alan Moore, graying, shaggy-hair bordering upon disheveled, with a beard so furious that it appears to be harboring mange, one might think that he somehow removed himself directly from the Paleolithic Age, traveled to England and, in lieu of available caves, began to scribble his "pornography" directly onto newly-discovered paper. And, by all accounts, with *Lost Girls*, that's exactly what he did. Dorman Schiller writes that, with *Lost Girls*, Moore sought to bring "legitimacy to the genre of pornography," a "revolution" similar, he argues, to the one that he brought to the comics industry.[3] Written by Moore and illustrated by his wife Melinda Gebbie, *Lost Girls* is, in Moore's own words, "an ongoing dialogue [on] the marvelous tradition of erotic art," akin, in many ways, to the work of Chaucer, D. H. Lawrence, and Shakespeare.[4] Started either in the late 1980s or early 1990s (Moore is not entirely sure himself), the book manifested as both a response to what Moore considered to be the dolorous state of contemporary pornography and a valorization of Edwardian and Victorian traditions of the art. As opposed to the contemporary product, Moore found pornography of that bygone era to be empowering towards women, intelligently composed, and, contrary to anything operating in the current climate, advancing, if not challenging, the dominant discourse of morality and etiquette.[5]

And if that focus seems perfectly rational, this next bit might not: *Lost Girls*, as much as anything else, is a quibble with Sigmund Freud. For Moore, Freud's argument[6] that all sex, to some extent or another, is incest is no better than the latter's belief that "all dreams of flying are dreams of sexual expression."[7] He continued, "There are a lot of scenes of flying in *Peter Pan*," and:

> Melinda mentioned that she always [sic] doing stories that had a dynamic of three women interacting. That somehow collided with the *Peter Pan* idea, and I suppose the logic went, if Wendy from *Peter Pan* was one of the three women were [sic] names talking about, who would the other two be? Of course, Alice and Dorothy are obvious once you've gotten to that stage.[8]

And the genesis of one of the more shocking re-interpretations of children's literary characterizations came into being. The *Pan* allusion is entirely significant as it plays well intertextually with Barrie's original construction of "The Lost Boys"—young boys who, upon falling out of their perambulators "when the nurse is looking the other way" and are not "claimed in seven days [...] are sent far away to the Neverland to defray expenses"[9]—and with the usage of Pindar's Pan, the horny, literally, satyr from Greek mythology. To consider the sexual implications of *Pan* is commensurate with Moore's style and a defining attribute that separates and elevates any consideration of his pornography from the more vulgar common denominator found on cave walls or online. Intertextualism in *Lost Girls* allows Moore to open a Pandora's Box of sexuality, taboos, and cultural paradigms set by literary history in one direction and set off in another by re-placing them all together in one locus at the Hotel Himmelgarten. In other words, Moore and Gebbie crafted an erotic re-interpretation of classic literary children's characters intertextualized in the late twentieth century that challenges entrenched puritanical perspectives on sexuality still prevalent and topical today. Seems reasonable.

And largely, it was: *Lost Girls*, while controversial, was appreciated for exactly what it was, "Edwardian Smut."[10] One critic stated, "The work voices an impassioned defense of artistic freedom that stresses that fiction and fantasies aren't the same as actual events and behavior."[11] Neil Gaiman hailed it, saying, "As a formal exercise in pure comics, *Lost Girls* is as good as anything Moore has written."[12] That last note, however, brings to mind some dissension. While Moore and the corpus of his work have largely been regaled as high art amongst a triumvirate of comic writers including Gaiman and Frank Miller, others within the industry have taken Moore to task as a bit of a hack who sought only to deconstruct the ideas permeating the genre of superhero comics. Noted comics writer John Byrne (*Superman, The Uncanny X-Men, The Next Men*) took to his own message board online to let loose an indiscriminate screed against Moore's work, particularly of how his work works:

> Moore inverted — I might say perverted — pretty much everything the superhero genre is all about. He was not the first to do so, but WATCHMEN was the first time we got it all in such a concentrated dose. Largely, this seems to have happened because Moore is very much a one trick pony. The one trick works for him and his fans, so no problem there, I guess.[13]

Byrne would go on to say that Moore's crime against superheroes, through his deconstruction and reinterpretation of them, was that he removed "HOPE" from the superhero which he determined to be the genre's main attribute.[14] To Byrne's credit, it seems that Moore agrees completely. When asked his opinion of the contemporary superhero in an interview with *The Quietus* in 2010, Moore blankly replied:

> I'm interested in the superhero in real life, but not the comic book version. I've had some distancing thoughts about them recently. I've come to the conclusion that what superheroes might be — in their current incarnation, at least — is a symbol of American reluctance to involve themselves in any kind of conflict without massive tactical superiority. [...] That's not what superheroes meant to me when I was a kid. To me, they represented a wellspring of the imagination. Superman had a dog in a cape! He had a city in a bottle! It was wonderful stuff for a seven-year-old boy to think about. But I suspect that a lot of superheroes now are basically about the unfair fight.[15]

While not exactly exhibiting the depraved indifference and hopelessness Byrne accuses him of, Moore does not necessarily take argument with the idea that his interpretation of the superhero skews vastly with the Golden and Silver Age models (even when he writes about them as he has with *Batman, Green Lantern, Superman* et al.). Not unlike Miller or Gaiman, Moore plays intellectual games with the motivating ideologies of the superhero. What drives them? What are the implications of their actions upon the people they supposedly represent through their vigilantism? To Moore, it seems, the superhero(ine) has as many layers as an onion, and, just as with any normal human being, they are just as flawed.

It is with one of his more recent works, however, *Neonomicom*, that Moore alludes to something radicalized that has underpinned his works in a manner not oft-discussed outside of this book: love, lust, and sensuality. And, in typically Moore-ian fashion, he undercuts his own work almost immediately:

> [*Neonomicon*] is one of the most unpleasant things I have ever written [...] it's got all of the things that tend to be glossed over in Lovecraft: the racism, the suppressed sex. Lovecraft will refer to nameless rites that are obviously sexual, but he will never give them name. I put all that stuff back in. There is sexuality in this, quite violent sexuality which is very unpleasant.[16]

Neonomicon is hardly without its share of love, lust, and sexuality, but, at face value, it would certainly seem to have, as its thesis, a concern examining the self-reflexivity and metacognitive awareness of the narrativity of comics. And, having said that, what Moore argues is true. The sublimated sexuality is there in all its veiled gore and glory. And, upon further investigation, it prompted us to reexamine the canon of this author of comics, Alan Moore: creator and destroyer of the expected, almost Whitmanesque in both visage and his argument that within his creations exists "always sex,/ Always a knit of identity, always a breed of/ life [...] / I am not the poet of goodness only, I do not decline to be the poet/ of wickedness also. / [...] (I am large, I contain multitudes.)"[17] What the writers in this collection have found is that the revolution that Alan Moore has founded and fostered is not as simple as removing hope from the superhero. That is merely a reflection of the day and age he wrote within, whether that be Margaret Thatcher's London in *V for Vendetta* or Ronald Reagan's America in *Watchmen*. Rather, Moore, from his earliest writings in the late 1970s through today, has been driven by the same impulses that drive the real life superhero: love, love lost, love found or rediscovered, and its myriad entanglements. Hope remains, but the ontology underpinning such hope is grounded in a significantly more complicated sense of ethics and identity.

* * *

As the authors in this collection consider the traditional comic hero — picture Superman or Doctor Manhattan — that hero transcends the mortal body and the world becoming something akin to the spiritualized aliens of Clarke's science fiction fantasy. In "Part I: The 'Low Form': Moore and the Complex Relationships of the Comic Book Superhero," our writers focus on

Moore's deconstruction of this mythic superbody. Brian Johnson's and Matthew Candelaria's work on *Swamp Thing* focuses squarely on these concerns. Johnson sees the Swamp Thing's eros and green politics ("ecological eroticism") as *grounded* in those things that the "humanist" superhero cannot countenance — the base, earthy materiality of bodies. Candelaria complicates this analysis of *Swamp Thing* by suggesting that Moore's early work — as opposed to *Lost Girls*— is deeply suspicious of sex. Human copulation, the meaty sex of the "red world," is exclusionary, as opposed to the rhizomatic inclusion of the "green world." Moore's lengthy tenure writing *Swamp Thing* allows him, however, to nuance this position greatly: Having given up his desire for power, Swamp Thing is able, by the end of the series, to bring the red and green worlds, or sex and love, together in a complementary manner. Similarly, Joseph Michael Sommers demonstrates how the Batman of *The Killing Joke* and Christopher Nolan's *The Dark Knight* is not a monad, separate from the world, but interwoven, homosocially connected to that which he despises — yes, even to The Joker. These forces of "good" and "evil," rather than being Manichean opposites, are identified as lovers of a sort, each intent on rehabilitating the other in terms of himself. Kate Flynn focuses on Moore's comic book space opera, *The Ballad of Halo Jones*, a comic that she sees as a direct response to, and commentary on, the conventionally superheroic narratives of *2000 AD*. Flynn sees Moore's critique of popular romance conventions in *Halo Jones* as limited; while, yes, he satirizes such conventions and illustrates their ideological dangers, he also ends up reifying women as "sexual gatekeepers." Karl Martin explodes this discussion of the superhero to the level of the nation and world. He demonstrates how *Watchmen* dramatizes the shift in our world from nationalism to internationalism, showing how the love of country or of the "international marketplace" (and the desire to preserve the "sacred space" of each) leads to violence. Martin ends by discussing how these two loves are complicit with one another and wrong-footed to the degree that such love does not confront the fact of historical change.

"Part II: The Vicious Cabaret of Love, Sexual Desire ... and Torture" extends the prior part through a discussion of (political) violence directed *toward* and *by* the body. Focusing on *From Hell* and *Lost Girls*, Zoë Brigley-Thompson frames her discussion of rape and sexual domination with the work of psychoanalyst Jessica Benjamin, who argues that masculine power controls women because, otherwise, male dependency upon women operates as an affront to male "freedom." Masculine power, aided by a dehumanizing "undifferentiation," is successful because women, too often, do not create themselves as "desiring subjects," but allow men to define their desire. Brigley-Thompson then shows how women locate freedom and an intersubjective relation through their frank, sexual play in *Lost Girls*. Mervi Miettinen interrogates a prominent theme in recent popular culture (e.g., *Saw* and *Hostel*) by demonstrating how William Gull in *From Hell* tortures and sacrifices (the now sainted) female body in order to attain a semblance of godhood. Against one prominent scholarly argumentative strand, Miettinen also argues that rather than being a deconstruction of male violence, *From Hell* formally constructs or mythicizes male violence. As in *From Hell*, the body is central in *V for Vendetta*. Todd A. Comer critiques what appears to be Moore's overt argument about freedom, describing how the opposition between fascism and terrorism is less an opposition of difference as it is an opposition of the same — in both cases, bodies are marginalized in favor of ideas. Comer then unearths a marginal narrative within the novel and constructs a theory of agency founded upon the mortal, female body.

Evan Torner deals with a new category of desire, asexual desire, and traces the "tropes" and "types" that are used to represent this asexuality. Torner sees Moore's comics as exhibiting a full range of sexualities and the films — based upon his work, though limited by the demands of "purchasing power"— as hesitantly following him in depicting a full range of (non)desiring positions. Nico Dicecco extends this discussion of the image to Moore's adaptive aesthetic, using the leitmotif of the mirror which opens and closes *Lost Girls* to discuss ways in which adaptation is less about a loving fidelity than autoerotic play. Adapted material is not foreign but already an integral part, a mirror, of who we are. Dicecco discusses how too strict a relation between a source text and its adaptation is akin to mental collapse, the inability to discern the difference between the real and imaginary (a problematic dramatized by Alice's character in the novel). However, despite this problem, he argues, an adaptation must still be connected, to some degree, to an original text in order for the metaphorical linkage of the two to generate new meanings.

And, finally, while the previous parts emphasized, in general, the ontology of the superhero, Moore's revision of the superhero, and the politics of desire and violence grounded in ideologically-derived bodies, "Part III: Victorian Sexualities and the *Écriture Féminine*: Women Writing and the Women of Writing" foregrounds women, conjuring up bodies, even embodied superheroes, and a body of writing which remains open and amorous. K.A. Laity, with Angela Carter's assistance, argues that de Sade never surpassed the class and sexual economics that restrain women. *Lost Girls*, using the marginalized (male) medium of comics, however, subverts gender roles and the "materialist economic system that perpetuates this tyranny of desire." It is, she writes, a "moral pornography" in which women are liberated from tradition and relate to the world and to one another in new, less despotic ways. Moore's experimental and strangely didactic gem, *Promethea*, takes this discussion of social reconfiguration to the next level by imagining a female superhero, Promethea, who triggers a (positive, non-violent) social apocalypse. Christine Hoff Kraemer contextualizes *Promethea* within recent scholarly work devoted to embodiment and sexuality as a means of knowing a God/dess. Against the traditional superhero whose care for the world originates from within well-defined ego boundaries, Kraemer argues that Promethea's love amounts to "the universe reaching out compassionately and erotically to every being." Sophie Bangs, the protagonist, is not only a vessel for Promethea, but also a trope for how wisdom is erotically charged and always embodied. Paul Petrovic complements the above through his formal analysis of *Promethea* as a deconstruction of the "heteronormative quality of sexual love," privileging instead a queer and matriarchal order with a decidedly different understanding of love. Orion Ussner Kidder critiques Promethea by focusing on a series of feminist and queer subplots, arguing that *Promethea*'s self-reflexive narrative is critically coherent and progressive in terms of the former, and sadly lacking for the latter. In light of Moore's legendary displeasure with adaptations of his own body of work, Lloyd Isaac Vayo asks, what, if anything, makes Moore's literary appropriations any more ethical than that of, say, Warner Brothers? Focusing on Moore and Kevin O'Neill's *The League of Extraordinary Gentlemen: Black Dossier*, Vayo delineates an "epistolamory" at work in a letter written by Fanny Hill and addressed to John Cleland, author of *Memoirs of a Woman of Pleasure*. Multiple relations between "writer and reader, woman and man, text and image, and language and meaning" are complicated. The glancing, transient relationality of mail journeying through the postal system becomes a metaphor for writing and for human bodies, lovingly passed through multiple hands.

Finally, Annalisa Di Liddo, author of the only major single-author text on Moore to date, provides our afterword in which she discusses a range of Moore projects, including *Unearthing* (a multimedia project), *Dodgem Logic* (a fanzine), and, naturally, his comics in terms of what she terms his "pansexuality" and anarchist politics. In particular she focuses on Moore's recent output, arguing that the graphic sex of *Neonomicon* may seem "gratuitous," but even here in this excessive revisioning of H.P. Lovecraft's Cthulhu myth, Moore is hardly arbitrary. The disgust and horror of the comic confronts the reader with his or her own voyeurism; furthermore, the comic explicitly indicates that such horrors are the logical end result of a humanity that has become little more than "vermin," to quote the comic. Moore, she argues, is a "tightrope" walker, willing to risk public concern and disgust with his art in order to usher in a freer, and more just future.

As we conclude, we find ourselves returning to what is arguably Moore's most famous and critically important text, *Watchmen*. Toward the end, New York is decimated but not by monoliths or betentacled Europaians. It is decimated by a fifth-dimensional construction, an Earth-born "alien" of Ozymandias's own design. Ozymandias asks Doctor Manhattan why he would leave the Earth for the far reaches of another galaxy when he has only now regained an interest in humanity. Off in another room, Nite Owl II and the second Silk Spectre lie naked and exhausted post-coitus, a *seemingly* absurd inclusion in light of the millions of New Yorkers who have just died. Manhattan replies that while he has indeed fostered a renewed interest in humans, he now seeks a place a bit "less complicated."[18] A place, perhaps, where he will start life anew and see how it all plays out. Ozymandias, experiencing a twinge of guilt, asks him if, "in the end," he did the right thing.[19] Manhattan reminds him that nothing ever really ends any more than it begins and then, seemingly, he blinks out of our galaxy for eternity.

Moore never writes it on the page, but artist Dave Gibbons draws what could only be described as a shit-eating grin on Manhattan's face as he departs, counterpointing Ozymandias' scowl. It is an ending almost as impossibly ridiculous as it is fascinating. Then again, considering Alan Moore, who by contrast to Manhattan, looks more Neanderthal than Adonis and, arguably, acts more like a raging id than the embodiment of the depilated, cold blue rationality of Manhattan, it appears as if the creator has slipped into his own creation. Manhattan, self-reflexively, has acquired a smidgen of Moore's earthy persona in his regained appreciation for humanity. It is a look that gives this book its shape and function as we try to comprehend the greater vicissitudes of a man of such constancy and drive who, not unlike Manhattan, looks at the complexities of human rationality *and* carnality and struggles to make just some sense of it all. Moore's purview is as ridiculous a juxtaposition of values and conclusions as the unfathomable number of bodies that have wriggled and contorted their way through coitus. When you really think about it, what's not to smile about?

Notes

1. Except Europa.
2. Something we humans discovered in the early nineteenth century in Japanese erotica.
3. "Alan Moore leaves behind his *Extraordinary Gentlemen* to dally with *Lost Girls*," *Moorcock's Miscellany*, 7 Aug. 2006, 3 Sept. 2010 <http://www.multiverse.org/fora/showthread.php?t=3930>.
4. Ibid.

5. Ibid.

6. Moore does not identify exactly which of Freud's theories he derives this notion from, but it is not a stretch of the imagination to believe he refers to Freud's notions of the Oedipal Complex from *The Interpretation of Dreams*.

7. Dorman Shindler, "Alan Moore leaves behind his *Extraordinary Gentleman* to dally with *Lost Girls*," *Science Fiction Weekly*, Aug. 2006 <http://www.scifi.com/sfw/interviews/sfw13282.html>.

8. Ibid.

9. J.M. Barrie, *Peter Pan* (Raleigh: Hayes Barton Press, 1992), 21.

10. Neil Gaiman, "*Lost Girls* Redux," *Neil Gaiman's Journal*, 19 June 2006, 3 Sept. 2010. <http://journal.neilgaiman.com/2006/06/lost-girls-redux.html>.

11. Gordon Flagg, "The Press on *Lost Girls!*" *Top Shelf Productions*, 24 Mar. 2007, 3 Sept. 2010 <http://www.topshelfcomix.com/news/147>.

12. Gaiman, "*Lost Girls*."

13. John Byrne, "Alan Moore and the Rights to *Watchmen*," *Byrne Robotics*, 1 Aug. 2010, 3 Sept. 2010. <http://www.byrnerobotics.com/forum/forum_posts.asp?TID=35901&PN=0&TPN=9>.

14. Ibid.

15. John Doran, "Hipster Priest: A Quietus Interview with Alan Moore," *The Quietus*, 13 July 2010, 3 Sept. 2010 <http://thequietus.com/articles/04603-alan-moore-interview-unearthing-2>.

16. Scott Thill, "Alan Moore Gets Psychogeographical with *Unearthing*," *Wired*, 9 Aug. 2010, 3 Sept. 2010 <http://www.wired.com/underwire/2010/08/alan-moore>.

17. Walt Whitman, "Song of Myself," *Leaves of Grass and Other Writings* (New York: W. W. Norton, 2002), 27–77.

18. Alan Moore and Dave Gibbons, *Watchmen* (New York: DC Comics, 2005), Chapter 12, 27.

19. Ibid.

PART I

The "Low Form": Moore and the Complex Relationships of the Comic Book Superhero

1. Libidinal Ecologies
Eroticism and Environmentalism in Swamp Thing
BRIAN JOHNSON

The theme of environmentalism is one of the most prominent and explicitly telegraphed features of Alan Moore's reimagining of *Swamp Thing* during his landmark tenure on that series from 1984 to 1987. In a range of stories focusing on toxic dumping, biological weapons development, environmental apocalypse, and the rise of green activism, Moore transformed *Swamp Thing* from a Gothic monster serial into an ecologically-conscious horror comic whose more conventional chills now became closely intertwined with Moore's scathing depiction of the environmental depredations wrought by everyone from non-recycling suburbanites to the American military-industrial complex. To ground this thematic retooling, Moore instituted a major ontological change into the protagonist. Subtly inverting Swamp Thing's origin by retroactively "killing" Swamp Thing's human alter ego Alec Holland, Moore transformed the title character from a man trapped within the body of a monster into a bio-genetically altered sentient plant haunted by the psychic residue of the dead man's ghostly consciousness. The subsequent revelation by a mysterious "parliament of trees" that Swamp Thing is also an "erl-king," an embodiment of the earth's own elemental being (4, 108), gave Moore a protagonist who could fully assume the allegorical green mantle of perpetually besieged *spiritus mundi* and thus provide the series with an anchor for stories about environmental issues that were achieving new notoriety in the early 1980s.

Although prior critics have noticed the "environmentalist thread" (Bushnell 36) in Moore's *Swamp Thing*, correctly seeing the protagonist as "a sort of green superhero, the incarnation of the primeval force of the elements, ready to rebel against man's violent invasion of natural spaces" (Di Liddo 51–52), the nature and significance of the series' environmental philosophy remain to be fully elaborated, as does the relation of Moore's ecophilosophy to the series' preoccupation with love and sex. Jack Bushnell's early feminist reading of *Swamp Thing* as "a re-visionist critique of comic book assumptions about male identity and its reliance on the controlling power available through science and technology" (31) is nonetheless highly suggestive on this point, and offers a valuable signpost to the direction such an exploration might take. Developing Bushnell's observation that Moore's critique of exploitative "masculine" science culminates in an idealized "nonphallic" union between Swamp Thing and his human lover, my object is to situate the Green politics of Moore's *Swamp Thing* within what I see as the series' equally substantial philosophical concern with post–Cartesian anti-humanism and several of its key poststructuralist cognates: transgression, eroticism, and death. In so doing, I hope to show how Moore's environmental advocacy in *Swamp Thing* converges with the series' sustained assault on ego-centric conceptions of subjectivity and depends upon a representation of erotic love whose implications are most fully legible within the Nietzschean tradition of antihumanist thought epitomized by proto-poststructuralist libidinal philosopher and fellow avant-garde "pornographer" Georges Bataille.

Central to my argument is Moore's construction of the series around Swamp Thing's developing romance with a human woman, Abigail (Abby) Arcane Cable, a narrative framework that is profoundly shaped by Moore's feminism and which both structures and enriches the graphic narrative's green politics. At one level, the love story between Swamp Thing and Abby functions within the political economy of the plot as the principal means by which Moore consolidates the series' ecological project. In this capacity, the idyllic depiction of transgressive love and sex between an "earth elemental" and a human woman functions allegorically to provide a pastoral counterpoint to the military-industrial complex's grotesque "rape" of nature, thereby providing an idealized erotic figure for the series' tacit ecofeminist endorsement of deep ecology — a holistic, anti-anthropocentric ecophilosophy that emphasizes the ontological interconnectedness of human beings and nature and "seeks a fundamental change in the dominant worldview and social structure of modernity" (Katz, Light, and Rothenberg ix).

More subtly, the ecofeminist love story in *Swamp Thing* is also paradigmatic of the series' intense preoccupation with "limit experiences" of transgression and eroticism that interrupt and potentially dismantle the rational subject of Cartesian humanism, opening up a space in which alternative configurations of posthumanist subjectivity become possible. Swamp Thing himself— in the wake of Moore's ontological revision of his origin and the creature's subsequent astral journeys through time, space, and metaphysical realms beyond ordinary reality — provides the focal point for Moore's development of this theme, gradually evolving into a florid version of what Julia Kristeva, citing Bataille, calls "the sovereign subject of inner experience [...] a new subject who, without renouncing the subject of knowledge [...] returns to the latter its heterogeneous negativity at the same time as its *jouissance*" (Kristeva 252). At the same time, it is the human protagonist Abby, whose own posthumanist transformation is achieved through her love for Swamp Thing, that comes to assume the central role in Moore's libidinal allegory of ecological renewal. In this way, I argue, Moore employs their loving partnership both to figure a philosophically-coherent convergence of ecology, feminism, and posthumanism and to allegorize the intimate relation between the practical work of green politics and the utopian horizon of the new earth it works to bring about.

Into the Green: The Deep Ecology of Swamp Thing

Moore's development of the environmentalist theme across forty-some issues of *Swamp Thing* is remarkably coherent and largely compatible with the philosophy of deep ecology developed by Arne Naess in the early 1970s. Distinguishing his project from the piecemeal, issues-based approach of so-called "shallow ecology," Naess defined deep ecology as a totalizing and normative ethical and political platform for the transformation of the "economic, technical, and ideological structures" (29) of global modernity. Unlike "shallow ecology," whose often utilitarian or market-driven interventions are not premised on any underlying ethical commitment to an ecological world view, Naess's antimodernist vision is rooted in a belief in the intrinsic value of nonhuman life, calls for a rejection of "standard of living" in favor of "life quality" (29), and foregrounds the importance of "valuation and emotion" in helping the individual to develop an ethical world view that will lead to transformative social action (32). Inherent in such a vision is an identification with nonhuman nature that would overturn the post–Enlightenment tradition of anthropocentrism in favor of an environmental ethos that values the interconnectedness of human and nonhuman life within the ecosphere as such (Katz, Light, and Rothenberg xiii) — a project that, as numerous critics have noted, has deep affinities with poststructuralism's deconstructive critique of hierarchical oppositions like "Man" and "Nature" that enforce the semantic division between "human" and "nonhuman" nature at the level of language and cognition.

Moore's commitment to the basic propositions of deep ecology and to their philosophical cognates in poststructuralist theory is evident from the first story arc in which the protagonist awakens from cryogenic sleep to discover that he has been captured and dissected by the Sunderland Corporation, a company "with strong and suspicious ties to a clandestine government 'dirty tricks' agency" (Moore, Introduction x) that is interested in the effects of Alec Holland's "bio-restorative formula" on humans (1, 41). Moore's evocation of the American military-industrial complex in the figure of "General" Sunderland as shorthand for the rapacious relation between capitalist modernity and nature more generally is made explicit in the subsequent action as another plant monster and ecoterrorist named the "Floronic Man," Dr. Jason Woodrue, revives and manipulates Swamp Thing into murdering Sunderland as part of what he calls "the revenge of the grass" (1, 112). When Swamp Thing ultimately foils Woodrue's genocidal plans to inaugurate "another green world" free of "screaming meat" by "destroy[ing] the creatures ... that would destroy the ecosphere with their poisons and bulldozers" (1, 107), he does so in the name of the ontological interconnectedness of human and nonhuman life, asking his opponent: "And what ... will change the oxygen ... back into ... the gases that ... we ... need ... to survive ... when the men ... and animals ... are dead?" (1, 124). Thus, thematically, the function of this confrontation between warring anthropomorphizations of planetary consciousness, in which Swamp Thing must face down his murderous double, is to establish the deep ecological ethos of interconnectedness between human and nonhuman life that will be the touchstone for Moore's environmental stories throughout the series.

Moore's organization of this confrontation around Woodrue's violent opposition between the "green world" of nonhuman nature and the "red world" of "the [human] meat" demonstrates his intuitive awareness of the compatibility between deep ecology and deconstruction; Moore pointedly rejects Woodrue's metaphysical distinction between human beings and nature and by showing how any simple opposition between green and red worlds remains caught within the binary logic of the very anthropocentric system that Woodrue's narrow identification with "the bitterness of the woods" (1, 107) seeks to displace. It is on this basis that Moore establishes "the green"— a literary paraspace representing the nonhuman dimension of the ecosphere to which Swamp Thing's conscious is connected and through which it can travel—as a model of interconnectivity that can serve as a microcosm for the belief in the more profound interconnectedness of the entire human-nonhuman ecosphere in which the tenets of deep ecology are rooted. As Swamp Thing tells Woodrue when denouncing his murderous rampage through a small town, "you ... are hurting ... the green.... This ... is not ... the way ... of the wilderness. This ... is the way ... of man.... You poison ... the green ... with your desires..." (1, 122–23). In this way, Moore has Swamp Thing present an elementary lesson in ecological deconstruction, showing how Woodrue's simplistic inversion of the human/nonhuman binary remains contaminated by the originary epistemological violence that David W. Kidner calls "the Cartesian separation of 'thinking matter' and 'extended matter' [that] does violence to the nonhuman world" (9). Swamp Thing's reprimand of Woodrue also suggests that a genuine apprehension of nonhuman nature's ontological interconnectedness ("the way of the wilderness") may in fact provide the model for an environmental ethics that would displace, and not simply invert, instrumental reason's anthropocentric subordination of nature to the status of raw material.

Back to the Bodily Swamp: From Ecofeminism to Libidinal Ecology

Supplementing and consolidating the deep ecological orientation of Moore's environmentalist stories in the series is a second thread that affirms the philosophical affinities between deep ecology and ecofeminism, both of which are premised upon a critique of Cartesian philosophy's attempt to found an "objective," autonomous, and implicitly male subject through "a program of purification and training — for the liberation of *res cogitans* from the confusion and obscurity of its bodily swamp" (Bordo, qtd. in Legler 24). Glossing Susan Griffin's thesis in *Pornography and Silence*, Gretchen Legler argues that "Cartesian objectivity is pornographic because it falsely separates the mind from the body" and has thus been instrumental in Western philosophy's "silenc[ing] and objectifi[cation]" of women and nature, both of whom are associated in this tradition with the unthinking matter evoked by Bordo's felicitous phrase, the "bodily swamp" (24). Against this "pornographic" tradition, ecofeminism has, like deep ecology, often been concerned with deconstructing the phallocentric language and discourses that sustain this relation of "the body of women in Western culture with the body of nature" and thereby perpetuate the domination of both (25). In the process, ecofeminism has sought alternatives to the Cartesian subject's pornographic gaze by following the lead of the libidinally-inflected poststructuralist "French" feminisms of Luce Irigaray and Hélène Cixous. This line of ecological thought has embraced a rhetoric of "eros," which, in the example of Griffin, comes to signify a collapsing of the barrier between mental and bodily knowledge, restoring to women "the capacity for speech and meaning, for culture, for memory, for imagination, the capacity for touch and expression and sensation and joy" (qtd. in Legler 24), while at the same time opening the incipient feminist subject to identification with the world of nonhuman nature in a way that overlaps directly with the environmental ethos of deep ecology.

In "Rite of Spring," the thematically and visually groundbreaking story in which Swamp Thing and Abby confess their love for each other and consummate their relationship in an unusual "nonphallic" (Bushnell 39) sexual/intellectual union, Moore decisively establishes the link between eroticism, ecofeminism, and deep ecology that unfolds throughout the remainder of the series. Ingesting a tuber with hallucinogenic properties that Swamp Thing grows for her on his vegetable body, Abby experiences both a literal consciousness-raising and an ego-dissolving flight into the sublime paraspace of the green where she and Swamp Thing's astral bodies merge in orgasmic rapture. The "content" of Abby's orgasm is in effect the ontological premise of deep ecology, for by absorbing some of Swamp Thing's consciousness and perceptions, she now experiences total boundary loss. "I am no longer certain where I end ... where he begins," she thinks, and is suddenly able to see what she had "never realized": that "everything's alive and ... it's all made of the same stuff" (2, 197–98). The tale's erotic and ecological registers thus become interchangeable during Abby and Swamp Thing's sexual "congress," as the eroticized boundary collapse between self and other becomes a vehicle through which Moore figures the collapse between human and nonhuman nature. Abby rhapsodizes,

> In him, I ride the amber sap, oozing through miniature labyrinths.... Through him, I sprawl with the swamp, sopping, steaming, dragonflies stitching neon threads through the damp air surrounding me.... The bark encrusts my flanks. The moss climbs my spine to embrace my shoulders.... We ... are ... one creature ... and all ... that there is ... is in us... [2, 200].

Her sexual transport with Swamp Thing tellingly recalls the eroticized landscapes of one of Moore's contemporaries in the mid–1980s, the American ecofeminist nature writer Gretel Ehrlich, whose "posthumanist vision of landscape" likewise "emphasizes erotic conversation between humans and the land" (Legler 23) in poetry and prose featuring an autobiographical female speaker who, like Abby, feasts on earth during a period of "honey-madness" as "a way of breaching subject and object worlds" (Legler 26). Abby's transformation into a female Swamp Thing in the artwork by Stephen Bissette, John Totleben, and colorist Tatjana Wood that accompanies the internal monologue of her merger with the earth signifies an identical ecofeminist breaching.

Abby's idyllic romance with Swamp Thing in the enchanted setting of the bayou in springtime, then, provides the series with its most powerful image of ecological utopianism. Therein, deep ecology's ethical injunction to love the earth is dramatically literalized in the figure of a human-vegetable couple who experience an earthly version of the sacred marriage, *hierosgamos*. As we have seen, the eroticism of this sacred marriage and its collapsing of the boundaries between human and nonhuman natures implies a dismantling of the rational, anthropocentric subject of Cartesian humanism, for it is only on the basis of what poststructuralism calls "the death" of this delusive and ideologically-determined subject-effect that the intimate identification of human life with nonhuman nature upon which the ethical judgments of deep ecology and ecofeminism depend becomes conceivable.

Swamped: Transgression, Sovereignty, and Death

Among the many theorists of antihumanism to narrate "the death of the subject," Bataille seems the most uniquely suited to accounting for the luxuriant conflation of eroticism, transgression, and sadism that defines Moore's epicurean combination of horror and sexuality (or "Love and Death" as the title of one story has it) in *Swamp Thing*. Widely regarded as one of the most influential precursors to poststructuralism (Botting and Wilson 6–8), Bataille blazed his own circuitous path across terrain first mapped by Nietzsche and Freud to develop a libidinally-charged rejection of the rational humanist subject that was rooted in the modern individual's awareness of death as the absolute limit of being. Beset by an anguished awareness of this limit, which defines the subject's essential "discontinuity" from the universe outside of its subjective experience, Bataille's subject is tormented by a nostalgic longing for the necessarily pre-linguistic, pre-symbolic "lost continuity" (*Eroticism* 15) of being that is announced by its never-quite-attained death and which preceded the moment of its birth and subsequent interpellation into the existentially dissatisfying human world of language, meaning, and work.

Such a subject, Bataille claims, seeks release from the prison of its discontinuous being and contact with the elusive beyond of "primal continuity" (15), an impulse that is manifest as a desire to push past the taboos (limits) that society has thrown up to defend itself against the self-immolating tendency of the life force's paradoxical drive to "complete" itself in death. "Eroticism" in its three principal (and often overlapping) forms — physical (sexual "perversion"), emotional (love), and religious (mysticism) — is the privileged signifier of this transgressive yearning to pass beyond the ultimate limit where "death means continuity of being" (13–23) since "[the] whole business of eroticism is to destroy the self-contained character of the participants as they are in their normal lives" (17). However, the manner in which eroticism "opens the way to death" (24) and makes the subject feel as though he is "tearing himself" (39) also leads Bataille to stress its "heavy, sinister quality" (19) and its proximity to suffering and violence. (He is thinking of the pathos of the lover as well as the perversions of De Sade.) Thus, in spite of a yearning for continuity, Bataille's conflicted subject still "blanch[es] at the thought that the separate individuality within us must suddenly be snuffed out" (16), that he must experience "a partial dissolution of the person as he exists in the realm of discontinuity" (17). Love and death are thus mutually implicated mirror images in Bataille, for there is no eroticism that does not call forth some form of violence upon the tenuous borders of the anguished but grateful subject.

Moreover, as this ambivalence implies, although the path to our lost continuity leads back though the bodily swamp and its *jouissance*, Bataille makes clear that "transgression is not the same as a back-to-nature movement" (36). That is because transgression (in the specific mode of erotic ego-shattering "violence" that Bataille envisions) "suspends a taboo without suppressing it" (36). In other words, such limit-defying experiences are fleeting because they do not actually "dissolve" the subject in any permanent way; eroticism is premised upon the transgression of a taboo, but transgression itself is only thinkable in relation to a limit that it traverses but does not obliterate. For this reason, Bataille defines the human condition of erotic longing as an endlessly frustrating one — an "assenting to life," but only "*up to the point* of death" (emphasis added 11). Bataille, in homage to Nietzsche, calls the tragic hero of his post–Cartesian account of being the "sovereign subject," and this figure has since been joined by a plethora of others who have followed in Bataille's footsteps, most notably the "subject-in-process" of Kristeva and the nomadic subject of Gilles Deleuze and Félix Guattari (Botting and Wilson 13–15).

Both Abby and Swamp Thing might profitably be read as belated entrants into this tradition of posthumanist superheroes, for their function, both collectively and individually, is to figure an "erotic" exit from the rational and autonomous Cartesian subject of knowledge in much the same manner as Bataille's ambivalent protagonist and in ways that evoke a similarly double-edged understanding of eroticism. This is most apparent in the way that Moore's stories move back-and-forth between Gothic and Pastoral — sadistic and romantic — articulations of eroticism. As in Bataille's account of sovereign man, the most sadistic and violent elements of Abby's narrative — her incestuous rape and spiritual "murder" by her demonic uncle Arcane in "Love and Death" — turn out to be recuperable within the larger thematics of subjective boundary dissolution that culminates in the erotic/ecological sublime of "Rite of Spring."

Meanwhile, Swamp Thing's own narrative of self-discovery, unfolding across the duration of Moore's tenure on the series, dramatizes the dissolution of conventional understandings of personhood and thereby provides a kind of allegorical "anatomy" of the process of egoic destruction that is analogous to Bataille's account of the birth of sovereign man out of the grave of the humanist subject. Such an anatomization begins, appropriately, with "The Anatomy Lesson," wherein, as we have seen, Moore rewrites the protagonist's origin, changing Swamp Thing from "Alec Holland, somehow transformed into a plant" into "a plant that thought it was Alec Holland" (1, 49). Although Moore has confessed to being fascinated by the "hard science fiction" premise of this ontological disturbance and interested in "investigat[ing] the possibilities of [Swamp Thing's] being a plant" (qtd. in Di Liddo 51), the symbolic function of dispensing with Alec Holland as the core of Swamp Thing's identity is very different. Rather than simply clearing the ground for an exploration of vegetal consciousness, Swamp Thing's ontological displacement of Alec Holland allegorizes the displacement of one form of human subjectivity with another; the death of Alec Holland comes to symbolize the death of an unethical and self-limiting mode of humanist self-understanding, just as Swamp Thing himself, freed from the corpse of this false self-image, comes to symbolize the emergence of a new (posthumanist) subject. Swamp Thing is, after all, a hybrid or borderline creature who generally retains his anthropomorphic form throughout the series, despite briefly flirting with the idea of withdrawing wholly into the green and becoming "a vegetable" after discovering that he is — ontologically-speaking — no longer technically "human" (1, 66). Similarly, when Abby expresses her unease over her romantic partner's inhuman ability to let his body "die in one place" and "grow [...] a new one somewhere else," leaving her feeling "as if you're somewhere else and I'm hugging your jacket" (3, 147), Swamp Thing reassures her that her feelings are "human" and subsequently decides that he must "restrain" his use of his new abilities, "lest I forget ... what I am..." (3, 150). His choice to identify with a humanity that is no longer the ontologically-given truth of his being tacitly affirms his narrative function as the figure for a defamiliarized human subject — one who remains discernibly "humanoid" and who is willing to let his lover call him "Alec" (a name that was never really his), but who is also manifestly nonhuman, who has access to the ego-shattering world of the green, and who gives body to Bataille's warning that "[e]roticism as seen by the objective intelligence is something monstrous" (37).

Within this frame, the entire unfolding of Swamp Thing's quest for self-knowledge may be understood as a psychological allegory for the death of the subject followed by his resurrection in a significantly altered form, as a version of Bataille's "sovereign man," the porousness of whose ego-boundaries, as we have seen, is especially congenial to the ethical injunctions of the series' libidinal ecology. As a representative of the Parliament of Trees informs Swamp

Thing, the origin stories of all earth elementals are fundamentally similar: "A man ... dies in flames ... a monster ... rises from the mire ... sacrifice ... and ... resurrection ... that is always ... our beginning..." (4, 109). From this point, Swamp Thing's journey involves learning to accept the loss of his conventional "human" identity by burying Alec Holland's bones and exorcizing his ghost ("The Burial"; 2, 10–32), while at the same time not falling completely into a "vegetative" state of total immersion in the green ("Swamped"; 1, 61–84). Such a psychological compromise perfectly instantiates Bataille's insistence upon the reign of the limit: the existence of a point (death) beyond which the subject cannot pass without experiencing annihilation. Like Bataille's sovereign man, in other words, Swamp Thing learns to embrace eroticism as a condition of his being: an affirmation of life "up to" but not beyond "the point of death" (11).

From Swamp Thing to Bog Venus: Libidinal Ecology Revisited

Moore's development of the theme of libidinal ecology that I have been tracing culminates in Abby's trial in Gotham City for "crimes against nature" (5, 8) after her sexual relationship with Swamp Thing becomes public knowledge. Anticipating Moore's later claim in *25,000 Years of Erotic Freedom* that "sex and sexual expression are political and always have been" (61), the story dramatizes the political implications of "loving the earth" in a fantastic allegory of an erotically-incited green revolution wherein Swamp Thing, enraged over the arrest of his romantic partner, transforms Gotham City into "some sort of savage Eden" (5, 52), only to find himself welcomed as a "cult deity"(5, 66) by a subculture of proto-revolutionary ecologically-minded Gothamites whom the media dubs "Swampies" (5, 67). A sly visual allusion to Michelangelo's *The Creation of Adam* (1508–12) tacitly affirms Swamp Thing and Abby's symbolic roles as the new God and new Adam/Eve of this glimpsed green utopia that constitutes the horizon of deep ecology's ethico-political ambitions, even as Swamp Thing's rose and thorn-covered body makes him into a striking combination of environmentalist superhero and walking Petrarchan conceit — an icon of libidinal ecology. Subsequently, Abby herself literally becomes the eco-feminist environmental activist that her erotic transport with Swamp Thing in "Rite of Spring" had symbolically prefigured, bringing the series' interlacing of eroticism and environmentalism full circle. Fittingly, then, in the final pastoral images of Moore's saga, the allegorical register of Moore's elemental utopianism is peeled back, as it is the human woman Abby, not Swamp Thing, who assumes the ethical duty of planetary stewardship.

Yet, even though I have emphasized the philosophical coherence of Moore's joint evocation of eroticism and environmentalism, I want to conclude with the caution that, despite its allegorical significance as a figure for the interpenetration of human and nonhuman nature, the presentation of eroticism in *Swamp Thing*, like deep ecology's account of the intrinsic value of nonhuman nature, remains, for Moore, an end in itself. As Moore has argued in *25,000 Years of Erotic Freedom*, the suppression of forms of erotic expression is psychologically damaging and perhaps even socially destructive. "Realized properly," Moore suggests, "pornography could offer us a safe arena in which to discuss or air ideas that otherwise would go unspoken and could only fester in our individual dark" (81), leading to "disastrous explosions of the sex drive — ugly eruptions into real life by what should have been a harmless fantasy" (76). For this reason, without denying its strategic function within Moore's ecological allegory, it is important to recognize that the relation of eroticism to ecology in *Swamp Thing* is also in some sense reversible — that what *Swamp Thing* presents is not simply a libidinal allegory of deep ecology, ecofeminism, or environmental activism, but also, simultaneously, an environmental allegory of healthy human sexuality and an actual achievement of the privileged form of liberating erotic art that Moore refers to as "'good' porn" (80): an "ennobled" form of sexual expression that would allow pornography to "take its place once more as a revered and almost sacred totem in society" (81).

Moore's reference to porn as a "sacred totem" gestures towards the reversibility of eroticism and environmentalism within the libidinal ecology of *Swamp Thing*, for the "totem" to which Moore alludes in *25,000 Years of Erotic Freedom* is the Venus of Willendorf (or "Bog Venus"), a prehistoric stone fertility goddess who is Moore's archetype for a "good," "primal pornography" that celebrates rather than shames its society's "erotic dreams" (84). Swamp Thing's emergence as a fertility god and nature deity in the green Gotham storyline and later again in "Loving the Alien" (6, 72–94), where his space-faring consciousness fuses in sexual union with an alien planet, clearly marks him as a version of the "Bog Venus" that Moore later celebrates as the model for "good" porn. It is thus not a coincidence that Moore's figuration of ecological themes in *Swamp Thing* is frequently supplemented by critiques of what Moore regards as "'bad' porn"— a term he reserves for the ubiquitous and "rudimentary" pornography of the video store and internet era that, because it encourages private consumption, seldom functions as "an affirmation of common humanity" but instead "affirms only our alienation and our distance from each other" (77). The destruction of an adult video store by a female werewolf in "The Curse" (3, 137–38) or Swamp Thing's turn as the deranged director of his own pornographic fantasies of Abby, which he constructs out of animated vegetable matter on a "blue" planet when he is exiled in space in the ironically entitled "My Blue Heaven" (5, 131–52), amply attest to Moore's dual investment in ecology and erotica as objects of intrinsic interest in *Swamp Thing*. Moreover, the terms of Moore's critique of "bad" porn — its promotion of alienation and solipsism — correspond directly to the graphic narrative's critiques of the self-enclosed Cartesian subject and its anthropocentric world view that would separate human from nonhuman nature. This is a connection that is highlighted by the fact that the solitary nightmare-world of vegetal pornographic simulation in "My Blue Heaven" is a wintry inversion of the sublime and ego-defying pastoral idyll of "Rite of Spring." "Good" pornography, in other words, like ecology and posthuman subjectivity, is defined by a paradigm of interconnection that subverts the classical subject-object distinction.

Within this context, the lyrical and visual beauty of sexually-themed tales like "Rite of Spring" and the still more experimental "Loving the Alien" make them emerge as claimants to the title of "'good' porn" whose aim is "to restore Bog Venus to her natural and proper place in culture" (84). This is not only because these stories exemplify Moore's call to "bring such a degree of artistry to our pornography that [the] immediate link between erotica and dire social embarrassment are severed" (81), but also because Moore has provided these erotic flights with a socially-redeeming and shame-diffusing alibi by linking their intrinsically arresting sensualism to the social project of environmentalism. Moore's achievement in *Swamp Thing*— which he shares with his extraordinary collaborators — is thus to have articulated the liberatory potential of eroticism and the ethical program of deep ecology together in such a way that eroticism cannot be dismissed as merely the husk of his environmental allegory. Like Sade and Angela Carter, the latter of whom is the subject of a warm appreciation in *25,000 Years of Erotic Freedom* (80), Moore is a "moral pornographer" (Carter 22); in *Swamp Thing*, he has developed not only a sophisticated and philosophically coherent work of libidinal ecology, but also a visionary example of what he might be pleased to call ecological eroticism.

2. Green Love, Red Sex
The Conflation of the Flora and the Flesh in Swamp Thing
MATTHEW CANDELARIA

Working on *Swamp Thing* was the beginning of Alan Moore's relationship with DC Comics. Moore saw it not just as a debut, but as an opportunity to show off the full range of his creative and imaginative powers. In the series, Moore displayed virtually all of the creative gifts that would make him the most respected name in modern comics: lyrical control over language, an ability to construct plots that are intricate without seeming contrived, and an ability to interrogate and reinterpret long-established characters — all are present in *Swamp Thing*. Having composed more than 40 issues, *Swamp Thing* represents one of Moore's longest sustained comic arcs. Yet, many critics dismiss *Swamp Thing* as marginal work, worthy of mention only in passing. For example, Geoff Klock, in *How to Read Superhero Comics and Why*, dismisses *Swamp Thing*, stating that it belongs among works that "while powerful and important, are only part of the superhero genre for marketing reasons: for the purposes of this book, they can hardly be considered superhero narratives at all" (18).[1] *Swamp Thing* does run counter in some ways to much of Moore's work because it is a mainstream serial. Once it is removed from critical discussion, creating a unity from Moore's work becomes much easier. *Swamp Thing* may not seem as interesting to many readers as the prurient violence of *From Hell* or the utopia-seeking worlds of *Watchmen* and *Marvelman/Miracleman*. And, admittedly, there is something about the initially old-fashioned relationship between Abby Cable and the Swamp Thing that may seem bland to readers who enjoy Fanny Hill's further adventures in *The League of Extraordinary Gentlemen: Black Dossier* as well as the endless romps provided by *Lost Girls*. Those accusations aside, however, Abby and Swamp Thing's frolics are definitely rated PG by comparison to these others mentioned, one manifestation of the series' almost-puritanical attitude toward sex in its early issues.

From the beginning of his time with the series to its end, Moore establishes a narrative of transformation from the human (or even subhuman) into the divine,[2] many of these themes already familiar in Moore's other works.[3] However, his span on *Swamp Thing* allowed Moore to transform love and sex from symbolic opposites into a harmonious union while tying both into a statement on freedom and the appropriate use of individual and social power. Contrary to many of Moore's other works, *Swamp Thing* not only eschews explicit sex, but initially equates sex with the evil, the ugly, the violent, and the disastrous. From his first issue of *Swamp Thing*, Moore establishes a dichotomy between what he labels as the red and green worlds. The "green world" is peace, growth, plants, and sap, while the "red world" is violence, destruction, insects, and blood.[4] Into this dichotomy, Moore places platonic love inside the green world and sex in the red. This dichotomous placement of the two phenomena creates an explicit critique of sex as destructive, dangerous, and violent, while love finds cherished, protected places in the narrative. It is not until Swamp Thing has achieved his full godly status and wisdom that sex can be brought into the green. Before Swamp Thing can bring sex into the green, he must learn the most difficult lesson of all: that to defeat the red world, he must stop fighting it.

Establishing the Red and Green Worlds

Moore establishes a dichotomy between a red world, characterized by violence, presence, and death, and a green world, characterized by healing, absence, and life. This dichotomy is evident since Moore's first issue of *Swamp Thing*, "Anatomy Lesson." In this chapter, Moore accomplishes the essential work of remaking the Swamp Thing by first emptying him of his history, accomplishing a *kenosis* similar to the one Klock associates with *Watchmen* (Klock 63). Moore turns his protagonist into nothing through a series of emptyings which begin in "Anatomy Lesson." First, Swamp Thing is emptied of his organs which are removed by Jason Woodrue, the Floronic Man.[5] Then, he is emptied of his original backstory when the reader learns that Swamp Thing is not Alec Holland transformed by his plant formula. Instead, Swamp Thing is a plant that believes itself to be Holland, like a planarian worm that learns to run a maze by consuming the brain of a worm that had run the maze. Swamp Thing is stripped of all characteristics except his "raw, wet, implacable greenness" (21.16), and his unstoppable ability to grow and not be killed by conventional methods like a gunshot to the head.

By contrast, the red world begins with the appearance of blood: "Lots of blood. Blood in extraordinary quantities" (21.1) or so imagines Woodrue.

However, as Woodrue informs us, "The blood doesn't matter. Just the dying" (21.22). Just as the green world's essential characteristic is growing life, the red world's essential characteristic is violent death, the power to take life. In this chapter of *Swamp Thing*, Woodrue is associated with the red world, through his imagination of blood, his glass of red wine, the ferocity of his red eyes, and his power over the life of Sunderland.

The red world is explicitly established in book three, "Another Green World." The chapter opens, "There is a red and angry world ... red things happen there. The world eats your wife ... eats your friends ... eats all the things ... that make you human ... and you become a monster. And the world just keeps on eating" (23.1). Within these panels a red centipede swoops down from outside the frame to devour a cricket. The frame pulls out to reveal that the action is taking place at the base of the throat of Swamp Thing, now rooted and gape-mouthed. Swamp Thing explains further, "I couldn't take the red world. So I walked out ... and I left my body behind ... and I'm somewhere else now" (23.1). This "somewhere else" is the green, a vast green emptiness separate from the body's physical presence. In this introduction, the red world is established as a presence, the green world, an absence, a leaving-behind.

The dichotomy between green world as absence and red world as presence is reaffirmed on the next pages. As the narrative moves inside the green, we see it as a vast empty space populated at the edges and shot through with long fibers. By contrast, when Swamp Thing senses another mind in the green, Woodrue's mind, it is drawn as a huge red mass, sending out fibers, and Swamp Thing describes it: "It crawls like cancer ... painting everything with the sticky darkness of old blood" (23.7). Woodrue embodies the red world, and he helps establish its characteristics. Swamp Thing confronts Woodrue with his sins during their conflict: "You Poison ... the green ... with your desires." Desire is the essence of the red world, and sex falls within its borders.

The Red World and the Fabrication of Sex

Sex does not necessarily have to be associated with the red world. Initially, the red world is linked with arthropods, blood, violence, power, and eating. Sex could be characterized apart from the red world, but instead Moore chooses to portray sex as something red indeed. This association comes first through Matt Cable when Abby[6] returns to their motel room to hear voices coming from inside. Before Abby opens the door, we see Matt alone with his creations, what Moore describes as "erotic homunculi" ("Introduction," 11). These creatures of Matt's imagination are yellow forms on a vivid red background. The forms are bizarre combinations of feminine and arthropod features: women with butterfly masks, a millipede with a woman's torso, a centipede whose every segment has a pair of full feminine lips (22.10). The red backdrop and the arthropod forms both tie them to the red world.

The association between the red world and sex is firmly established after Matt has been possessed by Arcane, who enters his mouth in the form of a fly. In "Love and Death" (29), the reader finds Abby passed out on the floor. She has been scraping her skin for over twenty minutes with a wire brush, trying to remove the smell that emanates from her, the smell of "the bad thing" (29.12). "The bad thing" is not explicitly stated, only hinted at. The panels show Matt and Abby inside the house, in the bedroom, show him kissing her naked shoulder, then their lips about to lock, and Abby's denial that it ever happened, then the reflection of her sleeping with Matt's corpse. She finally acknowledges that, yes, it did happen: "She didn't want to think about it, but there was that bug taste in the back of her mouth, and…"(29.13). As she makes this admission, her naked body rests on a bed of red insects, spiders, and centipedes, as others flitter around her. Even before this, we see her curled up on the ground, and superimposed on the shadow of her flank is an abomination, a composite form of a skull with insect and other animal parts, its head near her womb, but uncontainable, spreading its form through her leg and beyond. The "bad thing," then, likely, is sex with Matt as possessed by her uncle Arcane. His presence is signaled by red figures, mostly arthropods, that swarm around Abby as she is curled up in disgust and fear, and when his identity is revealed, Matt's possessed body stands under the spider-form of Arcane.

Sex is further tied to redness through "The Curse," and the menstrual blood concealed in the red lodge. This chapter begins with Phoebe, "the good wife" (40.2) reflecting on the indignity of being sequestered in the red lodge with other menstruating women, being banned from touching anything, eating "from sticks, like lepers" (40.6), and "their anger, in darkness turning, unreleased, unspoken, its mouth a red wound" (40.2). As these thoughts run through her mind, they are juxtaposed against the symbols of contemporary women's oppression: "Good news for housewives" (40.1) in the form of a display of steak knives, "Autumn Morn disposable douche" (40.2), and an adult book store, where women are bound in S&M publications. And when Phoebe transforms into a werewolf, she goes back to the places of oppression that, to a bridal boutique, to the adult bookstore, and to the grocery store where she impales herself on the display of steak knives. Thus, although sex is not initially part of the formulation of the red world, it becomes characteristic of the red world through repeated associations with the color, with arthropods, with violence, and with the subjugation of women.

The Green World and the Construction of Love

The relationship between the green world and platonic love is more complicated than that between the red world and sex. As part of Moore's reformulation of his character, Swamp Thing divests himself of everything "human," which occurs in a dream sequence in "Swamped" (22). The dream sequence begins with a version of Alec and Linda's wedding. When Linda sinks into the ground, Alec is told he has to put on his "mud suit" to get her, which is like his Swamp Thing form. Then he goes through several iterations of losing himself. First, in the mud suit, party guests scoop away the suit until nothing is left. When we next see the Swamp Thing in his dream, he is carrying Linda's limp body, still clad in her wedding dress. He is invited over to a barbecue by "Plain Aryan worms" (22.12). The worms not only have a bad sense of humor, but they are tucking in to a meal of Alec's body. They eat everything but the skeleton. When the Swamp Thing protests that nothing's left, the worms reply, "We left you the best part. We left you the humanity. Try not to lose it" (22.13). After considering Alec's skull and Linda's face, Swamp Thing decides to abandon Linda, saying, "I'm ... so sorry, Linda ... but I just can't ... carry ... both of you" (22.13). It is significant that the cry of "Alec? Alec come back" (22.13) comes not from Linda, but from Abby, who is kneeling over the rooted body of the Swamp Thing, and will soon take Linda's place in a retelling of this scene.

It makes sense that if Swamp Thing is vegetable, not human, then he would have no place for a human emotion such as love, but Moore chooses that Swamp Thing should be not only capable of love but driven by love. Love not as we might imagine it in human terms, but as a manifestation of our interconnectedness with all things, in which the loved one becomes a catalyst who enables us to surrender our self to become one with the world, as becomes evident in "Rite of Spring."

When Swamp Thing faces off with Arcane (now bolstered by Matt Cable's strange power, which Matt had squandered in the creation of his erotic homunculi) in "A Halo of Flies" (30), he first seeks to rescue Abby. In this moment it is as if Moore has looped us back to the moment in "Swamped" when Swamp Thing leaves Linda behind. Swamp Thing lifts Abby's limp body the way he carried Linda in his dream, her arm, hair, and dress trailing.

That she is even wearing a dress seems calculated to further invoke the similarity — she was wearing a t-shirt and jeans when Arcane pulled her under. The menagerie of deformed creatures around Swamp Thing's feet includes a planarian worm to only further drive home the parallel between the scenes. Now, Swamp Thing, free from his human burden (having left it behind for good in "Burial" [28]), can focus on love, and instead of leaving Abby behind, he carries her away from Arcane's house and rests her in his place of power, a green sward in the midst of the snows created by Arcane. However, the most direct juxtaposition between the green love and red sex occurs in Abby's dream as she lies passed out on the floor after trying to scrub herself clean of "the bad thing." Abby dreams of a romantic encounter with the Swamp Thing. He tells her she can call him "Alec," the two look into one another's eyes and they embrace. She describes the experience, "He whirled her around and her feet were no longer touching the ground. She buried her face in his chest and breathed in a scent of life and loam and autumn. It smelled good" (29.5), contrasted in the next panel with the smell of "the bad thing," the smell of sex. In one panel, her face is pushed up against Swamp Thing's green chest, and in the next she separates it with her fist from a bed of red insects.

To understand how green love works and is different from red sex, it is crucial to understand "Rite of Spring" (34), the chapter in which Swamp Thing and Abby consummate their relationship. Although this chapter has been described as "cosmic sex" (Peters 316) and "mainstream comic's first issue-length psychedelic sex scene" (Wolk 231), it is perhaps better called "rhapsodic, hallucinogenic intercourse" (Hatfield), as long as we understand that it is *not* sexual as human beings generally consider sex. There are hallucinogenic images and colors, and a rhapsodic marriage of minds, but nothing that is literally sexual.[7]

There is no reason why Swamp Thing and Abby could not have a sexual relationship. We know from her dream that Abby considers the smell and touch of the Swamp Thing to be sensuous and stimulating. This positive association is strengthened by the couple's first kiss. After the two confess their love for one another, Abby says that they have never kissed, and Swamp Thing says, "It ... would be ... unpleasant for you. Abby ... we are so ... different" (34.5). When the two kiss, we not only see the rhapsodic influx of romantic sunlight to know that it is not unpleasant, Abby says, "Oh. It's like lime ... but not as sharp" (34.6), a flavor she confesses to be her favorite. When we combine this sensual pleasure of physical contact with Swamp Thing's almost limitless physical variability,[8] fulfilling sexual contact seems not only possible, but easy to achieve. Abby resigns herself to a sexless relationship, however, Swamp Thing says, "There ... should be ... some form of communion" (34.8), and he gives Abby one of his fruits to eat. She absorbs some of his consciousness and not only sees the world as he sees it, but becomes part of him, part of the world, as she declares at one point "we ... are ... one creature ... and all ... that there is ... is in us" (34.15). Though they clasp, kiss, and hold one another, it is clear that there is no sexual activity, no physical penetration. Abby appears a figure that transcends clothing, but in actuality remains clothed, in contrast to the true psychedelic sex scene that appears a few issues later in "Windfall" (43.16).

The Rules of the Green

Even without sex, there is a good deal of "communion" and discovery in "Rite of Spring." In fact, it seems there is a great deal more within them than one might expect, some of which seems contradictory to the earlier dichotomy. Such as:

> Tenderness. Passion. Violence.... My enemy's blood erupts to fill my mouth with molten copper. I circle with the hawkmoths at their conjugation, breathless at the alien desires abstracted in their dance ... there is no contradiction ... only the pulse. The pulse within the world. Within us. Within me [34.16].

Violence, blood, insect mating, all within the green? If these are not the artifacts of the red world, what is, and what is the difference between the two worlds? To understand this, Swamp Thing must visit the Parliament of Trees and understand the wisdom of the Erl-Kings. When the Swamp Thing finds the Parliament of Trees, the gathering of plant elementals that have come before him, he is told several rules of the green, which include:

> "Power tempts anger, and anger is like wildfire. Avoid it."
> "Flesh doubts. Wood knows."
> "Where is evil in all the wood?" [47. 18].

Then he is thrown out because he is not yet "mature" enough to join the Parliament. Swamp Thing struggles with this wisdom, and he does not accept it. Even when he presents it to the "original darkness,"[9] it is full of qualifications and self-doubts. He says of evil, "I have not ... understood it" (50. 28), and later concludes, "Perhaps evil ... is the humus formed by virtue's decay ... and perhaps ... Perhaps it is from ... that dark, sinister loam ... that virtue grows strongest?" (50. 29).

How can one take this wisdom in context with the previous distinctions that have already been represented? If evil is the soil from which goodness grows, why fight Arcane? What is the objective context in which Swamp Thing can condemn Woodrue's actions? The Erl-Kings' wisdom serves Swamp Thing well during the "crisis," as the "original darkness" accepts his conditional explanation of evil, but this wisdom does not yet answer the dichotomy with which this essay has been struggling. Some critics take the success of the Erl-Kings' philosophy against the "original darkness" to imply it is the message of *Swamp Thing*:

> Nature and culture, vegetable reality and human morality, must be used to make sense of each other. Good and evil are dialectical contradictions: opposites which are identical, part of the same ongoing process of renewal. In revealing himself as a dialectical interpreter of reality, the Swamp Thing saves the universe, or rather enables its renewal [Carney].

At "The End" (50), it seems this may be the case, since this philosophy triumphs. However, it is worthwhile to note here that the palette of evil has changed. No longer are we talking about a red/green dichotomy, but a black/white (yellow) one. In "The End," the black hand and the yellow hand clasp in a way that we never see in any of the red/green conflicts.

Despite the issue's title, this is by no means the end of Swamp Thing's original plot arc. One more plot remains to be resolved that will take Swamp Thing from experiencing the Rules of the Green (as in "Rite of Spring"), being told them (as in "Parliament of Trees"), and guessing at them (as in "The End") to living them. In order to successfully make this move, however, Swamp Thing must learn to uphold his values, whoever he is, even when faced by a society that does not understand him but nonetheless seeks to judge him and his love.

Permissive Nature vs. Juridical Culture

During the time that Swamp Thing faces off against the "original darkness," Abby is arrested on charges of "crimes against nature" (51.4). The basis of the charges are photographs of Abby and Swamp Thing that have been published in a tabloid at the end of "Parliament of Trees" section. After her arrest, Abby suffers such torment by the community that she jumps bail, heads to Gotham, where she is arraigned for deportation, and then used as bait by General Wicker of the D.D.I., the shadowy government agency that has long pursued Swamp Thing. Once Swamp Thing discovers where Abby is, he utilizes a rose to make a dramatic appearance in court. He threatens violence unless Abby is turned over to him within an hour. Needless to say, the courts deny him his request.

Swamp Thing then transforms Gotham from "a defiant surge of stone and steel and glass that forces back the surrounding wilderness, jealously establishing its rigid gray territory" (52. 19) into "a fabulous bouquet" (53. 5). There is no synthesis, only one thing supplanting another as Swamp Thing's narrative contrasts the old (such as "stalled cars, ugly with buckled wings and broken antennae" [52. 20]) with the new ("monuments of fabulous and surreal beauty"). Commissioner Gordon describes the conflict: "This is unbelievable. Two hundred years of civilization reduced to jungle in as many minutes" (53. 3). When a nicely-caricatured Detective Bullock protests, "Gotham's always been a jungle, Commissioner," Gordon retorts, "No, it hasn't. It's teetered on the brink, but we've always managed to hold it there" (53. 3). Here we have the two irreconcilable opposites: nature and culture. Are these the red and green worlds, the world of nature and the world of man, as Swamp Thing states when confronting Woodrue, likening his violence to "the way ... of man" (23. 13)?

It may seem so, based on the statue of Gotham's founder, a lumberjack, with its bright red base (52.3). Annalisa Di Liddo uses this scene as the foundation for her interpretation of *Swamp Thing*: "Swamp Thing [...] becomes a sort of green superhero, the incarnation of the primeval force of the elements, ready to rebel against man's violent invasion of natural spaces" (52). What Di Liddo describes here is the conflict between the red world and the green world. However, note how Swamp Thing describes the green overtaking Gotham: "All over town, from sudden cracks and fissures, the sidewalks begin to bleed emerald" (52. 20). The green has become as blood, because Swamp Thing's abuse of power has violated the rules of the green, and he has become part of the red world. Di Liddo misses the point that what Swamp Thing does here is evil, or at least illegal, and not good, and he has become in this issue not a "green superhero," but a red supervillain, akin to Woodrue.

Swamp Thing is, like Woodrue, driven by desire, and not merely desire for Abby. If he had simply wanted her release, his powers could have granted this. Instead, he desires the subservience of the people of Gotham, who are to turn Abby over of their own accord. Where Woodrue claimed he was told to "destroy the creatures that would destroy us, that would destroy the ecosphere with their poisons and bulldozers" (23. 21), Swamp Thing now berates the citizens of Gotham: "You blight the soil ... and poison the rivers. You raze the vegetation .... And then you boast ... of man's triumph over nature" (52. 16). He has succumbed to anger and, as his memory reminds us, "Anger is like wildfire" (51. 21). The eventual fire consumes him after his dark victory in the form of a plan designed by Lex Luthor. Swamp Thing is believed dead, but has in fact been sent to another planet. In trying to make his way home, Swamp Thing travels to many worlds that impress upon him the need to eschew power in favor of following the rules of the green.

Not Quite Heaven But a Lesson Nonetheless

Swamp Thing finds himself on a planet covered with blue vegetation. Although the planet has some primitive animal life, it has no sentient life. Swamp Thing is alone, and in time his loneliness inspires him to construct a second body like his original body and then Abby. Although it is love that inspires Swamp Thing to create a replica of Abby, there is nothing of love in what he shares with it. Even as he is crafting it, he says, "I am tempted to laugh to dismiss this puppet show for the madness it surely is" (56. 8), but when he looks at her beauty, he confesses himself lost. How far Swamp Thing progresses with the illusion, we do not know. In the panels, we see little difference from their typical kisses and embraces, but we see enough hints to tell us that more may exist unseen. First, the Abby puppet is naked, unlike any of their real-life encounters. Second, the narrative of the Swamp Thing's first night with the puppet is described as "a kinetic progression ... of stopmotion glimpses ... sensual and inevitable in their sequence ... a blue movie" (56. 10). Finally, when the puppet attempts to re-entice him after he has seen through the illusion, she assumes more pornographic poses than the real Abby ever did. Of course, without Abby's mind, the only thing left to him is her body, so he would seek to do everything to it that he could, but this is not sex any more than it is love. It is cool blue madness. It can be likened to the creation of homunculi by Matt Cable, but differs because what he is creating is not others, but only additional parts of himself, which is part of the reason why he cannot mimic Abby's smile. Here, free of the dichotomies of earth, experiencing not love and not sex but mere madness, Swamp Thing learns the important lesson that simply because he can create a new world does not mean that he should.

Next, Swamp Thing visits Rann, a desert planet whose sole vegetation now seems to be a kind of red cactus. The association is not accidental, for Rann is a world with a sex problem. Rann has so overmastered nature that the world and its people have become sterile, and red is used as a mark of the power of fertility, both for the costume of Adam Strange, who is being used as a stud, and Swamp Thing, who eventually uses his power to restore fertility to Rann's soil. Red is even used as the color for the sheet in which Alanna wraps herself when she discovers her pregnancy. Here, Moore is taking advantage of the alien context to begin the work of realigning red and sexuality toward a positive valence, bringing it more in line with the philosophy we see in Moore's other works. He does so by creating a situation in which red sex is also associated with love. Alanna seems to love Strange, and he her, but the real truth of the matter is complicated by Keena Roo's accusations that the Rannians, including Alanna, are callously manipulating Strange. Keena Roo's accusations are lent strength by Strange's sudden (presumably controlled) return to earth and Alanna's ambiguous response (58. 22).

When Swamp Thing reunites with Abby in "Return of the Good Gumbo" (64), his body is with her, but his mind is not at first. While the two of them exchange pleasantries and enjoy a boat ride, his mind remains on Rann, thinking about what he did there and how he could do the same on Earth. He wonders whether he should do to the rest of Earth as he had done to Gotham, transforming it into a fertile Eden and freeing Humanity from toil.

Abby and Swamp Thing's reunion is accompanied by another communion, and this time the scene is far more sexual than before. We see Swamp Thing's hands reaching inside Abby's blouse and moving obscurely over points south, as he narrates, "It is not lust alone ... speeds my Magellan hands, fills out their sails ... Yet lust is there. I am ... still man enough ... to know its charms" (64. 12). In the psychedelic art there is something that might be interpreted as fellatio, though the text tells us, "she's howling like a zoo ... she's screaming like a jungle fire" (64. 13). And of course the panel is very, very red. Over the course of these final issues, Moore has undone the work achieved in the early series. Sex is still red, but it is not of the red world. The central issue is not love, not sex, but power and freedom. Abstinence is not part of the absence that characterizes the green world. Instead, the crucial absence is emptying oneself of the desire to seek and exercise power. The wisdom of the Erl-kings abides: "Power tempts anger, and anger is like wildfire. Avoid it." It is in light of their ancient history and repeated refusal to establish utopia that Swamp Thing also refrains. Instead of stretching out his hand, Swamp Thing sits back and watches, leaving Humankind free to fail, like the Judeo-Christian God, whom he has mimicked just pages before by wrestling Leviathan as evidence of his omnipotence.

Swamp Thing represents one of Moore's longest sustained comic arcs, one of sufficient length that it can contain within it a powerful reversal without suffering the contradictions that Moore finds so abhorrent (Khoury 86). Whereas sex and love begin as points in opposition, components of the red and green worlds, learning to eschew the desire for power allows Swamp Thing to defuse this dichotomy and live in harmony with the world. *Swamp Thing* provides a refreshing context to his other work, especially his recent work. Looking at a text like *Lost Girls* or even *The League of Extraordinary Gentlemen: Black Dossier*, it is easy to think that Moore is concerned with sex for its own sake. While Moore does have some important things to say about sex and sexuality, the importance of the subject is found in the way in which it can be used to address his central concern with power and freedom. Moore's belief is that "our most basic right" (64. 18) is to be able to live with the companion(s) of our choosing, free from the oppressions of those who seek power for its own sake as well as the exertion of unwelcome social influence that perverts our personal desires. The closing prayer of Cajun faith healer LaBostrie is for all of us: *"Laissez les bontemps rouler."*

Notes

1. Klock is one of the more generous critics. Most of those in my bibliography did little more than nod to the "Rite of Spring."
2. As we shall see, Moore's first act is to strip away Swamp Thing's humanity, turning him into a purely vegetative creature, and later in the series Moore transforms him into a vegetable god.
3. For example, the conflict between personal freedom and social power (*V for Vendetta*), whether a superhuman should use its powers to solve humanity's problems (*Watchmen*), and the relationship between sexuality and identity (*Lost Girls*).
4. This is a dichotomy that stands out visually in issues 22, 23, and 29.
5. Woodrue is a minor DC villain originally introduced in 1962 in *Atom* #1. He is an alien scientist who later transforms himself into a walking plant.
6. Matt Cable is Swamp Thing's longtime friend, who has been given the power to create matter with pure thought by a military experiment. Abby is his wife and the niece of evil sorcerer Antoine Arcane.
7. This is especially clear if you contrast it with the "Stravinsky" chapter of *Lost Girls*.
8. Consider his "natural" variations with local vegetation vividly displayed in issues 47 and 48, as well as his ability to consciously assume different sizes and shapes displayed in issue 53.
9. The "crisis" referred to in the upcoming sentences is *Swamp Thing*'s contribution to the DC Universe–wide "Crisis on Infinite Earths." After his obligatory participation in the overall storyline, Moore transforms this plot into a confrontation with a primordial "original darkness" that rises from beyond the watery bounds of Hell, rather than the DC–created supervillain, the Anti-Monitor.

3. When "One Bad Day" Becomes One *Dark Knight*
Love, Madness, and Obsession in the Adaptation of The Killing Joke *into Christopher Nolan's* The Dark Knight

JOSEPH MICHAEL SOMMERS

At the heart of the Christopher Nolan's motion picture epic, *The Dark Knight*, lies two particular comic book narratives: Jeph Loeb's *The Long Halloween* and Alan Moore's *The Killing Joke*. Nolan's screenwriting partner, David Goyer, specifically chose the former as it explores and expands the back catalogue of Harvey Dent's transformation into Two-Face, Dent being *TDK's* great locus of hope for Gotham and, eventually, the greater locus of tragedy in the film. Moore's 46-page one-shot, *TKJ*, however, aims for neither hope nor tragedy; it has loftier ambitions. It dares to try and pin down the intimacy of the relationship between the Joker and Batman by interrogating Bill Finger's 1951 origin story of "The Mystery of the Red Hood."[1] More specifically, through the Joker's torment and the reader's investigation of the torment of Commissioner Gordon, Moore examines the Joker's origins through traumatically-induced analepsis. Moore's almost invasive diegetic construction of the Joker's flashbacks[2] in the *TKJ* is actually quite important to understanding Nolan's considerably more linear construction of the arrow of time in *TDK*. In the *TKJ*, Bruce Wayne openly wonders how after "all these years.... I don't know who he is any more than he knows [me]. How can two people hate so much without knowing each other?" (11). The Joker knows. At least, until he knows it in another fashion. In fact, in *TDK*, Nolan's Joker does the somewhat unthinkable (for him): he outright answers Batman's question. Nolan's Joker tells the Batman that he neither hates him nor wishes to kill him. He states: "I don't want to kill you. What would I do without you?... You complete me."

Putting aside the Joker's affection for *Jerry Maguire* momentarily, bear in mind that the Bat just tried to fracture the Joker's skull, break his hand and possibly his back during an interrogation designed to ascertain the whereabouts of Bruce Wayne's love interest, Rachel Dawes, and the man who he deems to be his successor, Dent. The interrogation fails: two of the Batman/Wayne's closest allies, two people in his incredibly rarified circle of five comrades in the Nolan-verse,[3] die while the clown dances with the Bat high above the city in what amount to little more than a game or "social experiment" to them (Nolan, *TDK*). For a man like Wayne who is haunted by the meaningless slaughter of his parents as a boy, the loss of any further loved ones should have been enough to push him over the edge, or at least drop the Joker over it, and he has the opportunity to let the Joker fall to his death from the top of the Prewitt Building at the movie's climax. His established ethics in the Nolan-verse certainly would not have prevented it. He had a far less personal stake when he let Ra's al Ghul take a bullet train into the afterlife in *Batman Begins*. But, here, Batman saves the Joker. It doesn't escape the Joker's notice:

> You. You just couldn't let me go, could you? This is what happens when an unstoppable force meets an immovable object. You truly are incorruptible, aren't you? You won't kill me out of some misplaced sense of self-righteousness ... and I won't kill you because you're just too much fun. I think you and I are destined to do this forever [Nolan, *TDK*].

The Joker is not being glib. Nolan does not construct him as such. Neither did Moore. Douglas Wolk once noted that "virtually every comic Moore has ever written is inspired by some kind of pop-culture source of the past that he can elaborate and improve on [...] He's got a particular knack for probing those [pre-established characters] for their soft spots, then squeezing firmly" (230–1). It appears that Nolan agrees with Wolk as, out of all the backstories for the construction of their relationship, he chose the one that articulates that the Batman and the Joker do not hate each other near as much as they actually love,[4] or obsesses over, each other as only two sides of the same coin (shown through the interlocution of the Harvey Dent narrative) might.

In this essay, I will explore the interpolation of Alan Moore's *TKJ* narrative into *TDK* in an effort to explore the mutual obsession the Joker and the Batman have with each other. *TKJ* appeals to Nolan's sense of dualism[5] and mirroring[6] (Sarchett 78), creating the Joker and the Batman as opposing sides of the same two-headed coin, one dark and the other darker, cut from the same narrative of the loss of family. Like the Batman and unbeknownst to each other, Moore constructs the Joker as the cumulative effects of "one bad day" (Moore, *TKJ* 38). He challenges the reader's construction of both characters by showing that, apart, they are both fractured, two separate heads of one Janused, fear-inducing lunatic: one striving for the chaos brought about by the fear of the clown and the other driving to enact order through the fear of the Bat. The characters become interdependent: one cannot exist without each other, and both writers plumb the idea that this particular hero and villain need each other to be whole. Nolan, using Moore as inspiration, makes his Batman incapable of rescinding the mantle even if it causes him to lose those he loves ... in lieu of finding intimacy, in a volatile companionship, with someone just like him. Interestingly, as Nolan's Joker observes that the Batman is incorruptible, he makes a tacit claim that the narrative of the entire movie has been built around him trying to convince the Batman that they are one of a kind. Moore's Joker agrees, however, his Batman *also* agrees and wants to "rehabilitate" the Joker so that he can be just like him (44).

The Tain of a Mirror: Adaptation? Reinvention? How About Transmedia Dialogue?

To even begin to explore the idea of the adaptation or interpolation of an Alan Moore text as something of an dialogue between writers on the subject of "Batman" is somewhat challenging. Moore has a long entrenched history resisting the filmic adaptation of his work. Rex Krueger and Katherine Shaeffer, perhaps, sum it up best when they state that

> throughout his career, Alan Moore has shown both a penchant and a skill for reweaving the elements of earlier texts into new works and new worlds of his own. In doing so, Moore has walked a dangerous line. To adapt a text is, paradoxically, to both embrace and to let go of that text. Much like analysis, adaptation is a simultaneously creative and destructive act, which produces new material from the often-fragmented pieces of a source.

True enough. However, though Moore frequently borrows and rearticulates most anything he touches (from *Swamp Thing* to *Superman* to the Whitechapel murderer, to the childhood fairy tales heroines of *Lost Girls* et al.), he is far more reticent to allow others to rework his creations. For example, when he was once approached by director Terry Gilliam on how to adapt, arguably, his magnum opus, *Watchmen,* Moore responded:

> I had to tell him that, frankly, I didn't think it was filmable. I didn't design it to show off the similarities between cinema and comics, which *are* there, but, in my opinion are fairly unremarkable. It was designed to show off the things that comics could do that cinema and literature couldn't [qtd. in Wegner].

The "Batman narrative," however, is but one construction of an ongoing conversation between many different writers who have picked up the Kane and Finger characters; thus, while Moore may be one of the first to truly interrogate the relationship between Batman and the Joker, he does not hold a proprietary interest in them. That does not necessarily mean that Moore doesn't have an opinion on *TKJ* or its cultural impact. He states: "Its [sic] talking about Batman and the Joker, and says that yes, psychologically Batman and the Joker are mirror images of each other" (Stone).

Seeing the Bat and the Clown as mirror images of each other, at first glance, seems to be a bit of a spurious construction. Perhaps the Joker is but the collection of shards from a fractured mirror recomposed as a mosaic. However, comparing the Batman, in his tireless construction after construction after reconstruction as a figure built as an uncompromising crime fighter, to the Joker as mirror images of each other seems a stretch. Or is it? William Uriccho claims that "sometimes crime" in the Batman narrative "serves as the vocabulary of [...] equally obsessed counterparts" (120). Uriccho, among many others, views the Batman as a construction on Wayne's part of a misplaced childhood trauma. (124–25). He writes:

> Batman continuously avenges his parents murder by apprehending those perpetrators who blight Gotham's landscape, in the process metaphorically reenacting the primal scene. Terms like obsession, revenge and trauma are central to the character's brand of justice [...] those episodes that pit the Batman against costumed supervillains such as the Joker [are] distinguished by the fact that all of the characters mirror the Batman [124–25].

Other critics focus on the Joker as Batman's counterpart less on the side of trauma but more on the side of the fear of loss[7]: "From the start, the Batman mythos has been about the pressing of gothic fear into the service of heroic Justice" (Fisher). Others, such as Steve Brie, do not necessarily see any difference between the two: "The Batman persona developed as the result of a traumatic childhood experience [...] The boy, possibly suffering from Post-Traumatic Stress Disorder (PTSD), becomes the plaything of memory persistently re-experiencing the murders [of his parents]" (204). Brie argues that "memory, as the Joker suggests [...] can be a cruel process" (204) that can elide the distance, as Moore writes in *TKJ*, from "a carnival of delights with poignant childhood aromas [to] somewhere you don't want to go" (21). It is, as Brie suggests, Moore's genius to model the Joker's origin in *TKJ* after a similar loss and PTSD, "a personal tragedy," he calls it, while "inextricably intertwin[ing]" it with Batman's history (206).

Wolk seems to concur with this idea of a duality in the character's origin stories, seeing *TKJ* setting up the Joker as having "Job-like suffering" that "made him want to become a cruelly laughing force of random suffering inflicted on others," while the Batman suffers from a similar "madness [...] one the madness of assuming you can turn the chaos of urban life into order, one the madness of human frailty and violence without meaning" (98). To this argument, I would concur with the caveat that the actually seen, and not conjectured, exploration of the characters' inter-reliance upon each other begins with Moore and concludes decades later with Nolan as he constructs a conversation between his movie and the Moore source text. Nolan's acute realism co-mingles with Moore's devout fantasy and, as has been suggested, "the Joker serves as [a] double, a psychotic funhouse mirror image of the somber and obsessed hero [...] the eerie whiteness of the Joker's face signals its opposite; it's the 'dark' version of Batman's removable disguise" (Bukatman 206). When read together, Nolan and Moore both construct the two characters as "survivors" who are "both bizarre and psychologically over-determined" (Brody). Nolan begins this project in *Batman Begins* where he "digs much more deeply into the issues of childhood trauma" (Hassler-Forrest 37), but Moore settled the idea into the Joker's back story in *TKJ* prior to its inclusion into the Nolan films.

Riddle Me This: What Came First? The Bat or the Clown?

Before going too much further, the question really ought to be asked: What exactly is the Joker? J. M. Tyree has openly pondered what motivates his antics in *TDK* (32). Likewise, Todd McGowan has rightly claimed that "the Joker is the ethical center of *The Dark Knight*" for the somewhat spurious reason that the Joker challenges the "hegemony" of the calculated schemers of Gotham. And many others have considered what the Joker means to Batman and vice versa, but, I want to pose a simple question of ontology: What *is* the Joker? It is the question that the *TKJ* tries to explore. The late Heath Ledger stated that "*The Killing Joke* was the [comic] that was handed to me. [...] I guess that book explains a little bit of where he's from but not too much. From what I've gathered, there isn't a lot of information about the Joker and it's left that way [in *TDK*]" (Epstein). Nolan went a bit further to state that he did not want to do an origin story for the Joker in this film: "The Joker we meet in *The Dark Knight* is fully formed [...] He bursts in just as he [originally] did in the comics" (Horowitz). So, when the movie-goer meets the Joker five minutes into *TDK*, he is fully-formed, but a fully-formed what? A clown? Hardly. We learn from the opening heist that he wears "war-paint [...] to scare people," (Nolan), but he hardly seems that interested in being funny in anything less than the darkest sense and only to himself. Perhaps he is a knave or a jester, akin to the playing cards he often leaves behind as his calling-card. Again, possibly, but not likely: classically, knaves and jesters are servants, unprincipled, undisciplined, and dishonest. The Joker serves no one. The Joker's jokes only make him laugh, and usually much to his own chagrin. But examining the idea of the playing card grants access to greater insight: The Joker is a metonymy.[8]

Karin Kukkonen explains it best when she says that comic characters like the Joker are both "the part and the whole" of the semiotic meaning, the "tressage," or the "tied-up meaning[ful] tresses of the comic" character (91–92). In this particular case, the Joker literally is a tangled mess of greasy, unwashed, and poorly-dyed hair; he is a mass of overlapping metaphors: the clown, the dual-meaning of the comic as artifact and comedian, the jester or fool, the bad joke that no one laughs at, the man who is "faced with the inescapable fact that human existence is mad, random and pointless," yet seems to be the only one to notice, etc. (Moore 33). Moore may write it best when his Joker tells Bats, "When I saw what a black awful joke the world was, I went crazy as a coot [...] It's all a joke! Everything anybody ever valued or struggled for ... it's all a monstrous, demented gag!" (39). There's nothing funny or even ironic in his statement. Brian Bolland's illustration of him shows his characteristically upturned smile painfully bent into a frown. There's only pain, regret, sadness, and, possibly, introspection. Jamie Hughes has posited that superheroes and supervillains of this sort are simply creations "caught up in their own ideology" (548). Looking at the Joker in *TKJ*, I tend to disagree. What the Joker describes here is not an ideological "apparatus" (547); it is an identification. It is an identification built out of the fractures of a man into a metonymical persona of what the fractures mean to him: Life is a joke, a sick, black joke and to try and order it with rules, schemes, plans, and order is "repulsive" (33). Nolan's Joker tells us that "the only sensible way to live in this world is without rules," as Moore writes that "any other response would be crazy" (33). The dialogue between the book and the movie allows for the fragments of the mirror of identity to be pulled together into some semblance of comprehension.

We find this metonymy in *TDK* constructed into the Joker's face paint and scars. The Chelsea Smile cut through his face is the only catalyst to his backstory and the grease paint he wears both exacerbates the garishness of his wounds and focuses the gaze of his victims upon them so he can tell his story. It may appear that Nolan's Joker uses the face paint to mask the scars much like Batman hides his identity behind a cowl seemingly to protect his identity and loved ones. However, the Joker has no history[9] or secret identity

(McGowan). At least, he doesn't have a consistent one. He has become a walking identification of the bad joke he perceives the world as, the hypocrisy of those who would try to order the chaos and the mirror of the corruption he perceives around him. And yet, that doesn't mean he does not want people to ask him what's wrong, so Nolan gave him a physical manifestation of the psychological trauma that Moore provides.

Nolan's Joker gives us two possible origins for the smile permanently etched into his face. In the first, he tells a soon-to-be-filleted Gambol:

> My father was a drinker and a fiend. One night, he goes off crazier than usual. Mommy gets the kitchen knife to defend herself. He doesn't like that. Not. One. Bit. So, me watching, he takes the knife to her, laughing while he does it. He turns to me, and he says "Why so serious?" He comes at me with the knife — "Why so serious?" He sticks the blade in my mouth — "Let's put a smile on that face" and...

That's the end of Gambol. At Dent's fundraiser, Rachel gets a slightly different version:

> You look nervous. Is it the scars? [...] I had a wife, beautiful, like you. Who tells me I worry too much. Who tells me I oughta to smile more. Who gambles, and gets in deep with the sharks. One day they carve her face, and we've got no money for surgeries. She can't take it. I just want to see her smile again. I just want her to know I don't care about the scars. So I stick a razor in my mouth and do this to myself. And you know what? She can't stand the sight of me. She leaves! See, now I see the funny side. Now I'm always smiling.

The validity of either origin is completely inconsequential to *TDK*. Nolan constructs his clown in order to allow the comic book Joker, skin impossibly-bleached white by the vats he fell into at the Ace Chemical Processing Facility,[10] realization in a world filled with real-life mobsters and real-life monsters who possess no super-abilities but are the grotesque hyperbolic constructs of things that terrify people who don't exist in comic books. The Joker, here, is a metonymy of the fear of the irrational, the chaotic, the disorder that threatens one with madness or worse.

When One Bad Day Becomes.... Interlocuting Narratives

For Nolan (and Moore), fear and madness come from the loss of things irreplaceable, in this case, loved ones such as family, and the trauma of that loss becomes the metonymic construction of our protagonist and antagonist. The films are actually built on and out of the concept of fear. In *BB*, Ducard cum Ra's al Ghul asks Wayne during his training what he fears. Nolan takes this opportunity to trigger a flashback unraveling the years of trauma that is losing one's parents that is beset upon young Bruce Wayne. Ducard later teaches him that "theatricality and deception are powerful agents" and that Wayne must "become more than just a man in the mind of [his] opponent." Upon returning to Gotham, the Batman becomes a germ in Wayne's mind as a lone winged-rodent flutters up trapped against the crown molding of Wayne Manor. As Wayne crafts the outfit that would become the outward visage of Batman, he tells Alfred that "as a symbol I can be incorruptible. I can be everlasting — something elemental, something terrifying"; Wayne chooses the Bat, the thing that scared him as a boy, the memory that Nolan has precede the death of his parents in *BB*, to become his symbol "to turn fear against those who prey on the fearful." Bruce Wayne becomes fear through the adoption of a symbol.[11] As for the Joker, however, Nolan intentionally veils the mirroring between the Joker and Batman in *TDK* that Moore constructs in *TKJ* illustrating the unique parallelism that binds them together, but he does, however, gives the Joker his scars.

The scars operate as a visible metonymy of veiled analepsis Nolan withholds from the audience of *TDK*: however, they are placeholders for Moore's story. In it, the Joker tells an owner of a dilapidated carnival he wishes to purchase that "money isn't really a problem [...] these days," the insinuation being that it will not be a problem as Joker will be obtaining that carnival by dispatching the owner as opposed to paying for it. Yet, just as Ra's Al Ghul triggered Wayne's flashbacks, the carnival owner's request for payment triggers the Joker's. Interestingly, for a man who claims that he sometimes remembers his past one way and sometimes another, he remembers this flashback in crisp black and white.[12] In these flashbacks, we find the expanded narrative of Nolan's Joker's collapsed metonym: in this interpretation, we don't have to rectify the fact that the Joker had a father who was a drinker and was a fiend because, in Moore's Joker's previous life *HE* was the father (7) who couldn't hold his drink at the lunch hour (15) while *HE* was getting in deep with the mobster sharks (15) on a calculated gamble of helping them try to rob a playing card company next to the chemical plant where he once worked. This Joker did have a beautiful wife (7–8) who, in his own interpretation of the memories of his origin, he was fiendish to: he snaps at her simple rejoinder of a concerned "Oh" upon her wondering whether he had found any work to support their growing family (7). He did not. In the Joker's own mind, he is a failure as a comedian and as a provider for his family, and, even when his wife consoles him, Bolland begins to literally draw the darkness and the madness growing inside him in the visuals of the panel before the flashback returns to the main narrative. Bolland shows him losing his sanity first in the eyes (which are the

Joker's) as reflected in a kitchen cupboard and then, later, the Joker's trademark smile is actually impossibly cut into his wife's mouth as "she" reminds him that "you know how to make me laugh" (Moore 7).

Moore actually attributes the death of the Joker's wife, at least in his own memory, to electrocution from a faulty bottle warmer (22), but the manner in which he discovers the tragedy is accomplished with a callous brevity by the police and makes absolutely no difference to the mobsters he is lunching with who have plans for him (23). The robbery will go off as planned, and, as you might expect given the nature of the pre–Joker's misfortune, it fails miserably. However, Moore's final construction of the scene collapses time, memory, loss, and obsession into one brilliant miscalculation: already not invested in the job,[13] especially considering the mobsters who forced him into it have already been killed by security, the pre–Joker's final memory of his former life is of the Batman trying to capture him at the chemical facility (31). Batman is actually trying to stop him from being killed by security, but the Pre-Joker whose vision is obscured under the Red Hood and is terrified at being caught or killed by mobsters and cops and has been traumatized by the loss of his family, would rather jump to his own death than endure any further "punish[-ment]" (31). Anyone who has ever read a Batman comic knows what happens next. Whoever jumped into the chemicals dissolved in them, and the man who Alan Moore has catching his reflection in a rain puddle after rising from the muck, now no longer remembered in black and white but constructed fully-formed and in full-color, conflating his memories of the past with what's going on in the present timeline, is the Joker as we know him from the first time we have ever met him in *Batman* #1. Moore's visual trigger in the master narrative for this last set of flashbacks happens to be a clipping from Gordon's scrapbook showing the Bat taking the newly formed Joker into custody from the Ace Chemical Job and the Joker staring at himself in a puddle of rainwater while he waits for Batman to come and get him (12, 28). In *BB*, Ra's tells Wayne that he knows the "rage that drives you — that impossible anger strangling the grief until the memory of your loved ones is poison in your veins" (Nolan). While Nolan uses that construction for Wayne in *BB*, anyone looking at the famously-illustrated panel of the Joker's birth surrounded amidst a visual field of "HAHAHA"s realizes that the same holds true for the Joker as well (32).

...Becomes One Dark (K)night: Conclusions

Thus, as much as Batman is the focus of Nolan's first movie, interpolated with its source material, *The Dark Knight* is, consequentially, the Joker's film:

a dark fun-house mirror of occluded details, on-screen, but similar character trajectories hell-bent towards each other. Interestingly, whereas the Joker in *TDK*, believes (rightly) that he is kindred to the Bat, in *TKJ:* he tells Batman, "All it takes is one bad day to reduce the sanest man alive to lunacy [...] you had a bad day once, am I right? I know I am [...] Why else would you dress like a flying rat?" (39). The truth hurts. In the climax of *TKJ*, Batman actually admits that the Joker is right. Bats has come to him because he wants to "help" him. He tells the Joker, "I could rehabilitate you. You needn't be out there on the edge any more. You needn't be alone" (44). The Joker considers it before politely declining and telling Batman the eponymous killing joke.[14] Afterwards, they actually share a laugh and embrace each other as if they were old friends (45–6). Moore constructs his Batman on the premise that Batman occasionally visits the Joker in Arkham after spending long hours thinking about him and begs the Joker's complicity in trying to let him help order and tame his mind and body (4). Just like Bruce Wayne had to in order to overcome the madness of his loss. Even more interestingly, Nolan inverts that idea; his Joker tells Batman: "Don't talk like one of them [meaning the police]; you're not, even if you'd like to be. [...] You're just a freak. Like me." The Joker goes on to tell Batman that he "has all these rules," and he thinks they'll save him. "The only sensible way to live in this world," the Joker says, "is without rules." As Moore's Batman tried to rehabilitate the Joker, Nolan's Joker tries to rehabilitate Batman. Tyree posits about them, "The hero and the villain require each other completely, so that one cannot exist without the other, and the cycle of escalating acts of good and evil is a perpetual motion machine set to continue for all eternity" (28). Acts of good and evil oversimplify the tenuous ideological motivations and differences between the Joker and the Batman, "vigilantes," as one critic has called them, separated only by official endorsement, "rules," and "boundaries" (Dubose 918).

Towards the end of the *TDK's* second act, the Joker cruelly asks Commissioner Gordon: "Does it depress you, Commissioner ... to know how alone you are?" The Joker pushes this line of questioning because he is confident that he is not alone, and he is not; he has a sparring partner. A *better* half. Someone who completes him entirely and fills the void his family once held. One critic of the films has gone so far as to state that "Nolan's revisiting of Batman is not a re-invention but a reclaiming of the myth, a grand syncresis that draws upon the whole history of the character" (Fisher). While that might be somewhat of a stretch, Nolan and Moore certainly seem to operate in dialogue with each other, trapping the Batman and the Joker in a vicious cycle of antagonism as each other's nemesis. Moore and Nolan both seem to feel that they wouldn't have it any other way. Gotham City is their playground, or perhaps, better, the carnival for the Batman and the Joker to "exist outside the calculating morality that predominates among the police, the law-abiding citizens, and the criminal underworld" where they try to save or destroy the city ... or destroy the city by trying to save the city as part and parcel to the madness that is their obsession with each other (McGowan).

Notes

1. Detective Comics #168.
2. It's hard to call them memories since the Joker himself can't vouch for their authenticity. (Even if the story was written specifically with the 1951 Finger narrative in mind.) Moore himself said of *TKJ* as an origin piece:
> The fact that you can use them to tell allegorical stories or whatever, that doesn't mean you should. "Batman: The Killing Joke," which still sells, and I believe [...] it has been accepted that it was the main influence on the first Batman film [Stone].

The "first Batman film" referenced here is actually the Tim Burton *Batman* from 1989.

3. The others being Commissioner Gordon, Alfred Pennyworth, and Lucius Fox.
4. I would be remiss if I were not to mention that I am not the first person to consider that Batman and the Joker have a history of homosocial/ sexual affection towards each other. Jessica Kowalik mentions that Frank Miller, author of *The Dark Knight Returns*, "did manage to make the real Joker gay," in spite of DC Comics' reservations towards homosexuality in the mid–1980s (390). Likewise, she indicates that, if it were possible or interesting, Miller "would have found a way" to make Batman gay (390).
5. Barry Sarchett actually couches this idea in the work of Barry Barnes and David Bloor's "dualism" in his essay "The Joke(r) Is on Us: The End of Popular Cultural Studies" (78). In it, Sarchett uses Barnes and Bloor's deconstruction of axiological-based rationalism to undermine basic concepts such as "truth" (79). These remarks seem to confirm Zimmer's notion's that Nolan's Joker is the only character in *TDK* the audience can trust as he is the only character unafraid of the truth (Bentley).
6. See note 2. Likewise, even Nolan's metaview of the Joker extends to his score for *TDK*. Hans Zimmer, who scored both films with Newton Howard, indicated that when he was trying to "represent" the Joker sonically, he constructed a particular "two-note signature" that might "symbolize the Joker's penchant for anarchy" (White). Of course, in order to allow the juxtaposition, or rather to illustrate the synthesis and antithesis, between anarchy and order, you cannot simply rely upon a single note. Zimmer said:
> I really wanted to do the whole thing just with one note. I had this idea that rather than what a note is in the context of the notes surrounding it, what could I do emotionally through a performance within one note? How much can I stretch the meaning of a single note and get it down to such minimalism. I failed slightly. I had to use two notes in the end.... You know, the actual Dark Knight theme, Batman's call, is two notes and the Joker has the other two notes. You put them together and it makes a mess [Bentley].

The result of which illustrates the idea that both Batman/ Wayne and Joker/ Pre-Joker occupy dual positions within each's singular identity while *simultaneously* being two halves of one single identity.

7. It is no coincidence that the Scarecrow is a main villain in *Batman Begins* given his connections to fear-inducing toxins and experiences.
8. For the sake of argument, others have also viewed the Joker as both a "synecdoche [...] a pastiche of prefabricated styles and quotations in true post-fashion" (Sarchett 76) and as having a complete lack of a "symbolic identity" (McGowan). To the first, I would

only argue semantics and to the second I would remind the reader that, unlike the comic book Joker, Nolan's clown wears a mask of grease paint that is just as easily removed as the Bat's cowl.

9. Possibly, as Moore's Joker declares: "If I'm going to have a past, I prefer it to be multiple choice!" (39).

10. Conspicuously located next to a playing card company (Moore 15).

11. It might be prudent to introduce James Reynolds' concept of the ideologem at this point. Reynolds claims that this "mechanism," a "textual and ideological unit that functions with a social, ideological, and *discursive formation*" (126), mitigates the fidelity/ adaptation crisis in comics by virtue of looking at "comic-to-film adaptation as it can bridge the gap between real and fictional frameworks, a facilitated transference between the media" (127). It is a fine notion that allows for the "updating or repositioning a text" in order to bring it up-to-date with the contemporaneous moment of the reader; however, realistically, it is not so much different than M. M. Bakhtin's notion of the chronotope (see Bukataman) or several other cultural studies theories regarding adaptation theory.

12. Save the spot coloring of red that Bolland tells us grows as he approaches the infamous day where he became the Red Hood and the Joker began.

13. The pre–Joker was leading the heist as one of the many men to supposedly don the Red Hood to give his burgeoning family "a proper life" (Moore 16). When his family is destroyed, he has no reason to continue, but, as the mobsters tell him:

Mobster #1: What's happening tonight, it's no little thing. Nobody backing out now remains healthy. No exceptions. [...]
Pre-Joker: B-But...
Mobster #2: No buts, man. Tomorrow, you bury your old lady in luxury. Tonight, you're with us. Get the picture? [23]

14. In the interests of completionism: "See, there were these two guys in a lunatic asylum ... and one night, one night they decide they don't like living in an asylum any more. They decide they're going to escape! So, like, they get up onto the roof, and there, just across this narrow gap, they see the rooftops of the town, stretching away in the moon light ... stretching away to freedom. Now, the first guy, he jumps right across with no problem. But his friend, his friend didn't dare make the leap. Y'see ... Y'see, he's afraid of falling. So then, the first guy has an idea.... He says "Hey! I have my flashlight with me! I'll shine it across the gap between the buildings. You can walk along the beam and join me!" B-but the second guy just shakes his head. He suh-says.... He says "Wh-what do you think I am? Crazy? You'd turn it off when I was half way across!" (Moore 45).

4. "Don't laugh, Daddy, we're in love"
Mockery, Fulfillment, and Subversion of Popular Romance Conventions in The Ballad of Halo Jones

KATE FLYNN

Alan Moore's *The Ballad of Halo Jones* was first published between 1984 and 1986 as a strip in the British comic anthology *2000 AD*.[1] Then, as now, futuristic dystopias were *2000 AD*'s stock in trade; Moore's tale of a fiftieth century, crime-ridden ghetto thus sat comfortably alongside better-known stable mates such as *Judge Dredd*. Yet *The Ballad* was, in another regard, highly distinctive. Moore suggests that among *2000 AD*'s array of ultra-violent male protagonists, Halo Jones stands out as "an ordinary woman such as you might find standing in front of you while queuing for the check-out at Tesco's" (Moore and Gibson 59). His focus on Halo as everywoman is entwined with a satiric strategy that has received, as yet, no critical attention. Halo's preoccupation with everyday hardship — including poverty, violent crime, and combat — is repeatedly contrasted with the clichés of popular romance. In particular, *The Ballad*'s characters frequently discuss current storylines in holo-soaps, a futuristic form of melodrama based on women's emotional lives.

By popular romance, I mean mass-produced love stories. My use of the term is informed by the work of Tania Modleski, who includes within the romance field soap opera melodramas, which she defines as open-ended moral fantasies concerned with the primacy of family (85); gothic fiction; and Harlequin publications. She argues that popular romance depicts the transformation of masculine motives — either from murderous aggressor to tender lover, or vice versa — as part of an ideology that denies "the reality of male hostility towards women" (104). Typically, the heroine follows a developmental arc from "loneliness and penury to romance and riches" (40), while the hero, whom the heroine seeks to understand, vacillates between the roles of "brute" and "puppy dog" (71).[2] Modleski refers to this latter trope as the "splitting of the male" (71). I contend that Moore invokes such tropes in *The Ballad of Halo Jones*, in problematic ways, for the purposes of social and political satire.

Halo's love life does not assume a central role in the plot.[3] But a bald synopsis obscures the sheer number of references Moore makes to mass culture in general, and popular romance in particular: such references are made at the margins of the text, in fragments of dialogue and fleeting visual allusions. Taking each of Halo's romantic admirers in turn, I will examine how Halo is positioned as "ordinary"[4] through their departures from the holo-soap ideal, in terms of their gender, sexual orientation, class, and race. My analysis will demonstrate that holo-soap content disrupts the main narrative in the service of two strategic functions. The first function is to provide gallows humor, and the second is to map the socio-political dangers of popular romance narratives. Movement between these functions produces numerous internal contradictions. Moore presents holo-soaps as propaganda: they distract viewers from structural inequalities and simultaneously marginalize a range of subject positions. But the humor Moore deploys to make his point also reifies female characters' positions as sexual gatekeepers, and colludes in problematic constructions of gender, race, and sexuality.

Toby and the Glyph: Embodying the "Regular Boyfriend"

From the earliest pages of *The Ballad*, holo-soaps are under discussion. Rodice is the first to introduce the topic. She tries to dissuade Brinna from going outdoors by commenting, "I thought you wanted to watch *Existential Romance* for your research" (Moore 376, 16).[5] Immediately, romance viewing is positioned as a safe alternative to what Rodice perceives as the danger of leaving their flat. The warning is misplaced, indeed functions as an ironic augury, because Toby, the robotic guard dog, will murder Brinna while she stays at home watching holo-soaps (382, 11–12). Brinna's violent death half way through the first book acts as a catalyst for Halo's efforts to escape the Hoop. In Book Two, Halo discovers that Toby murdered Brinna; he claims to have been motivated by "love" for Halo and the knowledge that she would inherit him in the event of Brinna's death (412, 4). References to holo-soaps leaven the darkness of Toby's actions but do so as a complicitous critique of popular romance tropes. In this second respect, *The Ballad* may form part of a parodic tradition in *2000 AD*, previously described by James How as postmodern ambivalence toward Hollywood mainstream film (236).

It is striking that *The Ballad*'s first allusion to romance focuses on Brinna's "research" (376, 16) because later episodes typically depict romance viewing as an unthinking, and possibly dangerous, pleasure. Brinna's research topic indicates she is a very voguish academic. In 1984, soaps, romance novels, and melodrama were relatively new areas of scholarly interest, attracting attention under the rubric of women's genres from critics such as Modleski and Jane Feuer. By introducing *Existential Romance* as, in the first instance, a subject for academic enquiry, Moore may be suggesting holo-soaps are culturally significant to the world established in the strip. He may, equally, be poking mild fun at the academic interest taken in what *The Ballad* constructs as cultural ephemera.

At Brinna's murder scene (382, 11), the poking becomes more savage. Rodice and Halo arrive home to find the programme she was watching still playing on a loop. Three panels show a group of doll-sized holograms enacting a family scene; one of the figures, holding out her hands imploringly, repeats a fragment of dialogue five times: "Don't laugh, Daddy ... we're in love!" The line's banality seems greater with each repetition and provides a bathetic counterpoint to the horror of discovering Brinna's dismembered body. Although Toby is not yet revealed to be the killer, his involvement is foreshadowed in the bottom left of the page, where Rodice is shown crouching among Brinna's notes. Her coat forms a shape remarkably similar to Toby's silhouette. The suggestion that Toby is an observer despite his alleged absence is continued on the second page, for the establishing scene that forms the top panel is drawn from his eye level. The room is shown to be in disarray, with no explicit gore. Rodice refers to blood (382, 12) but it is not visible in black and white. Rather, an impression of violence is created by the page layout; the use of overlaying panels with centimeter-thick black gutters is suggestive of forensic photographs. Across the centre of the page, four square panels hone in on significant details through an aspect-to-aspect sequence. The focal points include Brinna's shoe, and a close up of her naked foot. As feet are fetishized by men in the Hoop (379, 11), these images suggest a sexual attack.

The gap between the suggestion of sexual violence and the sentimentality of the looped holo-soap dialogue is closed several episodes later, when Halo discovers that Toby is the murderer (411, 7). Just as her friend, Toy Molto, listens to soaps using an audio implant, Halo is shown listening to the unfolding drama of Toby's "memory cassettes" (411, 5–7), which include a recording of Brinna's death cries. Four panels track Halo's realization as she is listening to Brinna's murder. The use of moment-to-moment transitions give the impression of freeze framing, creating a visual link between Halo and the static, imploring hologram at Brinna's murder scene. When Toby returns and sees her response, he cries out: "For love, girly ... I did it all for love!" (411, 7). His claim is, of course, drawn from the same register as the looped instruction "Don't laugh, Daddy, we're in love" — the hyperbolic clichés of melodrama.

This is positioned as ridiculous — and thus as gallows humor — because he is a mechanical dog. A mechanical dog bearing, no less, a name associated in Britain with cute pooches and middle class feyness, rather than brutal murder. He does not manifest Donna Haraway's liberatory cyborg (and certainly not her fleshly dog). Instead, he looks too "animal" to effect the disguise popular romance demands. His body, which is both bestial and a killing machine, belies the domestication of his puppyish name by concretizing metaphors for male violence — and this contrast is the site of intended humor. Let us return, for a moment, to Modleski, and her interest in "splitting the male" (71). Elsewhere in *The Ballad*, this split is portrayed with comparatively little irony, because the convention is not taken to its extremes. Note that Luiz Cannibal has physical characteristics, such as tusks, that allude to animality without becoming a source of humor. Toby's motives comply with, indeed amply fulfill, the convention of transforming murderous brutes into tender lovers; yet the convention is mocked through his extreme embodiment. Luiz's tusks might allude to animality, but Toby *is* an animal, and he cannot disguise it.

Toby is shown to dismiss the importance of his murderous tendencies, and instead — correctly — identifies his body as the barrier to his relationship with Halo. "We can go to Kapek's World and fit me with a new humanoid body," he suggests; "I'd be just like a regular boyfriend" (Moore 412, 4). Despite Halo's fear of Toby, her romantic choices also imply his personal qualities are not the problem. Rodice refers, jokingly, to Toby's personality type as "mysterioso" (482, 8). Mystery is the quality that Halo erroneously romanticizes in Mix Ninegold, whom she compares favorably to a holo-soap idol: "He looks quite similar to the way Rulph Apollo looked in *Ciao, Aldebaran*.... He doesn't say much, but he's probably incredibly deep" (406, 4). In a more overt comparison, Halo's only consummated relationship is with Luiz Cannibal, a man she not only fears but who is rumored to be a murderer and a "psychopath" (412, 3). Toby's claims are thus consistent with the behavior of other men in *The Ballad*; he is different from them in body, not in brutality, and it is the body, not his behavior, which contests his status as a "regular boyfriend." This interpretation is supported by the circumstances of his death. Toby tries to murder Halo, but is halted by the Glyph, a ship passenger who has been rendered invisible through a succession of surgical modifications (408, 4). The Glyph precipitates an explosion that kills both of them. The self-sacrifice is significant because the Glyph's story, too, is concerned with embodiment. Specifically, the Glyph's story is concerned with the body as a site of gender role conformity.

A three-panel flashback reveals the Glyph embarking on a "body remould" in search of gender congruence (408, 4). The first panel depicts the

Glyph as a girl. The next depicts the Glyph as a boy. The third depicts a doctor beckoning from beneath a "Before" and "After" poster. While the Boy Glyph and Girl Glyph are barely differentiated from each other in their morphology, the poster shows a broad shouldered, pot-bellied "Before," next to an hour-glassed "After." The remolded "After" image bears a clear resemblance to Halo. The Glyph's unhappiness points to this binary's inadequacy. After forty seven attempts at body remolding the Glyph feels no more at ease. "Eventually, I wasn't a boy or a girl," the Glyph concludes. "I wasn't anything. I couldn't even remember what I'd been originally. The doctors were equally confused. Also, my personality had been completely erased. That's why I'm so boring" (408, 5).

The Glyph's presentation contributes in intriguing ways to *The Ballad*'s subversion of popular romance. Not only do Toby and the Glyph die simultaneously, they assume opposing but related functions in undermining romance conventions. Toby's failure as "a regular boyfriend" might be posited as one of excessive visibility: as detailed above, his animality is embodied for all to see. Conversely, the Glyph is invisible; invisible culturally, and invisible physically. One revealing sequence shows the Glyph trying to catch Halo and Toy's attention while they watch holo-soaps. They ignore the Glyph to excitedly discuss who is "secretly seeing Zuza's husband's girlfriend" (408, 7) and to wonder what will happen in the next episode of *Hearts in Orbit* (408, 7). The ironic juxtaposition between Toy's interest in "human drama" (408, 7) and her inability to hear the Glyph's pleas constructs the holo-soap as, primarily, a dangerous distraction from human suffering. As the Glyph forms a silhouette in the background of the last panel, the holo-soap characters form a mirror image in the foreground, emphasizing popular romance's erasure of subjectivities that fall outside the gender binary. Moore resists a similar erasure by depicting the Glyph as Halo's rescuer; in fact, the Glyph's invisibility enables the rescue, suggesting that there are opportunities for resistance even within the most marginalized positions.

The Ballad is not, however, a wholly subversive text. The conflation of personality with gender role conformity, for example, is problematic. *Why* should "not being a boy or a girl" make the Glyph "so boring" (408, 5)? Additionally, the explosion raises troubling questions: why should the Glyph's only agency reside in an act that proves to be self-effacing? Finally, and most conflictingly for the text, Moore's use of mockery enacts similar exclusions to the popular romance he derides. By laughing at Toby's embodiment, we may in turn laugh at popular romance; but at least one of the genre's conventions is upheld. For if the body is the basis for eligibility as "a regular boyfriend" (412, 4), Halo's eligibility as a "regular" girlfriend is implicitly linked to the body, too. Specifically, her "regularity" rests in her compliance with the idealized "After" image once aspired to by the Glyph. Moore's pursuit of an "ordinary" heroine constructs "ordinariness" as compliance with narrowly defined bodily norms.

Toy Molto: "Looking completely ordinary"

When Halo begins work as a spaceliner hostess, she expresses discomfort with her new uniform: "Showing my feet and everything. I mean, on the Hoop, if a woman did that, I mean ... well, we just didn't do it" (Moore 406, 4). Halo's comment is positioned as amusing, because her cleavage, thighs, and skin-tight leotard are at the forefront of the panel, while her feet are out of the frame. Her cabin mate, Toy, is dismissive: "Don't be stupid. You look completely ordinary" (406, 4). What does "ordinariness" entail? It has already been established that the body's compliance with gendered norms is part of Halo's "regularity," as well as a requirement of the popular romance she consumes. I intend to show that because *The Ballad* adheres to related norms by positioning women as the gatekeepers to heterosexual sex, "ordinariness" is also problematically situated as heteronormative.

During Toby's attempt to kill Halo, two parallel panels present close-ups of their eyes (412, 4). While Toby's pupils reflect an image of Halo's face, there is no comparable reflection in hers. The illustration neatly encapsulates that in Halo's society, women are for men to look at, and the direction of that gaze is emphatically one way. Disturbingly, to make sense of these pictures, the reader must adopt Toby's perspective of looking without being looked at. Invitations to look at Halo, for the purpose of exciting the implied (male, heterosexual) reader, occur regularly. Halo's discomfort with her uniform is an opportunity for titillation as well as humor. It is fascinating that Ian Gibson, when defending *The Ballad* against charges of sexism, redefines the gaze as "falling in love":

> I have been harangued by "womens' rights activists," accusing me of "using" Halo, and consequently all women, to glorify myself or some such. I really don't believe they have read the story or even looked at the pictures properly. Halo is NOT eye-candy. The reason so many young men fall in love with her is because she has a reality ["Halo"].

In fact, Halo complies neatly with the requirements of eye candy. She is fair, slender, youthful, and possesses bee-stung lips. Her appearing real is contingent on familiarity with *2000 AD*'s usual modality, which tends towards the more-than-real.[6] Of the thirty seven issues featuring *The Ballad*, the majority display aliens or futuristically-garbed soldiers on the cover. A semi-naked character from *Sláine*, smiling out at the reader and proclaiming, "My Hero!," is the only woman besides Halo to appear beneath the *2000 AD* masthead (Pugh). Halo looks remarkably "real" in this context. Her first outing as a cover star depicts her in a roll neck jumper, trousers, and trench coat, sporting a Princess Diana-like hairstyle (Moore 376, 1). Thus, she simultaneously appears more "ordinary" than, and paradoxically exceptional among, *2000 AD*'s usual cast of characters.

Halo's contingent "reality" represents a meaningful departure for *2000 AD*, but it does not challenge a femininity that consists in passively attracting male attention. Throughout *The Ballad*, women's opportunities for resistance are often limited to a tired rebuffing of unwanted advances. Deflecting harassment in bars is part and parcel of Halo's everyday life (460, 1); indeed, several female characters are assailed in public places. On the street, a man calls out to Rodice: "Hoy, Squeeze! Squeeze with a bare arm! Wanna go out with me?" (376, 20). Similarly, a man traveling on the Clara Pandy with Toy thinks nothing of threatening, "Don't play hard to get" (412, 5). Rodice's attempt to pick up a local singer—by offering snacks and proposing marriage!—is tame in comparison (377, 11). Nevertheless, her fandom positions her as "looking" rather than "looked at." The singer wears an over-extended, phallic loincloth when he performs, indicating that his appeal to his fans is primarily sexual (377, 10). Rodice's interest queers *2000 AD*'s male gaze, but only tentatively; for unlike Toby's ogling of Halo, the reader is not invited to take part. The object of her attention is repeatedly drawn in the background, and his body is vaguely defined due to a pattern of painted shapes on his skin. To use Gibson's terms, he is not eye-candy. Nor is he intended to be, for the implied reader is male and heterosexual. At least, *2000 AD*'s letters page would construct the reader as such.

It is, perhaps, the tension between the male heterosexuality of the implied reader, and the depiction of Rodice's relative assertiveness, that produces a queering of her relationship with Halo. When either Halo or Rodice speak of desire, it is for men, for the singer Box, for Mix, or for Luiz. Nonetheless Halo and Rodice's friendship is portrayed romantically. Their failure to meet in Charlemagne ends with Halo instructing the barman to "Play it again, Yortlebluzgubbly" (415, 7), suggesting her friendship with Rodice mirrors Rick and Ilsa's romance in *Casablanca*. The prologue to Book Two depicts a sixty-fifth century history lecturer debunking the myth Rodice was Halo's male lover (6). These references create a space for queer subjectivity that does not threaten the implied reader's primacy: outwardly, Halo and Rodice are "ordinary" women, where "ordinary" means the passive object of heterosexual desire.

Toy, her unusual height notwithstanding, also appears to be "ordinary." She dates men, and encourages Halo to do likewise (411, 4). She speculates regularly and at length on the heterosexual intrigues of her favorite holo-soaps. Unlike Brinna's intellectual note taking, Toy's engagement with holo-soaps is emotional and escapist. She discusses holo-soap relationships to distract herself from the Glyph (408, 7); to evade discussions that bore her (412, 3); to survive the bleakness of her army training (453, 5); and, finally, to cope with the fact that she is dying (456, 7). In prog 457, published the week of Valentine's Day, there is also an implication that soaps distract Toy from a denial of her sexuality. She is wounded in combat, but her audio implant continues to receive holo-soaps. When the holo-soap comes to an end, she makes an unforeshadowed declaration of interest in Halo. "I sometimes think I'm not a very honest person," she tells her. "I'm big, and I'm loud, and I never let anybody know what I'm feeling. Sometimes it's so difficult ... I ... I really like you, Halo" (457, 4). Toy's fatal wound is to the foot — the Hoop's favorite sexual symbol — so the scene inevitably carries the meaning of a spoiled sexual identity.

Toy's preoccupation with holo-soap marriages and extra marital affairs stresses the heteronormativity of the texts that she consumes. Her subjectivity is excluded from popular romance, as effectively as the Glyph's is; small wonder then that Toy is shown, at her death, hallucinating the smell of "the Robot Dog, still alive inside the furnace" (457, 5). Although Moore presents Toy sympathetically, killing her at the scene of her confession contains any threat she might pose to the implied reader's gaze. Her desire for Halo subverts popular romance conventions — but only temporarily.

"Ordinary civilians": Lux Roth Chop and Romantic Propaganda

We might surmise, uneasily, that *The Ballad* constructs popular romance as safe provided one engages with it from a position of privilege. Brinna is "so rich she doesn't need to live on the Hoop" (Moore 382, 10). Toy is an "ordinary civilian," defined by the army as "bored and lacking in direction" (452, 6). Her "ordinary" status is shared by Halo, who, like "everyone else and their uncle's pet parakeet" (376, 21), dreams of escaping poverty and degradation. In this context, popular romance — and specifically the manner with which it is enjoyed — is constructed as a site of class difference. It is clear that Toy's escapist involvement with holo-soaps is framed very differently from Brinna's scholarly interest. Bearing in mind Luiz Cannibal's comment that "only one being in a thousand still writes" (464, 5), Moore's portrayal of feminine mass culture may owe something to another story with a "mechanical hound," Ray Bradbury's *Fahrenheit 451*. Like Mildred Montag, Toy pursues an engagement with soap characters to avoid her life circumstances. Does Moore, like Bradbury, imply that emotional engagement with feminine mass culture is risky and a suitable target for criticism?

The view from Halo and Toy's social position, rather than Brinna's, endows holo-soaps with potency. Taking a cue from *Dallas*' early eighties dominance of the British televisual landscape, Moore suggests that holo-soaps tantalize their viewers with glamour. The holograms' clothing appears closer to that of the rich travelers on the Clara Pandy than it does to Halo's attire on the Hoop (377, 14; 408, 7). Equally, a phrase like "Don't laugh, Daddy, we're in love" appears American and indicative of affluence to British comics readers; the British soap lexicon, coming from a tradition of social realism, was and remains more likely to favor regional dialects in the vein of *Coronation Street*.

The attainability of glamour is entwined with holo-soaps' focus on romantic relationships, because relationships are positioned as a means of social advancement. In popular romance, according to Modleski, the heroine's usual trajectory is from "loneliness and penury to romance and riches" (40). Halo's encounter with the algae baron Lux Roth Chop subverts the conventions of a class-inflected romance. During her stint as a hostess on his spaceship, Lux asks Halo to dance at a party (414, 7). The dance looks comical — and thus appears to be mocked by Moore — because Lux is several years Halo's junior and clearly still a child. However, Halo is flattered and her memories of dancing with Lux return to her while fighting in the army. She watches him appear in a piece of "hologanda" (463, 5) circulated among the troops for morale:

> The main item is the marriage of Lux Roth Chop, aged twenty three. I danced with him once, when he was eleven and I was eighteen, and everyone applauded. Was that really me who did that? Yes. Yes that was me. This isn't [463, 5].

Halo's memory assumes the quality of an escapist text in which dancing with Lux, rather than her current existence, is emblematic of her real identity. Her conviction that it was "really [her] who did that" does not close the gap between her "ordinary" experience and the glamour Lux symbolizes. Whatever her fantasy, the dance did not fulfill its promise: she is not a Cinderella figure to be lead from poverty. Even worse, Lux is partially responsible for Halo's traumatic experiences as a soldier, because he funds the war effort (407, 4). The tenacity of Halo's fantasy is closely linked with a tendency to confuse escapism with literal escape.

Moore's conflation of propaganda and popular romance conventions is enabled by historically specific discourses, particularly those surrounding Royal Weddings in eighties Britain. Halo watches Lux's wedding in prog 463, which was published by *2000 AD* just two weeks after Prince Andrew's official engagement to Sarah Ferguson. At that time, the most watched television item of the decade was still Prince Charles' marriage to Diana Spencer ("Britain's"), which had taken place amidst accusations that the wedding was a strategic distraction from unemployment under Margaret Thatcher's government (Itzin). The success of the Royal Wedding as propaganda was not solely rooted in a respect for monarchical authority; rather, the eighties was characterized by a growing tendency to see Royal affairs as an engrossing "supersoap" (Olechnowicz 279). Blaine and O'Donnell remark on a "misplaced depiction of Diana as 'ordinary' compared to the rest of the monarchy" (21) which, I would argue, fulfilled propagandistic needs by drawing on popular romance tropes. As government policy perpetuated social inequality, Diana's alleged "ordinariness" minimized the impression of a class divide, and suggested that social mobility was possible. By subverting romance conventions, Moore is thus able to comment obliquely on matters of social justice.

General Luiz Cannibal: The "Ordinary" and the "Exotic"

While the Royal Wedding distracted onlookers from social inequality by drawing on popular romance's more sentimental conventions, the seamy underside of romantic tropes became grist to the mill of contemporaneous military propaganda. Robert Hamilton's essay on representations of the British Task Force notes that when male soldiers returned from the Falklands War in 1982, they were encouraged to see sex as a reward for combat (137). The idea that military aggression secures sexual rewards is a corollary to the split male trope of popular romance. It is therefore unsurprising that Moore's antipathy to the glorification of military power is expressed, partly, through Halo's desire for a military man.

Halo embarks on her affair with Luiz as part of a chain of rebellious, but self-destructive, actions. After Toy's death, Halo cuts her hair in an act of self harm that she describes as "wanting to do something ugly and painful and stupid" (Moore 458, 5). This urge coincides with her realization that she can no longer identify with "ordinary civilians," and an attendant awareness that she can no longer limit her aggression to combatants once she is relieved from duty (452, 6; 458, 6). Her new point of identification is a suicidal fellow soldier — known by the nickname "Life Sentence" — who asserts that their habituation to the army means they are no longer suited to "civilian life" (461, 3). It is in this context that, left numb and brutalized by the end of the war, Halo claims an affinity with Luiz, a man whom she is explicitly drawn to because he "scares" her (465, 4). "You're bad news," she informs him, "and I want to be with you anyway. You think that means I've got an unhealthy attitude?" (465, 4). An attraction to the split male is thus attributed, in Halo's case, to an enculturated dependence on military life which serves colonial projects, but not the interests of "ordinary" people.[7]

There is, however, an intersecting factor in Luiz's capacity to scare Halo, that Modleski's theory does not help to address. Gina Marchetti observes that critics such as Modleski have overlooked melodrama's treatment of racial difference (13), especially the ways in which romance narratives position "whiteness" as emblematic of Western moral purity (45). Luiz is a character of color, and until Halo surmises the extent of his war crimes, his martial fearsomeness is denoted by racially-loaded imagery. At Halo's first meeting with Luiz, she responds to his appearance by fainting in awe (454, 6). His attire, which incorporates the armor of Samurai warriors and an Arab sword, is ambiguously Eastern. His enlarged canines, in combination with his name, evoke caricatures of cannibals; he is a "giant with tusks" who wears live snakes threaded through his earlobes (454, 6). These characteristics indicate that he is a pastiche of the sexually compelling Asian warlords and captors that Marchetti identifies in films such as Frank Capra's *The Bitter Tea of General Yen* (46–66). Typically, when the split male is racially othered, his vacillation between brute and puppy dog is positioned as a sign of moral inferiority. He becomes an "exotic" figure, imbued with sensuality and danger, who must be annihilated to contain any moral threat to the heroine. *The Ballad* invokes this convention when Halo learns she has been unwittingly complicit in Luiz's crimes; she attempts to murder him before escaping into space (Moore 466, 6). Unlike its source material, *The Ballad* locates the threat to Halo's moral integrity within her military superior rather than a foreign adversary: Luiz is ostensibly on Halo's side, rather than an enemy captor like General Yen. By subverting popular romance tropes in this manner, Moore is able to re-emphasize his mistrust of military institutions and their treatment of the people they claim to protect.

Subversion notwithstanding, *The Ballad* perpetuates some of the raced exclusions enacted by popular romance. Halo's overawed response to Luiz still positions him as an "exotic" other to her "ordinary" heroine, where "ordinariness" is equivalent to "whiteness." We are invited to take his exoticism as an accurate indication of his moral inferiority, because his deceit and bloodlust are confirmed by the story's end. If his portrayal is intended to be tongue-in-cheek, as, say, Toby's clearly is, then there are unintended implications for

Halo's development as an "ordinary" heroine. For if Luiz spoofs rather than merely replicates the Asian warlords of Marchetti's study, the seriousness of his betrayal is undermined, and the poignancy of Halo's escape is lost.

Halo's escape concludes *The Ballad*, but I have chosen to complete my analysis by considering a slightly later appearance. At the end of 1986, Halo returned in a one-off, tongue-in-cheek story for *2000 AD*'s celebratory 500th prog. Drawn as a parody of Gibson's aforementioned "women's rights activists," Halo forces one of Gibson's other characters, Sam Slade, to strip in a poker game. She then assaults Tharg, another *2000 AD* regular, and, presumably alluding to publication disputes, complains of being sold "to white slave traders or dirty book dealers" (Moore 500, 32). The scene forms a glum coda to a complex and ambitious text, but helpfully illustrates some of the problems underlying Halo's representation as an "ordinary" woman for readers to fall in love with. Namely, Moore's use of humor ensures that when characters' actions genuinely diverge from popular romance conventions, they stop being "ordinary" and become a joke.

Notes

1. I will refer primarily to *The Ballad* as it first appeared in *2000 AD*. Several editions of *The Ballad* are available in graphic novel format, and the strip has also been re-printed in periodical form by Quality comics. These publications comprise separate texts due to differences in layout, color, and narrative content. An interest in the historically specific meanings attached to love and romance at the text's first publication underpin my preference for the original. *2000 AD* has its own argot, which I have adhered to. An individual issue is called a "prog." Weekly installments of the *Ballad* are referred to as "episodes." Each annual series of *The Ballad* is referred to as a "book."

2. The frequent use of animal metaphors in popular romance to suggest the hero's potential for violence, and conversely his domestication, is identified but not fully accounted for by critics such as Pamela Regis (119, 120, 176, 196). It seems to me that descriptions of the hero's animality project human behaviours onto other species, with the aim of essentializing gender roles through naturalistic fallacies. Andrew Goatly provides a helpful analysis of how animal metaphors in wider society are used to legitimate particular ideologies, including sexist ideologies, in precisely this fashion (125–58).

3. *The Ballad* was published in three serialized books of ten, eleven, and sixteen episodes respectively. The first book focuses on the teenage Halo. Without family, she lives with her friends Rodice, Ludy, and Brinna, in a ghetto for the unemployed known as the Hoop. The next book is concerned with Halo's attempts to build a life outside the Hoop by securing hostess work on a spaceliner. The final book takes place a decade later in Halo's timeline and tracks her experiences as a soldier in active service.

4. Moore does not further define what he means by "an ordinary woman," but it is my contention that his phrase is shorthand for a normatively feminine and working class woman. Throughout the essay I enclose "ordinary," and concepts that I see as related such as "regular," in quotation marks to indicate the constructed nature of the term.

5. Citing *2000 AD* poses a number of difficulties. The comic has neither volume numbers

nor pagination. Although *The Ballad* has its own book and episode numbers, these are not displayed consistently from week to week or year to year. For the reader's ease I have therefore used the short form Issue ##, Page ##. Pages have been counted manually, inclusive of the front cover.

6. "Modality" refers to the socially-determined truth value or credibility of visual representations; see Gunther Kress and Theo Van Leeuwen for a fuller explanation (154–74). They use "more than real" as a relative term to describe the amplification of "colour, representational detail, depth, tonal shades" in visual imagery (252).

7. Halo fights on the side of Earth, who seek to control mineral exports from the Tarantula Nebula (Moore 460, 5).

5. The Love of Nationalism, Internationalism and Sacred Space in *Watchmen*

KARL MARTIN

Alan Moore and David Gibbons's *Watchmen* is a remarkably rich text inviting readers to reflect on the nature of love, heroism, human freedom, and the future of human life on Earth. The graphic novel can also be read alongside the works of historians examining the emergence of international capitalism and its eclipsing of the nation-state. The three central characters in this reading of *Watchmen* are the Comedian, Ozymandias, and Dr. Manhattan. That the Comedian, Edward Blake, focuses his loyalty on a particular nation-state while Ozymandias, Adrian Veidt, claims a love for humanity marks a significant twentieth-century paradigm shift in both the world of *Watchmen* and our own. In *Death of a Nation: American Culture and the End of Exceptionalism*, David Noble characterizes the shift as one from narratives arguing for the protection of the "sacred space" of the nation-state to narratives abandoning the nation as sacred but proclaiming the sacred space of an international capitalist market (xxiv).[1] In spite of the differences between Blake's love of nation and Veidt's love of humanity, they share an element in common. Both men believe in the illusion of a sacred space beyond the reach of the chaos of time and historical change (Noble 14).

Above both their perspectives looms Dr. Manhattan who, with his perspective from outside the human experience of time and space, is given the last word before he disappears from the novel and, apparently, from Earth itself: "*Nothing* ends, Adrian. Nothing *ever* ends" (12. 27, emphasis in original unless noted). One possible interpretation of Manhattan's claim is that no space can be protected from historical change. What Moore and Gibbons demonstrate through the presence of Dr. Manhattan is the foolishness, even impossibility, of the violent projects of both Blake and Veidt. By the time readers meet him in the early panels of *Watchmen* where his death is recounted, Blake is a broken and bitter man, a cynic formed by the violence required to maintain the nation-state and the failure of his nationalist dreams to bring about an ideal society. By the end of the novel, Veidt's internationalist dreams are also shattered. The massive violence Veidt enacts in order to protect an internationalist space where goods can be exchanged without disruption from conflicts between rival nation-states belies his humanitarian claims. Readers are left with a strong indication that Veidt's plot will be revealed and his actions judged harshly. To better understand the way in which *Watchmen* interacts with the scholarship of post-nationalism, a brief introduction to that scholarship is in order.

From Bourgeois Nationalism to International Capitalism

Noble's scholarship is in conversation with Benedict Anderson's work in *Imagined Communities* where he argues that members of modern nation-states are not bound together by kinship or ethnicity but by an adherence to a common set of ideas (xxxvi). The young Edward Blake, for example, apparently shares a set of ideas concerning the exceptional nature of the United States; thus, dressed in a costume marked by national symbols (2. 9–11), he willingly serves the interests of the state. By contrast, Veidt becomes disillusioned with the chaos caused by warring nation-states and shifts his adherence to the international world (11. 21–22); thus, as a newborn capitalist in opposition to the nation-state, he essentially becomes a "neoliberal," in the terms outlined by David Harvey. "Neoliberalism," Harvey writes:

> is in the first instance a theory of political economic practices that proposes that human well-being can best be advanced by liberating individual entrepreneurial freedoms and skills within an institutional framework characterized by strong private property rights, free markets, and free trade. The role of the state is to create and preserve an institutional framework appropriate to such practices [2].

The paradigm shift about which Noble writes is just this: a shift from viewing the bordered nation-state as sacred to viewing the international marketplace as sacred with the nation-state cast in the role of defender of the international space on behalf of the capitalist class (221). In the world of *Watchmen*, tracking this shift provides a way of understanding the division between Blake and Veidt.

For Noble, the bourgeois nationalists in the nineteenth and early twentieth centuries in the United States made a distinction between the organic — and thus rational — culture of their nation and the disruptive cultures originating from either outside the borders of the nation-state or from the tradition-bound, and therefore irrational, cultures within its borders (xxvii–xxviii). Rational men in the United States,[2] free from the superstitious, tradition-bound cultures of Europe, "were certain that their national culture had grown out of the national landscape" (xxvii). Founded upon this landscape, the national culture of the United States was believed to have transcended the warfare and class divisions of Europe. Noble claims that this paradigm grew increasingly unstable beginning in the thirties. Because many of the historical developments leading to this instability can be found in the history recounted in *Watchmen*, the action of the novel also occurs in the midst of the disruption of this nationalist paradigm.[3]

Noble argues that one reason for the instability of this bourgeois nationalist paradigm, especially in the decades following World War II, was the inherent tension between two commitments: "The bourgeoisie were imagining bounded nations built on the foundations of static nature, on the foundation of a timeless space. But the bourgeoisie were also committed to the constant expansion of a boundless marketplace" (xxviii). The "boundless marketplace" requires the protection, not of national boundaries, but of a sacred international space where goods can be exchanged without disruption from conflicts between rival nation-states who each believe they must protect their national borders and assert their national interests. Internationalist bourgeoisie, according to Noble, have not abandoned the idea of a sacred space free of the irrationality of historical change but have simply invested in a new sacred space, the international marketplace rather than the individual nation-state. This insight helps explain Veidt's willingness to take advantage of the tension between nation-states as recounted in the corporate memos found between chapters 11 and 12.

What these nationalist and postnationalists share is a belief in their ability to establish and protect a rational, timeless space. Blake finds Veidt's actions in defense of an international space shocking, not only because of the scope of the violence but also because Veidt's actions do not fit the nationalist paradigm.

Edward Blake as a Defender of the Nation-State

According to his headstone, Blake is born in 1924 (2. 28). Thus, he is only fifteen when he is pictured with Sally Jupiter, the Silk Spectre, at the first Minutemen Christmas party mentioned in the excerpt from Hollis Mason's *Under the Hood* attached at the end of chapter 2 (9). Portrayed as a fully-developed man rather than an adolescent, Blake is shown embracing

Jupiter and gazing confidently at the camera. Blake's attempted rape of Jupiter less than a year later marks him as a violent teenager willing to take what he wants by force. Of Blake, Mason writes, "He went on to make a name for himself as a war hero in the Pacific, but all I can think of is the bruises along Sally Jupiter's ribcage and hope to God that America can find itself a better class of hero than *that*" (10). Mason's hopes are dashed: the entry from *Under the Hood* features a photograph of a sneering, heroic Blake displaying a machine gun and holding a Japanese flag draped over his right fist, a symbol of conquest. With the nation's moral sanction, Blake becomes both an agent of violence and a potent symbol of American power. From Mason's perspective, the Minutemen crime fighting unit — named after early American patriots — "had worms in the apple eating it from the inside" (excerpt from *Under the Hood* 9). Blake's violence against Sally Jupiter is a prime example of the corruption he saw. Mason seems to better embody American ideals than does Blake, but he has neither faced nor participated in the violence at the core of the nation-state's identity in the way that Blake has. While Mason may indeed be the more appropriate heroic national symbol, he is a naïve one, and by the late forties he and his group have ceased to exist. Blake's career, by contrast, is wildly successful. The Comedian's role as a symbol of American patriotism is confirmed in chapter 5 of Mason's *Under the Hood* (excerpt attached to the end of chapter 3). Mason, reflecting on the fifties, writes:

> I remember thinking at the time that it was funny how the more serious things got, the better the Comedian seemed to do. Out of the whole bunch of us, he was the only one who was still right up there on the front pages, still making the occasional headline. On the strength of his military work he had good government connections, and it often seemed as if he was being groomed into some sort of patriotic symbol. At the height of the McCarthy era, nobody had any doubts about where the Comedian's feet were planted politically [11].[4]

As a consequence of this "grooming," the Comedian is clearly associated with the nation-state when Captain Metropolis attempts to reconstitute a band of crime fighters.

In 1966, when Metropolis gathers together a group of crime fighters (Dr. Manhattan, Rorschach, the second Nite Owl, Ozymandias, and others), Blake sets fire to a map of the nation and walks out, refusing to join the Crime Busters. As he does so, he announces, "It don't matter squat because inside thirty years the nukes are gonna be flyin' like maybugs..." (2. 11). Blake's statement explains why he would channel his energies into working only for the nation-state — it remains the only entity capable of sanctioning his violence while allowing him to see himself as heroic. But we can also see his growing despair. Before setting fire to the map, he proclaims, "What's going down in this world, you got no idea. Believe me" (2.10). Yet in spite of his growing cynicism, the Comedian continues his political involvement. He fights in Vietnam to help insure a continued American dominance and to keep the dominoes from falling in Southeast Asia. He may see little hope for the future, but fighting for the nation-state is all he knows to do.

As Dr. Manhattan stands by Blake's graveside, he recalls his time with the Comedian at the end of the Vietnam War (2. 12–13). In his interchange with Dr. Manhattan, Blake demonstrates a certain tension in his view of the world. He wants to maintain the posture of the nihilist, insisting that nothing matters and that everything is a joke. Yet, after proclaiming that the common people of Vietnam do not care who wins the war, he tells Manhattan, "I mean, if we'd lost this war ... I dunno. I think it might have driven us a little crazy, y'know? As a country" (2. 13). As they gaze out from the officer's club where they have been talking, they see President Nixon, both hands raised in a victory salute, standing on a platform adorned by an American flag before a cheering crowd. Seeing the president, Blake proclaims, "There he is. First press helicopter into Saigon since the ceasefire. He's got the next election in the bag for sure" (2. 13). While the primary thrust of the scene is the Comedian's accusation that Manhattan is "driftin' outta touch [...] God help us all" (2. 15), Nixon's presence also confirms Blake status as a servant of the nation-state. His criticism of Manhattan is at least partially rooted in Manhattan's refusal to remain committed to the American nation-state. Yet by this time in *Watchmen*, the Comedian has embraced cynicism, at least to some degree. In two frames showing the Comedian wielding a flame-thrower in Vietnam, Dr. Manhattan proclaims, "As I come to understand Vietnam and what it implies about the human condition, I also realize that few humans will permit themselves such an understanding. Blake's different. He understands perfectly ... and he doesn't care" (4. 19). Based on the above conversation, Manhattan is only *partially* correct about the Comedian.

After all of the violence Blake has perpetrated — sanctioned by the nation-state — his distraught reaction to Veidt's plan is at least somewhat out of character. It would seem that if the Comedian were convinced that the best interests of the American nation-state required the sacrifice of a large percentage of the population of New York City, he would, perhaps grudgingly, accept the action as necessary.[5] But Veidt's plan is unlike the plans Blake himself has been involved with, for Veidt's violence is done not under the authority of the nation-state, the only authority Blake has accepted, but in the name of something else.

Moloch recounts to Rorschach an odd visit he received from the Comedian shortly before his death: "I woke up, he was there, in my room, drunk, babbling, not making sense ... I sat in bed, scared stiff. He sounded crazy. I thought he was gonna kill me..." (2. 21). As the panels take us from Moloch's narration to a graphic representation of the visit, an obviously distraught Comedian, now aware of Veidt's plan and dressed in his symbolic nation-state attire, tells Moloch, "I mean, I thought I knew how it was, how the world was. But then I found out about this gag, this joke..." (2. 22). Part of what bothers the Comedian is the scope of the violence in Veidt's plan, for he tells Moloch, "I mean, I done some bad things. I did bad things to women. I shot kids! In 'nam I shot kids.... But I never did anything like, like..." (2. 23). The Comedian is incapable of even finishing his sentence, of articulating the violence in the plot. Yet, given his life of violence and disregard for human life other than his own, why should this be? One reason, I would argue, is that nearly all the violence he has known has either been sanctioned by the nation-state or overlooked by the leaders of the nation-state because of his service to them. Veidt's violence is of a different order altogether.

Adrian Veidt as a Neoliberal

When readers of *Watchmen* first meet Adrian Veidt, he is visually marked as a capitalist entrepreneur. Rorschach arrives at his penthouse office to inform him of the Comedian's death and to warn him that a killer may be targeting former vigilantes. Rorschach holds Veidt in contempt because Veidt quit fighting crime and "cashed in on his reputation" (1. 17). As Rorschach leaves, readers see Veidt in the background of the panel gazing out the window as the foreground features various Ozymandias action figures positioned around a newspaper with a headline proclaiming that the doomsday clock has moved closer to midnight. Not only does the panel foreshadow Veidt's unwillingness to allow the world to slide into nuclear war due to what he considers the irrational actions of leading nation-states, it also suggests part of what is at stake for Veidt personally: war will lead to economic chaos and interfere with the sale of the action figures on Veidt's desk, in addition to his other extensive business interests.

Veidt's primary concern with expanding markets is reinforced when Veidt returns to his Antarctic headquarters to view the events he has set in motion (10. 8). After donning his Ozymandias garb and being escorted by his three minions to a video screening room, his first order of business is to instruct his servants on how to manage his investments in light of the impending chaos. World anxiety, Veidt believes, will lead to increased erotic imagery in advertising which will in turn lead to increased birthrates. As his plan unfolds to kill millions of people, Veidt's instructions are to invest in "the major erotic video companies. That's the short term. Also, we should negotiate controlling shares in selected baby food and maternity goods manufacturers" (10. 8). Following chapter 10 readers find supplemental material indicating the far-reaching nature of Veidt's commercial investments. More than anything else, this material marks Veidt as a postnational neoliberal whose highest priority is to be free to conduct business without regard to national boundaries.

As Veidt prepares to kill his servants to erase any trace of the plot they helped to launch, he tells them his life story. Unlike Blake who by the time he is a teenager is already an agent of the nation-state, Veidt, left an orphan in the mid-fifties when he is only seventeen, sets out to travel the world. From this early stage in his life, he is already transcending national borders. Veidt takes as his hero Alexander of Macedonia whom, he believes, ruled "without barbarism" (11. 8)! Veidt judges Alexander's one failure to be his return home to "quell dissent." Alexander, in other words, displayed too much concern for his homeland and had not embraced a truly internationalist paradigm: "He'd not united all the world, nor built a unity that would survive him" (11. 10). Inspired by the wisdom of the ancient world, Veidt sets out on his quest: "Thus began my path to conquest … conquest not of men, but of the evils that beset them" (11. 11), including an irrational concern for one's own home.

Later, while battling Rorschach and Nite Owl, Veidt recounts his first meeting with the Comedian: "As intelligent men facing lunatic times, we were very alike, despising each other instantly" (11. 18). Ironically, it was the Comedian, Veidt tells Rorschach and Nite Owl, who opened his eyes to his true calling by predicting that if something wasn't done, Veidt would simply be the smartest man on a dead planet (2. 11). Veidt leaves the 1966 meeting of the Crime Busters with a new mission: "I swore to deny [the Comedian's] kind their last black laugh at earth's expense" (11. 19). Unquestionably, Veidt is referring to the Comedian's cynical violence, but he is also implicitly condemning the Comedian's role as servant of the nation-state. In the interview attached to the end of chapter 11, Veidt describes his differences with the Comedian: "It's largely a political difference. He sees me as an intellectual dilettante dabbling in national affairs that don't concern me. I see him as an amoral mercenary allying himself to whichever political faction seems likely to grant him the greatest license" (10). Veidt's characterization of the Comedian is somewhat unfair, for the Comedian has only ever served the leadership in control of his nation-state. What this description really masks is the fact that they exist in different paradigms.

Veidt wins, or appears to. The Comedian dies, and, through his use of technology, Veidt is able to create a new "enemy," compelling the nations of the world to cease their violence with one another and close ranks against the alien enemy. In his moment of triumph, however, Veidt is still haunted. In his final conversation with Dr. Manhattan, Veidt explains that he is not haunted by the deaths he has caused — indeed, he remains convinced that the deaths helped deter much greater carnage that would have surely resulted from a nuclear war between rival nation-states. He even tells Dr. Manhattan that he has caused himself to feel each of the deaths he is responsible for. In a wonderfully evocative bit of dialogue, Veidt explains his lingering anxiety: "Well, I dream, about swimming towards a hideous ... no. Nevermind. It isn't significant..." (12. 27). Of course, this dialogue is highly significant to the novel's readers, for Veidt's dream parallels the storyline of the Black Freighter pirate comic which was often graphically interwoven with the story of Veidt's internationalist plot. Like the Black Freighter's narrator, Veidt believes himself committed to stopping a great evil. And, like the narrator, Veidt destroys key elements of the world closest to him in order to accomplish his goal. The Black Freighter narrator kills his own family while Veidt does great damage to the largest city of the nation-state that he has long called home. The significant difference is that the narrator realizes that he, in fact, was the enemy all along (11. 6) and feels terrible remorse, while Veidt remains relatively convinced of the rightness of his actions. Even in his commitment to transcend the irrationality of the politics of nation-states, Veidt cannot seem to quell the sense of a betrayal of his homeland.

Everything Must Change

Watchmen's relevance as a commentary on the real world is indisputable. Following the final image of chapter 12, the reader is confronted with Juvenal's often quoted Latin phrase, "*Quis custodiet ipsos custodes*," a phrase most commonly translated, "Who Watches the Watchmen?" Moore points out that the phrase is, "Quoted as the epigraph of the Tower Commission Report, 1987." By placing the phrase in the context of the Tower Commission Report that brought to light the illegal activities of members of the Reagan administration, Moore highlights the political context in which the quotation is most often used.[6] In the context of the Report, the quotation refers to the difficulty of reigning in super patriots, the self-styled guardians of the modern nation-state or the timeless space of international capitalism, who often claim to have acted in the "best interest" of the people. Those involved in the Iran-Contra scandal were not concerned with repelling an attack on the borders of the nation-state. Rather, following a neoliberal political agenda, they were concerned with bringing rationality to international affairs where both instability in Iran and the threat of communism in Central America were perceived as problems for the capitalist class to be solved by Americans. Nixon, in fact, with the help of Dr. Manhattan as a living nuclear deterrent and Blake as an enforcer, is largely responsible for the transition from nationalism to postnationalism. Although Blake never makes the move himself, he ironically assists Nixon in the transition to a postnationalist foreign policy. Because these goods are being produced by multinational corporations such as the one headed by Veidt, Blake could even be said to be assisting Veidt's neoliberal agenda. It is only Dr. Manhattan's removal to the moon which reinvigorates the Cold War and pushes Nixon and his military advisors to contemplate nuclear war.

Veidt, using technological advances developed from the work of Dr. Manhattan, believes that by neutralizing the various nation-states he will succeed where the Nixon administration has failed. In other words, because he is willing to engage in a level of violence unimaginable even to Nixon and the Comedian, he will achieve the covert agenda of the bourgeois nationalists turned postnationalist who have long lived with the contradiction of trying simultaneously to protect the borders and identity of their particular nation-state, while providing ever-expanding international markets for the capitalist class of which Veidt himself is a member.

In our own world, presidential administrations since Kennedy have taken as a given what the latter would have proclaimed in Dallas. Even Nixon, in order to accomplish the transition to neoliberalism, must remain committed to Kennedy's quoted vision — whom it is implied, ironically enough, that he, with Blake's assistance, may have assassinated: "We in this country, in this generation, are by destiny, rather than choice, the watchmen on the walls of world freedom" (11. 18). Although they continue to use the language of a sacred national space in their political rhetoric, national leaders have largely abandoned the project in favor of the neoliberal project of the creation of a sacred international marketplace where the presumed rationality of capitalism will allow for ever-expanding consumption of the products and services produced by transnational corporations. In this transition, the liberty of its citizens — even its privileged bourgeoisie — ceases to be a primary concern of the leaders of various nation-states. David Noble summarizes the situation well: "In the realm of the new sacred international marketplace, there [is] only liberty. Self-interest [is] no longer disciplined by national interests" (288).

These neoliberals have made the same mistake made by bourgeois nationalists before them and by Veidt in *Watchmen*: they believe they created a timeless sacred space that will not be corrupted. They believe they have escaped history, that the equivalent of Rorschach's journal does not exist somewhere that will reveal their complicity in the violence that, masked as love of humanity, has brought the international marketplace into being. Perhaps, like the mighty Ozymandias, they seek assurance that the sacrifices they have imposed on humanity will be worth it all. With Ozymandias they ask, "I did the right thing, didn't I? It all worked out in the end." Perhaps they will find the final words of Dr. Manhattan instructive. Endorsing the truth that no human cultural creation can escape the ravages of time, Dr. Manhattan responds to Ozymandias: "'In the end'? *Nothing* ends, Adrian. Nothing *ever* ends" (12.27).

Notes

1. By "sacred space" Noble means a space ruled by rationality alone, a space untouched by the changes brought by time. See Chapter One, "The Birth and Death of American History" in *Death of a Nation*.

2. The gendered language is intentional, for in the view of bourgeois nationalists women were, by definition, irrational.

3. In the world of *Watchmen*, the most notable disruptions are the development of nuclear weapons and the war in Vietnam, two developments that Blake finds very troubling.

4. Mason suggests that Blake may be responsible for the death of the strongman known as Hooded Justice. If he is correct, the incident provides a good example of the way that Blake's violence is contained by the nation-state. No doubt Blake's primary motivation for killing Hooded Justice is personal — Hooded Justice interrupted his attempted rape of Sally Jupiter. But in the context of the fifties, Blake could kill Hooded Justice, rumored to be an East German named Rolf Müller, because he was a suspected communist.

5. The Comedian certainly has no qualms about firing into crowds of civilians during the police riots prior to the passage of the Keene Act (2.16–18).

6. Ironically, the original context speaks more to sexual relationships rather than to politics.

PART II

The Vicious Cabaret of Love, Sexual Desire ... and Torture

6. Theorizing Sexual Domination in *From Hell* and *Lost Girls*
Jack the Ripper versus Wonderlands of Desire
Zoë Brigley-Thompson

> *With symbols man casts woman down, and then with symbols keeps her there* [Moore, FH 4, 24].

In the comic book genre, women are routinely objects of violence. In 1999, the comic book writer Gail Simone set up the website *Women in Refrigerators* to document how women in comic book narratives tend to be "depowered, raped, or cut up and stuck in the refrigerator." The work of Alan Moore is no exception in presenting violence against women as a routine event. Moore, however, probes for the causes of physical, psychological, and sexual violence against women from the perspective of both male perpetrators and female survivors. In analyzing these power relations, Moore is not afraid to ask hard questions or to offer complex answers. Writing from the perspective of female survivors of violence, Moore is at his most appealing; though his writing about sex and brutality can verge upon the exploitative, he sometimes reveals an unexpected sympathy with dominated women.

Initially, Moore might appear to be an unlikely feminist, but his unexpected sympathy works, to quote psychoanalyst Jessica Benjamin, "to redeem what has been devalued in the women's domain" and "to conquer the territory that has been reserved to men for women" (*Desire* 1). Like Benjamin, Moore wants to expose violent sexual domination and present a more positive alternative; this twin agenda will be explored in this essay through the discussion of two significant texts: *From Hell* and *Lost Girls*. While *From Hell* exposes the ubiquitous nature of sexual domination in Moore's work, *Lost Girls* puts forward a different mode of being where women can be desiring subjects existing beyond traditional gender scripts of power. Before beginning a detailed analysis, however, it is worth providing a brief introduction to these texts, while mapping out the conjunctions and parallels of thought between Moore and Benjamin in regards to sexual domination.

From Hell presents Moore's version of the Jack the Ripper story. Set in nineteenth century London, the plot follows the upbringing and life of William Gull, the royal doctor, a man who becomes obsessed with controlling and subjugating women. His obsession with opposing forces of matriarchy and patriarchy may draw on visions of patriarchal domination from nineteenth century theorists like J.J. Bachofen, whose ideas were reproduced by J.G. Fraser and others. Drawing on Western antiquity, Bachofen theorized that before patriarchy, there were two significant periods in human history. The first was a hetaeristic era during which women were treated as common property; Joseph Campbell describes this period as composed by a sexual economy where women serve the needs of "a powerful male tyrant [...] able to make use of whatever women he chose" (xxxi). The second significant period was supposedly a time of peaceful matriarchy, but Bachofen emphasizes the primacy of the current order, patriarchy, which "brings with it the liberation of the spirit from the manifestations of nature, a sublimation of human existence over the laws of material life" (109). Benjamin's association of patriarchal domination and masculine power is highlighted when she outlines the causes of sexual domination: dominative men need "to make sure that [women's] alien otherness is either assimilated or controlled, that her own subjectivity nowhere asserts itself in a way that could make [man's] dependency upon her a conscious insult to his sense of freedom" (*Desire* 3).

Gull's urge to dominate is bound up with a macho philosophy of male dominance, which is in turn intimately connected to nineteenth century visions of history and progress. Benjamin suggests that, as an era that marked the rise of capitalism and rationalism, the Victorian period fosters sexual domination because such domination "is materialized in a way that occludes its gender roots — in the instrumentalism that pervades our economic and social relations" (*Desire* 4). As he tours London in a hansom cab, Gull does not recognize the humanity of the city, but reads the metropolis as a web of patriarchal conquest that represses women's power, especially maternal power. This abstraction is made real, however, when Gull is offered the state-sanctioned opportunity to violate and murder prostitutes. Benjamin argues that fantasies of domination are "not merely a wish, but a mental state, generally understood as one of undifferentiation," the inability to give proper recognition to the humanity of women (*Bonds* 86). This certainly describes Gull's attitudes to the prostitutes, who are merely tokens in exchanges of sexual power.

Leaving Victorian Oppression and Entering Modern Equality

While Moore uses Gull to expose dominative scripts of power in *From Hell*, *Lost Girls* offers sympathetic accounts of heroines questing to discover their own desires. *Lost Girls* tackles a harder question than *From Hell*: why do women comply with domination? *Lost Girls* tells the stories of three heroines from children's literature, Wendy, Dorothy, and Alice, now grown up, and it shows them questioning their tolerance of past sexual domination. Gull's philosophy of misogyny in *From Hell* has been experienced by the "Lost Girls" as psychological and physical trauma often inflicted by men and occasionally by women. Working with artist Melinda Gebbie, Moore questions what Benjamin describes as "the curious role of women in both criticizing and complying with the idealization of masculine individuality and the devaluation of femininity" (*Desire* 2).

In Benjamin's theorizing, idealization is key to women's inability to be desiring subjects. Benjamin's notion of ideal love relates to the "early love of the father" who "appears to be the solution to a series of conflicts that occur" and "represents freedom, the outside world, will, agency, and desire" (*Desire* 7–8). Benjamin argues that the mother's and the daughter's desires "always have to contend with this monopoly and the devaluation of femininity it implies" (*Bonds* 123). Having seen their mothers devalued and degraded, Benjamin notes that too often adult women seek to find their desire in "a powerful other who remains in control" (*Bonds* 123). Such a love is "the passive form of accepting the other's will and desire as one's own; from there it is just a step to surrender to the other's will" (*Bonds* 122). This kind of relationship occurs regularly in Moore's writing. For example, there are dubious, dominative relationships between Laurie Juspeczyk and Dr. Manhattan, as well as Silk Spectre and The Comedian in *Watchmen*, Evey Hammond and V in *V for Vendetta*; and Dorothy in *Lost Girls* harbors an incestuous love for her father. To Moore's credit, however, all of these women eventually reject their "ideal love" and seek a relationship where the scripts of power are more equal. To break the cycle of domination, Benjamin demands a relation that is not dominated by phallic power, but by an anti-phallic, intersubjective relation. Creating this relation requires that one desist from perceiving women as abstract symbols in a script of power, as Gull considers women, while expressing "a wish for a holding other whose presence does not violate one's own space but permits the experience of one's own desire" (*Desire* 19). Like Benjamin, Moore is interested in creating an anti-phallic space or relation where the lover becomes a source of erotic sustenance and play for the heroines rather than a dominative sexual predator, the "holding other" to which Benjamin refers. Discussing the spoken word performance of Moore's "The Birth Caul," Marc Singer argues that the birth caul "functions as a kind of anti-phallus, delivered to Moore through matrilineage" (44). Another anti-phallic symbol for Moore is the Willendorf Venus, which he contrasts to the anti-masturbatory "Nazi cock-ring" in *25,000 Years of Erotic Freedom*. The Willendorf Venus represents "good pornography," an art-form that offers a shame-free vision of sexuality (81). Moore's use of the Willendorf Venus and the birth caul gesture to the matriarchal power so reviled by Gull in *From Hell*, and foregrounds the possibility that daughters might be empowered rather than nullified by their mothers. Moore's "Lost Girls" seek this kind of intersubjective space, where they will be able to express their desires without fear of violation or exploitation. The discussion that follows considers power scripts of sexual domination, as they are exposed and subverted in *From Hell* and *Lost Girls*.

The Ripper and Sexual Domination in From Hell

Playing off the Jack the Ripper stories in *From Hell*, Moore represents the hypocrisy of Victorian Britain and "the bloated self-important arrogance that seemingly accompanies all empires" (*25,000* 38). His comment recalls Bachofen's imperialist affirmation of the "Occident, with its purer, chaster nature," which was supposedly given the task of "liberating mankind from the fetters of the lowest tellurism in which the magic of the Orientals held it fast" (99). *From Hell* tells a story of sex, empire, and purity, recalling Anne McClintock's thesis that "controlling women's sexuality, exalting maternity and breeding a virile race of empire-builders were widely perceived as the paramount means for controlling the health and wealth of the male imperial body politic" (47). Moore seeks to expose the hypocrisy of nineteenth century ideologies, challenging Bachofen's view of the West's "purer, chaster nature" (99). Painstakingly researched by both Moore and illustrator Eddie Campbell, *From Hell* is not a "whodunit," nor is the investigating detective, Inspector Abberline, able to bring the Ripper to justice. The tale of suspense begins with the birth of an illegitimate child whose mother, Annie Crook, is a prostitute and whose father is Queen Victoria's son, Prince Albert. Crook is later committed to an insane asylum, but a group of her friends — Polly, Mary, "Dark" Annie, Liz, and Marie — who are also prostitutes, learn of the illegitimate baby and set up a blackmail scheme which will lead to their deaths.

The prostitutes in the blackmail ring will later become the tragic heroines of *From Hell*, and Moore suggests that hetaerism (as described by Bachofen) still exists in the treatment of women in nineteenth century London, where the bodies of prostitutes are the property of any man with a few coins. The whole chain of events begins when the "Old Nichol Mob" tries to extort the women, and Polly explains in distress that "they said if I didn't pay more, they'd shove a knife right up my..." (*FH* 3, 11). Moore makes it clear that the life of a prostitute is a desperate battle for safety and survival.

The confined prospects of working class women who become prostitutes are reflected by Eddie Campbell's knotted black and white drawings, especially by his use of narrow boxes and frames that enclose the narrative. When Marie meets a customer in the street, she takes him down a back alley, and the narrow boxes which frame the narrative mimic the enclosed space of the yard where they have sex. The dialogue during this scene shows that the experience is not erotic for Marie; the punter admonishes her, saying: "It's not in. You're holdin' it between the tops of yer legs"; and, later, he becomes aggressive, violent even: "I know cunt when I feels it. Open yer legs an' I'll see meself as it goes up right. OPEN em!" (*FH* 3, 4). The punter uses the language of entrances and exits, recalling Jessica Benjamin's question about desire and force in "Revisiting the Riddle of Sex." "How often," she asks, "are our past and present sexual mythologies, our templates of masculine and feminine, shaped by this dynamic of invasion and shutting out, shutting out and struggling to get in?" (154). A sense of enclosure and entrapment is clear in Campbell's narrow boxes which pan back a little above the woman's distressed face, above the yard, and above the street. The illustrations avoid being titillating, refusing to show any nakedness; there are only two figures pressed together in a perfunctory business transaction. Even as the perspective widens, the boxes remain the same size, emphasizing the city's knowing ignorance of the crimes that go on within it. The unseen violence in the enclosed yard shows the lack of choice for the prostitutes. Moore's dialogue and Campbell's narrow images emphasize Marie's entrapment and lack of freedom.

This narrowness is emphasized again in the story of another prostitute. Rebuked by her lover, Michael, for reporting his domestic violence, Liz is thrown out on the streets. During their argument, the perspective shows Liz as a small figure, while Michael's body looms large (8, 6). When Michael throws Liz out, the final portrait positions itself looking through the open door; over Michael's immense shoulder is the tiny, distant figure of Liz on the street. This image of powerlessness only anchors the plaintiveness of her final remark, when she says that she is going to look for "somebody kind, who knows what women are like inside" (8, 6). Liz's comment is a plea for compassion, for men not to exploit women, but her phrasing also recalls Gull's routine of disemboweling his victims, so it becomes a sinister omen of her own death. Michael's callous act is a contributory factor in her murder, and Moore emphasizes that social attitudes to women in general are culpable. Campbell notes that Moore's theme is "the horror inflicted by a patriarchal system."

The agent of this system is Gull. An alternative narrative strand in *From Hell* follows Gull's biography and how he becomes a member of the freemasons, the royal doctor, and an agent of the British Empire. Later, Gull becomes Jack the Ripper himself, when Queen Victoria asks him to eliminate the prostitutes — Polly, Mary, Liz and Marie — who are trying to blackmail the queen's son. Gull, however, has his own motivation for killing the women in a brutal and misogynist way. Influenced by the patriarchal freemasonry, Gull's philosophy reflects nineteenth century ideas about matriarchy reminiscent of Bachofen, suggesting that human history has been a battle between men and women. Gull explains, "'Tis in the war of sun and moon that man steals woman's power; that Left Brain conquers Right ... that reason chains insanity" (4, 21). Gull's imagery recalls Bachofen's comment that "With the sunrise ancient religion associates the idea of triumph over the maternal darkness" (114). Like Bachofen, Gull organizes his ideas about matriarchy and patriarchy in relation to a series of binary oppositions which privilege masculinity and its associations with power, order, and reason. Moore, however, presents Gull physically acting out Bachofen's abstract ideas about subjugating women and the matriarchal. As Campbell notes, Gull actively seeks "to re-establish the domination [of women]." This desire to dominate women and re-establish male authority is at the heart of the murders, which are performed by Gull as brutal exhibitions of power.

As he and Netley drive around London, Gull explains how places like William Blake's grave, Cleopatra's Needle, and Saint Luke's Church symbolize the traumatic dismembering of female power. For example, Gull explains that Half-Moon Lane in Lambeth is named after Herne, "an antlered man" who "usurped Diana's role as leader of the Lunar hunt: a male pretender to her female throne" (4, 24). Inscribing the city with images of men dominating women, Gull suggests that London, its society and culture, are complicit with his murderous project; such violence is endemic.

London, however, still retains traces of women's power and Gull is particularly preoccupied by the figure of Boudicca. He describes how when she and her daughters were raped by the Romans, Boudicca waged war on London (4, 8). The boxes grow narrower when Gull tells Netley:

> Measured against the span of Goddesses, our male rebellion's lately won, our new regime of rationality unfledged, precarious. Our grand symbolic magic

chaining womankind thus must often be reinforced, carved deeper yet in History's flesh [4, 25].

For Gull, this symbolic magic involves the ritualistic murders of prostitutes, but his discussion of masculinity and creativity also recalls Bachofen's comment that "the source of immortality is no longer the childbearing woman but the male-creative principle, which he endows with the divinity that the earlier world imputed only to the mother" (111). Bachofen ominously contends that "even abuse becomes a lever of progress" toward this male order (93).

For Gull, the lever of progress is his series of ritual murders, the climax of which is the killing of Marie Kelly. Marie is the most sympathetic of the prostitutes and is the love interest of the detective, Inspector Abberline, which makes this murder especially horrifying. Campbell's illustrations, though black and white, are nonetheless disturbing in depicting the crucial moment: "[W]hen the knife is going into the heart cavity, we follow the knife in and we rush down through the capillaries, veins [...] and we're inside this enormous meat cathedral" (E. Campbell). Campbell's artwork emphasizes Gull's belief that he is making the prostitutes into something greater than themselves: "Do you know how I have loved you? You'd have all been dead in a year or two from liver failure, men, or childbirth" (10, 23). In Gull's philosophy, women's greatest purpose is "to endlessly reflect the harsh male brilliance of a father son" (4, 35).

As a symbol of omnipotence, however, Gull is more than an aberration of nineteenth century philosophy; he describes himself as a syndrome (14, 17), and he is associated with symbols of a primitive evil such as Doctor Jekyll and Mister Hyde, and William Blake's sketch of *The Ghost of a Flea*. At the end of *From Hell*, Gull continues to have visions of the future and he visits the Halifax Slasher, Ian Brady, and the Yorkshire Ripper, Peter Sutcliffe, establishing himself as the precursor for a long line of serial killers. Gull represents the sexual domination of women not by isolated madmen, but by "civilized" society in general. This message is clear when Abberline receives a deluge of anonymous letters all claiming to be written by the Ripper. Abberline asks, "[W]hat kind of men, Godley? What kind of men write stuff like this?" (9, 35). Campbell obliges when we turn over the page to show us the letter writers; the series of pictures shows a reverend at his desk writing beside the Holy Bible, a man in working clothes with a pint of beer presumably in the pub, a man in a library of books masturbating at his desk, and two teenage boys laughing together as they write (9, 36). Jack the Ripper's views may be extreme, but, according to Moore, they represent an undeniable aspect of attitudes to women in patriarchal society.

This reading of patriarchal society is undoubtedly bleak and extends into the future through the serial killers visited in Gull's vision. At the end, however, Gull's divine masters direct him to a farmhouse in Ireland in 1902, where a mother calls her children in from playing. The prostitute Marie was Irish, so the implication is that Gull may have mistaken his final victim and she may have escaped. When Gull envisions the Irish mother, he is afraid; he describes "within her eyes, that terrible ferocity," and she rebukes him, "ye auld divil I know that ye're there, and ye're not havin' these. Clear off wit' ye" (14, 22). Recalling the scene of Marie's sexual encounter with a punter in a London back alley, the narrow frames move up and out from the intimate space of the mother and her daughters to a perspective above the family: below, the mother angrily points a finger up. Unlike the cramped streets of London, the farm is surrounded by space, implying the freedom of women beyond the metropolis. Faced with such a "perplexing vision," Gull dissipates into a puff of cloud. There is hope for the mother and daughters at the end of the narrative because they have an anti-phallic power, like that of Moore's birth caul and Willendorf Venus. Moore gestures towards another mode of being where women are not subject to violent, oppressive domination. As Benjamin writes, "what possesses itself is free" (*Desire* 3).

Lost Girls and a Desire of One's Own

On the whole, *From Hell* offers a bleak portrait of exploited women, perverted sexual desire, and clinical callousness. More possibilities exist, however, in Moore's project with the artist Melinda Gebbie, *Lost Girls*, as it traces a path from abuse to women re-discovering their own desire. Benjamin notes that too often "women [...] seek their desire in another," turning to "a powerful other who remains in control" (*Bonds* 131). If *From Hell* takes us into the mind of the man who wants to sadistically dominate women, then *Lost Girls* offers the viewpoint of women coming to terms with different forms of exploitation and abuse.

The story is set in an era before the collapse of British and European empires, and the flourishing of women's sexuality is shown to be a momentary revelation in the general narrative of history. Events take place in Austria on the eve of World War One, specifically in the Hotel Himmelgarten, a space of intersubjectivity where the heroines explore their sexuality. The hotel resembles Benjamin's description of the "creation of an environment in which transitional experience is possible, where play and creativity can occur" (*Desire* 18). It is, however, a precarious space, which is threatened by retrograde notions of sexual purity as represented by Moore's account of the sadistic

"Nazi cock-ring," used to painfully suppress expressions of desire (*25,000*, 39). The Hotel Himmelgarten is initially presented as a safe space beyond fascist Puritanism, but there is always a threat of violence and homophobia. The book opens in colonial South Africa where a pair of bigoted maids discuss Alice's lesbian relationships in a troubling manner and, after the "Lost Girls" flee, German soldiers smash up the hotel and break Alice's magic looking glass. All these threats of violent domination create a convincing picture of the atmosphere before the outbreak of war, but they also reflect the violent histories of the three women, each of whom tells the others her story.

Both Dorothy and Wendy have to contend with guilt and shame, and to combat these feelings, they discover the authority of their own bodies, recalling the power of the Willendorf Venus. At the beginning of *Lost Girls*, Wendy is Benjamin's all-sacrificing mother, a sexless prop sacrificing her desire for the demands of propriety. As Benjamin suggests, "The mother's sexual feelings, with their threat of selfishness, passion, and uncontrollability, are a disturbing possibility that even psychoanalysts would relegate to the 'unnatural'" (*Desire* 6). Remembering her confrontation with the rapist, Hook, however, helps Wendy to regain her sense of sexual power. Wendy describes a story from her teenage years: how she fantasized about being raped, and on being confronted by a real rapist, felt guilty, almost as though she deserved to be violated. In this uncomfortable scene, Wendy describes classic rape myths where "no" means "yes" and sexually active or desiring women are never blameless for sexual crimes committed against them. Moore, however, allows Wendy to have a moment of revelation when she realizes the difference between fantasy and reality, and she refuses to take the passive role in dominative scripts of power: "I could think about what I *liked*. That didn't mean I wanted it to *really* happen. That didn't mean that anyone could force it on me" (emphasis in original, 27, 5). Wendy's fantasy of rape is very different from the reality of rape, an act of violence inflected by misogynist male visions of women as empty objects. While Wendy's fantasy envisioned a temporary surrender of power for sexual titillation, actual rape strips women of their desire and their very humanity as is shown in the undifferentiation of Gull in *From Hell*. Gebbie's artwork, however, confronts the rapist Hook with a powerful, vivid, and unashamed female body that dwarfs Hook and his sex. Wendy's body is reflected large in Hook's pupil, and, turning over, the splash page depicts Hook being swallowed by a crocodile *vagina dentata*. Wendy comments that Hook was "*scared* of grown-up women, thought they'd overwhelm him, swallow him" (27, 5).

Like Wendy, Dorothy uses her body to combat sexual domination. When the "Cowardly Lion" shouts lewd comments at Dorothy from a distance, she confronts him with her naked body, and he reacts "like I'd got the whole

Sioux nation down there" (18, 3). The association of female sexuality with a Native American army imbues her with an anti-patriarchal, anti-colonialist power. Like Gull in *From Hell*, Hook and the "Cowardly Lion" are terrified by an all-engulfing women's power and consequently feel the need to dominate them. The women, however, combat such violence with the power of the female body as symbolized by the anti-phallic Willendorf Venus.

Wendy's and Dorothy's stories challenge rape and sexual intimidation, but most significant of the three women is Alice. Following a tradition that has sexualized Lewis Carroll's narratives, Moore rewrites Alice as a withdrawn, narcissistic survivor of abuse. Moore was already thinking about Carroll's Alice when writing *From Hell*, and he compares Annie Crook to Alice. After Annie has the affair with Albert, she is committed to an insane asylum to hide the royal family's shame. When she escapes from the madhouse, her incoherent speech refers to Alice and the idea of a wonderland:

> All about a little girl, an' she went down ... down the hole. Rabbit hole. A — and there was a QUEEN, a horrible old QUEEN.... And the Queen said.... The queen said "Off.... Off with her...." "Off with her head!" [3, 17].

Moore compares the ominous Red Queen from Carroll's narrative to Queen Victoria, who represents not the power of women's desire, but the establishment values of imperialism, rationalism and patriarchy. Wonderland in this instance is far from liberating, representing the wrong-headed values of nineteenth century Britain rather than a sexually satisfying wonderland.

What Alice Crook and the Alice of *Lost Girls* have in common is a sense of their own violation and, consequently, a feeling of the nullity of their desires. In *Lost Girls*, Alice's first sexual experience is being raped by a friend of her father, "Bunny," who introduces her to a disturbing sexual wonderland. Gebbie uses oblong shaped frames that mimic mirrors to tell the rape, each featuring a reflection of events: for example, Alice's dismayed face in the full wine glass that Bunny offers her, and Bunny's face reflected large in Alice's silver buttons (9, 4). Wendy's provocative stance was enlarged in Hook's pupil, yet here Bunny dominates reflective surfaces, just as the abusive Michael dominated the frames with Liz in *From Hell*. Alice, however, develops a resistance strategy, entering the world beyond the looking glass, a world where she is the arbiter of her own pleasure: "a world wherein the most outlandish things were possible, bound by nothing but the logic of desire" (17, 5). In this mirror land, Alice learns how to submit. In school, when she has a liaison with a female teacher, she describes how "I wanted to become a submissive reflection of her every lust," signaling that there is a possibility of domination not only by men but also by women who mimic negative gender scripts taking on the powerful male role (26, 2). Alice develops what Benjamin calls an "ideal love" for her violators and describes how she "shared *their* sadistic pleasure" (emphasis in original, 26, 7). Alice, however, is ultimately freed by storytelling and the imagination, coupled with pleasurable, joyful, shameless sex at the Himmelgarten Hotel, a space of intersubjective relations. Alice describes their stories as a "victory" and she explains that "I once thought part of me was stuck inside [the mirror], but not now. We've rescued her" (30, 2–3). The sexual and imaginative relationships that Alice has with Dorothy and Wendy undo the damage of sexual domination, and it offers an intersubjective space where the women can engage in erotic play whether real or imagined.

This space of sexual freedom is impossible for the group of prostitutes in *From Hell*. Though these women have close relationships and find good sex to be a comfort, they cannot engage in the healing of *Lost Girls* because they are too terrorized by the reality of sexual violence, rather than titillating fantasies of surrendering power. The intersubjective space of sexual discovery at the Himmelgarten Hotel is always threatened, however, and the arrival of soldiers announces an end to sexual liberation. Burning Monsieur Rougeur's erotic books, soldiers enforce the Puritanical values of Western empires on the brink of collapse. Alice's premonition that the soldiers will be "dying in the mud when they should be fucking in bed" prefigures the final images of the book which show a disemboweled, castrated solider (30, 2). A single poppy remains blooming on the battlefield, recalling the visionary beauty of Alice's and Dorothy's opium-tinted first sexual encounter.

* * *

Just as sexual domination is the twin of sexual freedom, *From Hell* and *Lost Girls* are two sides of the same coin. *From Hell* offers a bleak vision of hetaerism and sexual exploitation in nineteenth century London, where "what woman lacks," as Benjamin puts it, "is a desire of her own" (*Desire* 7). Gull's misogynist fantasies of dominating women are merely an extreme version of attitudes belonging to many ordinary men in the narrative who need "to penetrate, to know, and to control [women's] desire" (Benjamin, *Desire* 19). The prostitutes do not have the luxury of discovering their own sexual needs, though the presence of the indomitable Irish mother at the end offers hope for new generations of daughters. Lacking sexually realized mothers, the "Lost Girls" must work through their trauma and, by reaching back into the pleasures of childhood, they pluck free a joyful and shameless version of sexuality.

In writing about sexual domination, Moore asks some uncomfortable questions, but his accounts of women's exploitation rewrite scripts of power, presenting the female body not as an object but a talismanic extension of women's desire. Moore calls for a shameless sexuality, where the erotic can be explored without fear of abuse or violation. For women to discover their own sexual needs is essential to this philosophy, because, as Benjamin concludes, "women must claim their subjectivity and so be able to survive destruction" (*Bonds* 221). Moore seeks to communicate this message in his representations of women, celebrating the moment when the Venus of Willendorf is set free: "Shameless and blind to all the outraged posturings occasioned by her presence, Venus promenades along the moral tightrope of her path, [...] sure — footed and invulnerable in her glamour as she wanders, one step at a time, towards the hoped-for glow of a more human and enlightened future" (*25,000* 89).

7. "Do you understand how I have loved you?"
Terrible Loves and Divine Visions in From Hell [1]

MERVI MIETTINEN

Jack the Ripper's London murders in the late-nineteenth century have lead to a vast proliferation of serial killer fiction from detective mysteries and gothic horror to slasher films and comic books. Unresolved, the Whitechapel murders continue to spawn innumerable theories about the person(s) responsible for these crimes to this day. Writer Alan Moore and artist Eddie Campbell tackle the subject in their ambitious 16-part graphic novel, *From Hell*. Published first serially in 1991–1996 and subsequently as a collected edition with appendices, the graphic novel features almost 600 pages of sooty black-and-white visuals, presenting the reader with a heavily-layered text filled with a web of occult references, intertextual clues, and historical detail. *From Hell* delicately blends fiction with non-fiction, and the plot traces the murders all the way to the throne, identifying Queen Victoria as the commissioner of these crimes, enacted by the Royal Physician Extraordinary, Dr. William Gull, in order to hide the scandalous marriage of Prince Eddy to a local sweet-shop girl, Annie Crook. The narrative focuses on the five victims that most "Ripperologists" agree are Ripper victims: Polly Nichols, Annie Chapman, Elizabeth Stride, Kate Eddowes, and Marie Kelly.

Unlike most works in the detective/mystery/horror genre (Cawelti 329–334), *From Hell* makes no attempt at creating a generic whodunnit? structure of mystery literature, opting instead to reveal Dr. Gull as the killer from the start, and depicting his private occult motivations behind the murders. Through the Masonic-infused visions of Dr. Gull, the narrative goes beyond the more traditional interpretation of the murders as linked to prostitution in which prostitution, the "diseased sexuality" (Gilman 264) of the immoral woman of the nineteenth century, comes to equal the corruption of national health. Within this framework of interpretation, the murders act as a perverse cure to the society and its corrupt elements and, as the Whitechapel women threaten to corrupt the monarchy (both literally and metaphorically) through their diseased sexuality, as a way of restoring the empire.

While keeping these themes visible, *From Hell*, however, ambitiously goes beyond them, combining discourses of love and violence in a highly disturbing way that emphatically functions to mythicize male violence. As Roland Barthes writes in his *Mythologies*, it is through the use of myth that "historical intention" is given "a natural justification" (142). By delicately administrating this kind of Barthesian naturalization to its mythical violence, *From Hell* can actually be read as a re-assertion of male hegemony through purifying violence rather than a deconstruction of it. While one could argue that the way Gull explains his murders as a deliberate work could act as a tool to denaturalize the narrative and violence it contains, the structure of the text itself actively tends to work against it, producing a very troubling text of mythicized male violence. Indeed, the very formal structure of the graphic novel supports this naturalization by taking the unresolved murders and giving them a resolution, a mythical (and natural) closure.

While some critics[2] have interpreted *From Hell* as aiming at deconstructing this particular view of male hegemony through masculine violence, one could argue that it also does the opposite. In mythicizing male violence within the text, the graphic novel goes beyond the traditional depiction of sexual violence and creates a more abstract level of signification that focuses on the killer's metamorphosis into a divine subject through an evisceration of the "sainted" female body. As the female body becomes the annihilated "bloody mass" of Klaus Theweleit's *Male Fantasies* (1987), *From Hell*'s depiction of the murders and Dr. Gull's divine visions create a disturbing discourse of terrible loves and divine visions incanted into existence through mythical violence.

The Ripper, Sexual Violence, and the Questionable Re-Assertion of Male Hegemony

"Hegemony," as Michèle Barrett writes, entails the values of the dominant classes becoming those of society without the use of force (238). In the late nineteenth century, the established masculine hegemony and its high Victorian standards on sexuality deemed any sexual behavior outside Christian matrimony as "deviant sexual behavior" (Hurley 72). Within this context, it can be deduced that the masculine hegemony of Victorian England was increasingly threatened by the East London prostitutes and their more fluid sexuality;

the hegemonic values of the British society were still very much characterized by the male norm, and, as Judith Halberstam writes, sexuality frequently arose as the "dominant mark of otherness" (7), of that which went against the hegemonic value system. The Whitechapel women were in possession of sexual knowledge and asserted themselves very much in the public domain, which meant that they presented a very visible and corporeal threat to the male hegemony (Walkowitz 183). This threat of sexual freedom is easily coupled with the notion that the western cultural discourses have traditionally reserved the place of the Other for the woman as opposite to the masculine normative self. The female comes to represent the negation of the norm, a disruption that challenges order, and it is only over "her dead body, [that] cultural norms are reconfirmed" (Bronfen 181). Logically, then, the female body must be repelled, destroyed, and controlled through violence in order to restore the masculine order.

It is not exactly new to read the murders by Jack the Ripper as a way of reasserting male hegemony. In fact, this view can be traced very clearly to such works as Jane Caputi's controversial (and dated) *The Age of the Sex Crime*. In it, Caputi approaches serial sexual murder as an act of ritual and myth, and, quite incidentally, identifies Jack the Ripper as instigator of the "age of sex crime" in the twentieth century (3–4). However, Caputi's argumentation throughout her book equates nearly all (and only) male-female sexual encounters as examples of sexual violence, ignoring all male-male or female-female relationships, which makes many of her views on gender relations dated and unsupportable. Klaus Theweleit's vast *Male Fantasies* approaches the issue of sexual violence from a more varied perspective, focusing in the first volume on the mutilation and murder of the female body. Theweleit locates two distinctive desires at work in the murders of women by fascist soldiers in early twentieth century Germany: a contradictory desire for proximity and distance; both of these "compulsions" are satisfied in the act of killing and mutilation where a man simultaneously "penetrates" the woman through his weapon and removes her from himself by killing her (196). However, Theweleit recognizes a level of lover's intimacy between the killer and his victim in the killing, made possible through a process where the woman is removed of her identity and "reduced to a bloody pulp" (196). This kind of psycho-sexual analysis of sexual murder surpasses both the simple view promoted by Caputi as well as the normative discourses of romantic love and develops into a more abstract, dehumanized vision of a transgressive and violent "love" that overcomes the physicality of the body by literally obliterating it.

It could be argued that *From Hell* aims at problematizing some of the violent discourses present within the case of Jack the Ripper and the entire discourse of male violence in the twentieth century (Caputi's so-called "age of sex crime"). While the murders themselves took place at the end of the nineteenth century, the assertion of *From Hell* is very clearly that the murders literally "delivered" the twentieth century, as Gull states it (10, 33). Thus, Moore and Cambell take on a nineteenth century crime to address a twentieth century issue, and they openly state their hope of producing a more realist and less misogynist reconstruction. For example, the representation of the Whitechapel women as "ordinary women" (Moore, Appendix I, 8) as opposed to either saints or whores clearly aims at a more realist and less stereotyped representation of the murder victims. However, there are complications and contradictions to this interpretation. In analyzing the misogynist violence of *From Hell*, Christine Ferguson for example argues that even though Moore and Campbell aim at distancing themselves from the obvious misogyny of the "Ripper nostalgia," they at least partially fail due to William Gull's "speculative etiology," which she interprets as mystical displacement that gives the murders a motive that derives from a supernatural "design" as opposed to mere misogyny (56–7). In other words, as Moore and Campbell devote several pages (even chapters) to Dr. Gull and allow him to present a detailed account as to why these murders have to occur, they simultaneously allow him to remove some of the blame.

This "mystical displacement" connects in with the earlier concept of Barthesian "naturalization" of violence through the use of a mythological framework, which begins to function as a natural justification for the crimes. While Gull's explicit narration of this mythological framework behind the murders may be seen as a way to de-naturalize the murders, the formal structure of the graphic novel systematically proceeds to do the opposite. The towering phallic structures of London loom heavily over the characters in the panels, the very "architexture," the shape of the text (Amar 686) of the graphic novel enhances Gull's words. The intimidating occult power prescribed to London and its architecture is depicted, both textually and visually, as something beyond human comprehension, and ultimately responsible for Gull's violent actions. The intimidating visuals of London's buildings, often shown from a lower perspective to stress their magnitude, visually enhance the powerlessness experienced by the Whitechapel women (and the reader, too, powerless at the magnitude of the text). As this occult power is closely intertwined with his visions, their relevance in re-assessing the misogyny of the text cannot be overlooked. The very structure of the text — its formal "architexture" — becomes the true culprit, as *From Hell* becomes a text of such a grandeur and force with its intimidating drawings and dense references that it goes beyond comprehension — and by going beyond comprehension via its formal structure, it simultaneously undermines any ability to cognitively understand male violence, too. Thus, the very formal quality of the text itself becomes an accomplice to the mythicization of the masculine violence it depicts.

Annihilation through Architec/xture — The Female Body Rendered Lifeless

The representation of female characters in *From Hell* provides a curious yet rarely discussed juxtaposition between the Whitechapel women and the other female characters. While Dr. Gull's violent attacks on the female body focus solely on the women who through their relative independence threaten the male hegemony, the text also "attacks" the upper-class women through its very form. The upper-class women come to represent the opposite of the prostitutes in every way, as the text depicts them as mostly static, silent, and sterile, concealed indoors. (No "good" women are really shown active outdoors at any point.) These "proper" Victorian women, such as Gull's mother, his wife, or even Queen Victoria, are all firmly suppressed into the appropriate location of the good woman: the domestic. They do not enjoy sex (as Gull's wedding night shows), nor do they act as sexual subjects, remaining rigid and with significantly fewer close-ups of their facial expressions and emotions. While these women remain physically unharmed, they, too, can be read as victims of the same male hegemony imposed by the text that annihilates the women in Whitechapel via Jack the Ripper. It is not enough to merely divide the threatening female body into Madonnas and whores and then brutally extinguish the whore, but the female element is in its entirety *"annihilated"* in a way that ensures that the "good" component, too, is "robbed of life, rendered lifeless" (emphasis in original, Theweleit 183). Queen Victoria becomes a cardboard cut-out of herself (2, 18–19 and 2, 28), and the images of the good wives and mothers indeed render them "lifeless," static, and confined whilst the women of Whitechapel, while free to roam the streets, are literally robbed of their lives and identities. This robbing of life, whether literal or abstract, is a key way of subtly re-asserting male hegemony in *From Hell*.

The architecture of London plays a central role in the narrative, visually emphasizing the phallic control expressed by Gull in his monologues. Campbell's sooty black and gray drawings of London loom intimidatingly over the characters while his "unique cross-hatchings" mirror Jack the Ripper's slicing motions with which he inscribes his history on the bodies of his victims (Ali 611). The phallic nature of London's architecture is closely woven into the urban landscape, anchoring the phenomenon of sexual murder firmly into the industrialized and overpopulated city as opposed to the countryside. Dr. Gull's masculine power as Jack the Ripper is inseparable from the city as his habitat; it could not have been born without it. This is underlined in the last vision of the dying Dr. Gull, as he sees a woman with her daughters (presumably Marie Kelly) on a vast, open field on what is most likely Irish countryside. However, at this vision Gull for the first time expresses fear, and she soon expels him from the scene: "Clear off back to Hell and leave us BE!" (14, 23). This clearly invites the interpretation that Gull/Jack the Ripper and his male power is constrained into the urban landscape of London, and the natural, open, and light (and feminine) countryside renders him and his masculine control powerless.

Contrasting/Obscuring Sex and Violence

London as a site of phallic architecture and the female body as a site of mutilation receive a curious juxtaposition in *From Hell*. As Di Liddo notes, Gull at several points refers to the city of London as "a body," which is contrasted with the living bodies of the women he kills: unlike the mapped and clear lines of London, the "female bodies of the Whitechapel prostitutes are seen by Gull as mysterious, and therefore represent too great a danger to the status quo the doctor has vowed to defend" (79). The fluid female bodies of the prostitutes are contrasted with Gull's controlled Victorian body, and this is most prominently executed in the graphic novel through the depiction of sex. Whereas all the five victims are depicted at various points in the narrative as having sex and often even enjoying it (the most mutilated of them all, Marie Kelly, even instigates a threesome with another female), Gull's only sexual encounter depicted in the narrative is his wedding night, illustrated in a sequence of completely black panels accompanied only with the speech balloons containing the dialogue between him and his wife, culminating in his wife's shrieking: "Oh NO! William, it's too BIG! William, stop it, you're hurting me. Take it out! Take it OUT!" (2, 12). Gull's failure to achieve a satisfying sexual union with his wife is all the more evident when contrasted with the Whitechapel women's numerous sexual activities. While no sexual interaction per se takes place between Gull and his victims, the sexual overtones and implications of the murders are obvious, highlighting the perversely amorous nature between the killer and his victims.

When murder is analyzed as analogous to sex, the most common assertion (as exemplified here by Caputi) bluntly asserts the male killer as penetrating the female victim (133) with little thought given to other forms of sexual murder (for example, gay murders or murders by women). This psychosexual analysis is carried out more thoroughly by Theweleit, who notes the relevance of the specific body parts, mouth, and genitalia, of women that most often are the focus of the attack; the mouth and the genitalia (the mouth symbolically representing the genitalia) are not attacked with bare hands but with penetrating objects (191). He does not ignore the obvious sexual connotations of this, but he also stresses that, ultimately, a man kills with "weapons, not symbols," and that the victims are "living human beings" whose death, when "translated into something else, obscures the sexual violence present at the killing" (194). While the depiction of the murders in *From Hell* at first sight seems to comply with the common assertion of sexual murder (and initially appear as if critiquing it), a closer analysis reveals how, in fact, this process of obscuring seems to take place — and through this process, the need for sexual violence is enforced as it serves as a gateway for the male killer's metamorphosis. While Ferguson's earlier argument on *From Hell*'s "speculative etiology" critiqued the mystical displacement that took place through the Mason-influenced designs of Gull, I would argue that it is this process of obscuring, located in the very act of killing as Gull deploys the act of violence to "trigger" himself into a new level of (higher) consciousness (10, 20), which produces a most uncanny mythicization of violence within the text.

So, for example, the murder of Kate Eddowes in Chapter Eight is depicted as a very physical act of murder, complete with near-orgasmic grunts from Dr. Gull (8, 38–39), which on the surface appears to conform with Caputi's sexual murder. The knife becomes the clichéd metaphorical erect phallus that penetrates her throat and abdomen as he removes her uterus, her "true wedding ring," as Gull earlier referred to the organ (7, 21). Of course, the focused attack and mutilation of the female reproductive organs testifies to the "vagina's castrating potential" (Theweleit 201) in a very Freudian sense, and the desire to remove and mutilate it signals a desire to control the female body. In this way, *From Hell* quite clearly underlines the connection between sex and violence Caputi sees as dominating all sexual encounters, which may help to explain why some critics of *From Hell* would conclude that the desired effect of the authors would be on some level to parody the entire discourse of murder as sexual intercourse. However, what should not be overlooked is the second level of meaning to the murder as defined by Theweleit which is also present in the "obscuring" of Eddowes' body: by brutally mutilating it, the destruction of her form becomes an entry point into Gull's powerful private vision of a twentieth century skyscraper. This vision, of which the reader, too, is allowed to partake, testifies powerfully to the idea that a desire to enter a "trancelike state" (which thereby obscures the actual violence) is indeed the ultimate goal behind the violence (204). It is this process of obscuring, enhanced through the visions shared to the reader, which actively functions to further mythicize the violence through the very structure of *From Hell.*

Terrible Loves, Divine Visions and the Female as "Bloody Mass"

The relationship between Dr. Gull and his victims is not just that of a sexual murder. Throughout the text there exists a bizarre, transcendent love affair between Dr. Gull and the women. During the pre-murder (indeed, pre-coital) discussion between Dr. Gull and his first victim, Polly Nicholls, she responds to his elaborate notions of time and history where their names shall go together: "Sir, you make it sound as if we're to be married!" (5, 27). Humorously, he acknowledges this to be true. Later, before the murder of Annie Chapman in Chapter Seven, he muses to her: "Oh yes. Oh yes, you're all my brides. Each one of you" (7, 22). These unholy "marriages," however, are soon consummated through an act of misogynist violence, and climaxed in the mutilation of the female body as Gull destroys the "true wedding ring" of his victims by slashing their genitals.

In Gull's mind, the real violence of the mutilation and death of the women becomes an allegorizing act, as their blood spills on the streets of London in an occult desire to control their sex. The women become abstracts, their individuality removed much in the same way torture victims become "nonpersons" through the act of torture (Denton-Borhaug 224). This loss of individuality is further enhanced by Campbell's choice of depicting all the Whitechapel women in a style that occasionally makes them indistinguishable from each other, as his "closely woven lines blur the women's facial features throughout the novel" (Di Liddo 81). While it can be argued that this is done primarily for the purpose of an ambiguous ending in the case of Marie Kelly's death (the Appendix clearly implies that she was not actually killed), it also collapses all five women into one, symbolic female, stripping them from their personal identities and enhancing their shared qualities.[3]

Through the destruction of the female bodies of his victims, Dr. Gull's true motivation goes beyond mere masculine re-assertion of power through sexual murder, as the killings paradoxically remove the borders between Gull and his female victims while his earlier monologues claim to do the exact opposite. This interpretation is further supported by Theweleit's recognition of the underlying motivation behind killing as going beyond the obvious interpretation of the murder as a penetrative sexual act, stressing instead the desire to see the female body as "a bloody mass" that enables "a specific state in the man himself—as if he were overcome by a sudden *absence*" (202). This "absence" refers to a hallucinatory state where the killer is not fully present, which also means that he does not really commit the murder:

> As a "bloody mass," the victim loses her outlines and her character as an object. The same thing happens here to the perceiving *subject*. He, too, finds himself in a state of dissolution. This process, in which both the killer and his victim lose their boundaries and enter a union, and in which the predominance of hallucinatory perception puts the man into a trancelike state, seems to be the ultimate aim of the attacks [Theweleit 203–204].

Both the victim and the killer become "dissoluted" in the killing (Theweleit 196); the boundary between them is lifted. In *From Hell*, Dr. Gull enters a trancelike state and experiences "visions" during the murders, inviting the interpretation that he reaches this state of "absence" precisely because he kills the women, and that, ultimately, his goal and motivation for these violent acts is not just the purging of the Empire from their disease (which does remain a subtext), but to himself reach a new level of consciousness (indeed, a new subjectivity) through an intimate (albeit violent) union between him and his female victims. Ironically, then, while Gull's monologues argue that his mission is to enhance the borders between men and women and to suppress the female, the collapse of these very boundaries is precisely what enables him to experience his visions and transcend as an omnipresent entity into the twentieth century—which he then ultimately denounces in Chapter Ten.

As Dr. Gull's bloody hands cradle the organs of Polly Nicholls, he experiences his first revelation: "Oh. Oh, look at it! It's.... What is it? I've never seen anything quite like.... Look at it, Netley. Can you SEE? Can you SEE it, Netley?—Light, Netley. Did you see? She was full of light" (5, 33). Dr. Gull experiences a private vision in the dark alley by the mutilated body, and neither Netley, his driver (and accomplice), nor the reader is allowed to partake in these visions yet. During the second murder, Dr. Gull experiences a brief vision with the reader, looking through a window and seeing a clearly twentieth century living room. This, the reader is allowed to see, too, receiving a glimpse of what is to come. As the murders escalate in Chapter Eight, Gull experiences a vision of a skyscraper during which Netley thinks he has disappeared: "I couldn't see you, I ... Oh my God, sir. Oh my God, where did you go?" (8, 41). His absence becomes literal as his boundaries disappear, yet he paradoxically seems to become present throughout history, as the final vision in the madhouse seems to suggest in Chapter 14. The mutilations of the women serve as access points into Gull's visions, and the more brutal the dismemberment, the more intense are the visions and the more the reader is allowed to see of these futuristic visions. As the reader is increasingly drawn into the visions through the shifts in focalization, the obscuring of the mythicized violence intensifies dramatically. After the murder of Kate Eddowes (whom he has mistaken for the final victim, Marie Kelly), Dr. Gull laments on the way he failed to reach this trance properly: "To come so far along a path and then turn back while having scarcely glimpsed your destination.... One more. Just one more would have done it" (8, 41). To Gull, the women and their "bloody mass" are a portal to a new level of consciousness, a key to his personal ascension. In the final murder of Marie Kelly, he fully reaches this trance as he experiences visions of the future and his past with every stroke of the blade.

The mystical nature of Dr. Gull's actions (his "speculative etiology") underlines the way the murders are not, in fact, personal, but universal, almost abstract: this becomes clear as Dr. Gull, at several points in the novel, proclaims his spiritual love for the women he kills, effectively blurring the distinction between reality and fantasy, seeing the women not as women, but as symbols of something greater, an abstract feminine entity. The mutilation of the female body means that the woman becomes "dissoluted," both as a love object as well as a bodily object (Theweleit 196). The desire to witness the female as "bloody pulp" overrides the more common notion of murder as "just" analogous to sexual intercourse, although that level of signification is not completely absent from the pages of the graphic novel. In destroying the bodies of real women, Gull may metaphorically expel the female from the masculine hegemonic state through their suffering in the tradition of ancient druid mythology (4, 27), but what he ultimately desires is his own metamorphosis which rather than separating the male and the female appears to dissolve the borders between them.

What ultimately motivates Dr. Gull as Jack the Ripper is his desire to reach a new level of consciousness, to reach a state of dissolution through the literal evisceration of the female body where the killer and the victim, through the victim's status as a "bloody mass," lose their respective boundaries and become "one" in an illusory union. Through the mutilation of the women's bodies, *Gull* the murderer is the one who is transfigured; Gull is the one who becomes *God*. The climax is reached during the final murder of Marie Kelly in Chapter Ten, which goes on for numerous consecutive pages without a single word or sound effect. As every detail of the mutilation is presented, the panel breakdown slows significantly, causing the killing to last much longer than the previous murders (Di Liddo 80). In complete silence over numerous pages of steady, silent, and blood-soaked panels, the reader is forced to witness the extensive mutilation ("evisceration," as Ferguson calls it [56]) of Marie

Kelly's body as Gull transfixes her into a saint. The panels depict close-ups of the blade slicing the flesh and organs, whilst Gull with visible affection arranges her body into the spectacle later captured in police photographs (Ho 99). As Marie Kelly becomes a mass of blood and tissue, she is transformed into a tool of Gull's metamorphosis, and thus herself a virtuous saint as the instrument of his ascension.

To seal the murders' nature as a part of a perverse lover's intimacy, Gull's mind transforms Marie Kelly into a virtuous saint, whereas he himself becomes her savior. Through his violent love, his actions, she is being transfixed, elevated as the instrument to his metamorphosis. Gull heralds himself as her savior, her redeemer; he has purged her diseased and corrupt body from its pollution through death:

> Do you understand how I have loved you? You'd have all been dead in a year or two from liver failure, men, or childbirth. Dead. Forgotten. I have saved you. Do you understand that? I have made you safe from time, and we are wed in legend, inextricable within eternity [10, 23].

As Ali notes, the words "I have saved you" become extremely paradoxical in comparison to what the reader has just witnessed (625), creating a terrible vision of love through transcending violence where Gull becomes the redeemer of the women's lives.

Conclusion

From Hell depicts a brutal "love affair" between Jack the Ripper and his victims, asserting both levels of Theweleit's act of murder: violence as sex and the dissolving of the female (195–196). As I have demonstrated, *From Hell* presents this rhetoric wrought in heavy occult mythology, which can be read as mere misogyny shrouded in "speculative etiology." Furthermore, as the murders are obscured by the intensified visions of Dr. Gull, the acts themselves are removed from the sphere of reality, becoming abstract. Indeed, it is precisely through this kind of Barthesian mythicization and the resulting naturalization of sex crimes the murders become "anything but the logical and eminently functional product of the system of male domination" (Ferguson 30). It is easy to read *From Hell* as deliberately setting out to display the murders as "logical and eminently functional," and in the process aiming at demythicizing the crimes, displaying them for what they are, laying bare the shameless misogyny behind it and indeed (pun intended) ripping it open. This reading can be challenged, however, through the analysis of the murders as emphatically mythicizing male violence. Furthermore, the formal structure of the graphic novel itself, despite its attempts at de-naturalizing the crimes, ultimately supports this mythicization process through its formal qualities (such as the elimination of the women's individuality through the artwork or the depiction of London), which reproduce the same affect as the dissolving of the female body as a "bloody mass" in the killing. *From Hell*, through its dense weave of quotations, allusions, and historical detail, in itself seems to create a divine text that cannot be de-naturalized or de-mythicized, but which despite its vast references and appendices, ultimately constructs rather that deconstructs the case of Jack the Ripper, and in the process mythicizes masculine violence in a highly disturbing way.

The violent and distorted images of love, sexuality, death, and power appear to combine in *From Hell*'s dark and sinister narrative to criticize its misogynistic violence, yet both the representation of the killings as a part of a larger plan to re-assert male hegemony and the trance-like state sought by Dr. Gull through the evisceration of the female body undermine this reading. The formal structure of the text further problematizes the reading of the graphic novel, as it seems to go beyond comprehension, and thus further evoke the reading of the text as emphasizing mythical violence as natural: love and death become inextricably linked, as the male killer's ascension into divinity is dependent upon the bloody mass of the female body.

Notes

1. I am grateful to Matti Savolainen and Maarit Piipponen for early suggestions and feedback in this essay. However, my deepest gratitude goes to Todd Comer and Joe Sommers for their insightful comments, support, and patience during the writing process. This text would not exist without them.
2. See for example Ho and Di Liddo.
3. The women's names, too, form a repeated point of confusion that further enhances their shared nature as the allegorical female of Gull's delusions. In Chapter 5, Netley reports to Gull the names of the victims-to-be: "Some big Swede they call 'Long Liz' … an older woman, name of Anne Sivvey … and another Mary; Mary Nicholls … though they calls 'er 'Polly'" (5, 10). "Annie Sivvey" refers to Annie Chapman, and Polly Nicholl's real name was in fact Mary Ann. Later in the text Kate Eddowes gives her name as "Mary Kelly" in Chapter 8 (which proves fatal), and Marie Kelly is reported to have several nicknames, including "Ginger" and "Fair Emma" (Appendix, 42).

8. Body Politics
Unearthing an Embodied Ethics in V for Vendetta
TODD A. COMER

V for Vendetta may be Alan Moore's most direct commentary on the (superheroic) body and its often fascist desires. While *V* was written in a period framed by the conservative policies of Reagan and Thatcher, intimations of fascism are everywhere in Moore's work. The German soldier who shatters Alice's mirror in *Lost Girls,* William Gull's bird-like transcendence in *From Hell,* Superman's repression of the too-earthy Swamp Thing in "The Jungle Line," Moriarty's cavorite-fueled flight toward space in *The League of Extraordinary Gentlemen*— all speak to Moore's critique of the fascist tendency to marginalize the world and others. Moore and illustrator David Lloyd's graphic novel is the most direct commentary on the body if only because the *body* of the villain, the fascist society, and superhero, V, are obnoxiously present, even as they strangely absent themselves. The fascist society erases or remolds individual bodies as it ideologically frames itself as an immortal communal body, and V's body is vibrantly alive even if always hidden behind cape, gloves, and mask.

The novel appears to ground agency to an *embodied* totalitarianism in V's (dis)embodiment. Just as power is very much an issue of a writing and ideology naturalized by the body, freedom also appears to be an issue of the body and representation. But Moore and Lloyd get it wrong, at least on one overt level, by misunderstanding the ultimate goal of fascism and reproducing a notion of agency that merely reproduces on another level the (ontological) state that it presumes to counter. Rather, in other words, than being an opponent to the state, the terrorist V embodies a repetition of the things he allegedly opposes — immortality, permanence, and exclusion. While in agreement with Moore and Lloyd's general politics, I offer a thoroughgoing critique of their method by showing how it does a disservice to that which most essentially defines us, and limits us: our bodies. But I do not end there.

In the last portion of the essay I uncover a narrative which shifts the locus of agency from V and Evey, his erstwhile partner, to two relatively minor characters: Finch and Valerie. The goal is to uncover a theory of agency that gives the body its due, allowing for the intimacy inherent in mortality, while offering an option to the fascist system that truly constitutes a difference and not merely an opposition of the same. The ultimate purpose in what follows is to use *V for Vendetta* to construct a theory which, by embodying writing, creates space for a way of being that undermines fascism in a more nuanced, ethical, and less contradictory manner.

Putting on the Face of Ideology

Ideology grounds itself in bodies in Moore and Lloyd's *V for Vendetta*. Each segment of the government is synechdochally-named after a part of the human body: the Eye is in change of surveillance; the Fingermen are the enforcers; the Nose is in charge of crime detection, and so on (15). Efficient working of each of these parts creates a social body that is both coherent and effective, at least for those who are its able and willing members. The "nature" of this power is nicely introduced in the first few pages. The opening pages show V placing a mask over his face and a desperate Evey heavily rouging her cheeks, creating what she hopes is the marketable face of a prostitute. The only words are broadcast over the radio by the Voice of Fate (9), a human voice meant to be understood as the voice of the computer Fate. The Voice describes the "*face* of London tonight" (emphasis added). In all of these cases, identity is being constructed, though not all constructions are created equally. In the last case, the Voice of Fate tells the population the time, date, road conditions, temperature, and information on food rationing and a "major terrorist ring." The voice even predicts the exact time that a rain shower will begin, "12:07 A.M" (14).

There could be *many* differing representations of London. But what we see here is a seamless linkage of Fate's words with reality — seamless because the text points unerringly to nature's reality (i.e, schedule), naturalizing one particular ideological representation of London. Ideology "is the system of the ideas and representations which dominate the mind of a man or a social group" (Althusser 120). Louis Althusser writes:

> It is indeed a peculiarity of ideology that it imposes (without appearing to do so [...]), obviousnesses as obviousnesses, which *we cannot fail* to recognize and before which we have the inevitable and natural reaction of crying out [....]: That's obvious! That's right! That's true! [129].

By this construction, Nature is immortal and if a power structure can link itself to that which is natural, it may also put on such an un-queried immortality. Power is seductive then to the degree that its construction of reality is understood to be *natural*, not a construct, and therefore the *only* "right" and "true" option available. The naturalizing effect described above — the Voice's linkage to weather patterns — then doubles back and naturalizes the notion of society as a body as well. (The fact that "Norsefire" [28] chooses to embody itself is a similar naturalizing move.) This is the "voice" of Fate, after all, and, if it is in sync with Nature, it makes sense that its representation as a self and body would also be naturalized.

Such ideological work naturalizes a very specific notion of what it means to be a social body, however. For example, the graphic novel's first panel represents the source of the Voice of Fate's broadcast as a skyscraper (9). In the absence of a representation of its foundation, the skyscraper — and the words that erupt spontaneously from within it — seems to transcend the earth. Similarly, the buildings around it stand back from it with the emptiness of air serving as borders. In the second panel, Lloyd draws a mass of people whose vague figures blur into one another. But, clearly, in this panel and in the two that follow, borders are being created between people. The mass of people are surveyed, separated, directed along certain routes, and molded into an individualistic social body. What these early panels suggest is that humanity's natural ontological state is to be *with* others (Nancy, *The Inoperative Community* 15), but here — through the systematic application of ideological and forceful mechanisms — individualism is naturalized. Despite the voice balloon which points to the skyscraper and encloses the words of the Voice, this building, *the* symbol of immanence in the opening, is not a person at all. And in the following panels, no identity seems to stands on its own. In every case, there is identity construction which is in relation to the world. Jean-Luc Nancy's *The Inoperative Community* defines the traditional community (founded on the metaphysical notion of the individual) as irrational, desiring the impossible, immanence. Immanence, as Nancy describes it, is "the absolutely detached for — itself, taken as origin and as certainty" (3). Fascism, as presented in this novel, concretizes the "atom[ic]" logic of individualism which says that it is possible to exist outside of relation. The society instituted by Norsefire desires immortality naturalized in the form of an individualistic social body. It is common to think of singular persons as "individuals." However, in terms of fascism, the exclusionary logic of individualism is expanded to the level of the nation, and built upon the erasure of the particularities of singular bodies.

At the center of this society is Fate, a non-human work of artifice, which Adam Susan refers to as his "bride" (38). His narcissistic love we are told is a reaction to the chaos of modern life and to the "empty gasps and convulsions of brutish coupling." Fate is a "god" for Susan who believes that his connection with it brings him into relation with the "whole of existence." The fascist leader falls back on heterosexual imagery to naturalize his own monadic love. Much the same can be seen in more traditional relationships, however: Helen, who constantly uses her body to cement power relations with men, propositions Finch in the hopes of building a new army and rebuilding the state (264–265). When he refuses her, she calls him a "queer," and he walks on alone. In this scene societal "order" and heterosexuality are directly linked. Love and sex in general are put to work for the state as bodies become mere tools in an exchange of power. The first panel of the novel represents a transcendent, phallic skyscraper because, ultimately, that is the essential *telos* of fascism: to transcend the body and gain the purity of an idea (9).

Blowing Up the Parliament, or V's "Grand Opening"

Fascist ideology holds that identity is a seamless process in which the world outside has little relevance to societal identity construction. The panels depicting Evey and V's construction of identity give the lie to this alleged immanence of identity construction; if a traditional story hides its creative process as it forms a seamless, realistic, and, hence, convincing portrait of how life "naturally" *is*, these panels demonstrate the denaturalizing process behind all identity construction. But they also show the reader, vividly, how it is the world and its others that assist in giving birth to identity (Nancy, *The Birth to Presence* 13). Evey, while young and healthy, requires a literal mirror to construct her identity (9). If fascism is concerned with immanence, Evey's need for an exterior mirror suggests a very different notion of identity in which the self finds itself by crossing borders. Evey's identity construction is, in fact, just an indirect, yet individual, version of what we saw above in the molding and direction of the masses. She is driven toward illegal prostitution by a government, a figurative mirror perhaps, which has made it impossible for her to live without additional income. Evey's "illegal" identity construction is then to some degree a product of the world *outside* of her. In the terms described above, Fate's broadcast is in sync with the "body" of nature; in this case, Evey uses make-up to construct a prostitute's face, but, assuming it was well constructed, the facial representation does not accurately the body which fails to perform as her text (make-up) suggests (10–11). There is too much of a gap — or, to use V's phrase as he blows up Parliament, a "grand opening" (13) — for her to convince anyone, especially a fingerman, of her identity. It is simply not a natural fit. For this reason, she serves as a useful foil to the naturalized identity of Norsefire.

V is more complicated. Years before, V had been rounded up with a number of other people rejected from society for reasons of race, sexual preference, politics, or disability, and forced to undergo hormone treatments at Larkhill Resettlement Camp (80). V's face is said to be horribly "ugly," and his body, following the camp's destruction, may be covered by burns (81–83). Unlike the fascist state's foregrounding of the body, V's body is lost behind his caped costume; and, on his face, he wears a Guy Fawkes mask with two brightly rouged cheeks. The very fact that his body is distant—that is, not easily mapped, isolated, or measured by what amounts to a regime based on Foucaultian biopower—and possibly disabled in the conventional sense demonstrates that it will not be able to cohere with his facial construction; after all, a naturalizing representation cannot be grounded in an atypical body. The facial construction itself is also excessive; unlike the Voice of Fate or Evey's construction which desires a version of realism, V's costume eschews all such seriousness. His representation and his body embody, if you will, an enormous gap in signification, and this is the source of V's agency.

Using Ferdinand de Saussure's more precise language, fascism could be seen as an attempt to take a signifier and signified, and seamlessly naturalize them in the "body" of the sign. V's agency amounts to a demonstration of the "arbitrary" link between signifier and signified, and the relational nature of the sign in general (Saussure 833). As V destroys one particular *meaningful* reality, the Voice of Fate is incapable of naturalizing a new meaning. It cannot keep up: there is an every-widening gap between what had been a naturalized, hence seamless, connection between the Voice's representation of reality and reality itself. As V continues puncturing this border, the population doubts the government, seeing that reality is open to interpretation and change. Susan states the problem succinctly when Prothero, who voices Fate, is kidnapped—"he's taken away the Voice of Fate. How shall I fill the *gap* it leaves? How shall my country fill the silence?" (emphasis added; 3. 189). As the preceding panels show, the people begin to fill the silence with anti-authoritarian graffiti. They write back to the Empire.

Do Ideas Copulate?

V loosens up the significatory process and reveals the meaningful play of existence. Bound up in one particular naturalized meaning of reality, fascists would, arguably, be less in touch with reality and others, leading to the alienation of love and sex. Everything, after all, in such a lockstep framework is grist for the fascist mill — in such a society, "reality" would be even less likely to be encountered, if it ever is, unclouded by a subjective representation. For V, the play of the sign should, therefore, logically lead to a greater degree of bodily encounter with the world and with others, to a love and experience of sexuality without the degree of alienation seen above. But to what degree is this true?

To begin with the obvious: V's agency against a body-hating state is contradictorily constructed on his own body's destruction. Since his body's destruction begins with the fascist state, this instance could be overlooked; however, the central narrative of agency, really, is that of Evey and she only achieves agency at the expense of her body as V (in the guise of the state) starves, tortures, and humiliates her toward freedom. V, in other words, reproduces the alienating nature of the fascist state, but takes it to such a degree that this objectification tips over into something allegedly antithetical to the state: freedom. Freedom happens at the moment that the body and its desire for intimacy and love is overcome; freedom only happens when Evey marginalizes her love of Gordon. This reads like the age-old distrust of the body found in any number of texts from Plato's *Phaedo* on: once the body and its desires are marginalized, the spirit, soul, or mind, is free from the restrictions of its specific body but also, in this context, the national body as well. When V tells Evey that she was in a "prison" (when she was with Gordon) which "deformed" her (170), he is using an ableist metaphor to speak not of the body but of the soul's perversion. The body does not matter to him; in fact, the body may be tortured because it is the body that is partly at fault. The body is weak and desires comfort and cannot therefore be trusted.

If fascism is really a desire for immanence, for permanence and immortality, then V's erasure of his own body becomes questionable. While, yes, he may confront fascism with the *artificiality* of the representational process, V also ends up implying that, yes, it is possible to reach immortality. When Finch fatally shoots him, V says, "Did you think to kill me? There's no flesh or blood within this cloak to kill. There's only an idea. Ideas are bullet-proof" (236). His transfiguration into the "badass" idea that cannot be killed occurs at the moment that V escapes from prison with his body covered by burns. In the figurative erasure of his mutable, finite body, he ends up reproducing the sort of fixity that he supposedly fights against — a body that is not a body, but is superhuman, god-like in its disembodiment.

Arguably, V is engaging in a version of strategic essentialism ("Essentialism"). V uses the fixity of ideas — despite his alleged aversion to fixity of all sorts — as a short term tactic on the way to a world in which any such fixity can be eliminated. In a specific sense this "essentialism" is undeniable. To bring Evey to her body-denying freedom, V must put on the essentializing body of the nation, only to dispose of it when a particular empowering work has been achieved. This remarkable process begs many questions. Not the least of which is the practical question of how one can find this experience separate from a totalitarian regime? Even V, after all, requires the system to transform the young woman in his hands. And it is important to note that she found this freedom (162) *before* V's charade was unmasked; it was not, in other words, a confrontation with a naturalized fascist structure alongside V's lie (i.e., his unveiling of the playful nature of the signifying process) that changed her. Evey became free primarily through the brute force of power.

The above argument leaves out any analysis of those pages dealing with Ruth and Valerie's narrative, a crucial part of Evey's "prison" experience. But even when figured into my argument, the overt message of the episode gestures toward the permanence of essentialism. Valerie writes, "I know every inch of this cell. This cell knows every inch of me. Except one" (160). This "inch" of personal "integrity" (156), this kernel of her essence, is that which must not be "deformed," to repeat V's predicate (170). While V's strategic essence (as a fascist actor) is anathema to that of Valerie, they both remain akin as essences; they both deny the body and the play of existence. They both, for that reason, do not find a way outside of the closure of the fascist state which also denies the body on its way to becoming some *ideal* iteration of the "Thousand Year Reich."

V's theatricality and playful use of representation do also connect to a stereotypical gay identity, though his desire, if he has any, is never shown. Along with the Valerie and Ruth's lesbian romance, non-straight sex appears to be privileged; however, this privileging is *almost* in passing and there is no clear link between an embodied sexuality and agency which would truly counter fascism. It is possible that gay sexuality offers an answer to the fascist coupling of men and women in part because such sex is less easily yoked to biological reproduction and the process of naturalization. But, if so, such a theme has not been overtly foregrounded. V's idea-driven agency does not make room for an agency, a way of being that would allows to humans to meet as finite figures open to the world. Ideas do not love, and they do not copulate.

Finally, in terms of the very *form* of Moore and Lloyd's novel: David Mitchell and Sharon Snyder's work on the representation of disability demonstrates how ideas, political and otherwise, are grounded in bodies to "help[...] secure a knowledge that would otherwise drift away of its own insubstantiality" (214–215). Norsefire, then, uses a metaphorical body to "materialize" and stabilize its social idea which would, otherwise, be mere "textual effect[s]."

V's obliterated body, similarly, operates as a metaphor for the idea of anarchy because, after all, nothing fascist can be naturalized by such a body. Moore and Loyd's text suggests that this opposition of a national body and a non-body is a real opposition when, contradictorily, Norsefire's obsession with the body masks an ultimate desire to leave the body behind and become an incorruptible idea. To the degree that they discard the body and reach for the fixity of ideas, Norsefire and V are essentially the same: they create a world of binary oppositions and exclusions and an endless cycle of violent repetitions. By *formally* posing this battle of idea-bodies, the authors could be said to be falling into the same impasse.

V for Vagina: Toward an Embodied Vendetta

There *are* gestures toward an embodied agency that are, arguably, not overtly or coherently brought within the fold of V's own theorization of freedom. What follows constructs a theory of agency around Valerie and Finch rather than V and Evey. This is helpful for two reasons: First, in light of power's link to men and representation in the above, Valerie embodies a different style of writing which does not reproduce the violence of fascism. Second, V and Evey's agential process is self-oriented, even if it is focused around the erasure of the self's ideological desires. A focus on Valerie and Finch, allows for a theory of agency which begins, not with a focus on the self, but with space, the world outside of the ego.

The new spatiality and grounding for agency that follows is triply hidden — within the body of Valerie, in a wall, and in the novel at large. Though the word boxes do not provide the text, the toilet paper that Evey rescues from a crevice in her cell wall does (154). Valerie writes, "I am me, and I don't know who you are but I love you. I have a pencil. A little one they did no[t] find. I am a woman. I hid it inside me." This obscure text yokes together love, sex, and identity in complex ways. In light of the emphasis on representation within fascism, it is difficult not to see the placement of this pencil as an implicit critique of the male writing described above. If so, Valerie's writing reframes representation by (unproductive) sex, and the shit and piss of mortality. Such a writing represents a deeply embodied and, hence, mortal agency. Due to the location of this pencil, the "invaginated" (Derrida 97) writing and identities that follow operate according to a new notion of spatiality. Nancy, in an interview, states:

> Sex doesn't cut the body any more than the mouth or the anus, or any bodily orifice cuts the body. It is an opening, which is something different. This is

why, regarding eroticism, I like to say there is no penetration, that penetration in a certain way has no proper meaning. To penetrate is to enter into the internal structure of the matter, but in physical love as well as in spiritual, it is the same — there is no penetration *into*, there is everywhere only a *touching* [emphasis in original, "Love and Community"].

A masculine, fascist state understands sex as a "penetration" between an inside and an outside, as an assimilation of the other, and requires such a binary notion of space to orient its identity and its literal and ideological work. Nancy shows how the vagina is not something that is penetrated from the outside, but that it is in its essence an exposure of the "inside" to the "outside." It is, to use his metaphor from another text, like a glove "turned inside out" (*Inoperative Community* 33). The "self" finds itself spaced-out and into the other. Valerie's love would not make sense within an individualistic world in which the self constructs itself through othering and objectification. Valerie writes, "I am me, and I don't know who you are but I love you" (154). While she lacks knowledge of the other, she retains a sense of "self," and thus puts forward an unthinkable love. In a fascist ontology knowledge and representation allow for a closure that stabilizes the self, but not for Valerie who denies knowledge any purchase on her lover; love is for her akin to Nancy's "touching." Love is central to the representational work of Valerie who underwent precisely the same prison experience as V. In V's case, however, love is the first thing that he challenges in his conversations with Evey regarding freedom.

Freedom is frequently drawn as an issue of spatiality in *V for Vendetta*, though it does not always conform to the invaginated spatiality described above: When Evey is freed from V's prison, she finds herself in the Shadow Gallery, drawn as a full page panel. In Evey's case, the mobility of borders is represented in the absence of any thoroughgoing critique of borders. Those panels representing Finch's drug-induced experience at Larkhill, however, offer just such a critique: Finch states, in a direct reference to the distancing effect of ideology, that he wants to put himself in the position of V by making the experience of the camp "real" to him (210–212). While Finch does ingest L.S.D., he also says, "But they say L.S.D. only magnifies what's already there" (212). What is already there in this scene — as it is in the pages of Thomas Pynchon's *Gravity's Rainbow* from which this scene was lifted (433) — is death, a *voluntary* confrontation with the death of the other. As he walks through the camp, ripped bags hanging on barbed wire dissolve into decapitated corpses (211–213); fences that had been spatially nearby now disappear on the horizon. And, then, crucially, Lloyd draws one panel full of ghosts, dead people who, while breaking the fourth wall, look squarely at the reader.

There is a strange, oscillating spatiality in these panels as these figures (ontologically) draw near to him (and the reader) and then disappear as Finch finds himself, once again, behind a wall. Faced with the death of the other, Finch's fascist self finds itself outside of itself and with others. This metacomic moment — in which walls are panel borders and panel borders are walls — denies "closure," to use Scott McCloud's word, as meaningful possibilities, which are denied by the (un)conscious work of interpretation, erupt into space (63); this moment dramatizes the work of panel borders and the work of interpretation, but it finally leaves its reader puzzled, not quite sure how to find close this *gap*, or, more importantly, if closure is something to be desired in light of a world of concentration camps. Nancy calls this experience an "inoperative community," the experience that follows when the sense-making work and representations of a community falter and the borders between self and other are down (*Inoperative Community* 15). Brought together, Finch and Valerie's experiences add tremendously to our understanding of an anarchic community that is not based on a monadic idea, but grounded in an exposure to the death of the other as Finch confronts the death of others at Larkhill, as Valerie loves the unknown, finite person on the other side of her prison wall, and as V and Evey confront the death of Valerie.

This interpretation, which yokes together Valerie and Finch through the spatial metaphor, is based on Finch's voluntary confrontation with the death of others and Valerie's embodied writing. Such an analysis also answers many of the misgivings described above, while recentering agency in the novel. Peter Y. Paik summarizes, for example, an online debate on James McTeigue's 2006 film in which Evey's transformation is understood in terms of Slavoj Žižek's "subjective destitution" (168–170). The latter involves a "symbolic suicide, in which the act of giving up what is most precious to oneself is followed by the second renunciation whereby one recognizes that one has 'nothing to lose in a loss.'" Evacuated, someone like Evey or V is now able to fight a system that had relied, most importantly, on their investment within society. As Paik points out, the biggest problem with this argument is that such an utter destitution would also undermine the moral coordinates necessary in the first place to directly combat the system (171). Recentered around Valerie's *écriture féminine*, the real agent of change is not V or Evey, but Finch squarely confronting the death of others, for it is Finch that freely experiences the *space* of Valerie's writing, while undergoing no "subjective destitution." What remains is an identity that is not (re)productive, but endlessly playing, endlessly writing, and open to the world and its others. Destitute subjects, to say the least, do not play: Evey assumes the position of V (easily, because after all V is not a body), and devotes herself to politics. Finch, by contrast, leaves it all behind, work, society, and sex, as he moves on to a future not predefined by the fixity of ideas.

Is V's "idea" to be found in a graphite "inch" of "integrity" hidden in the vagina of a dying lesbian? The vast majority of young male readers — thrilled by V's "badass" status as an un-killable idea — would find this connection to gay sexuality and body fluids disturbing, foregrounding how important and how marginal this other theory of agency happens to be in the text for those most conservative readers, the readers of superhero comics. In my reading, *V for Vendetta* deeply questions the myth of the superhero, while complicating and extending the conventional reading of agency and love in the novel. *V for Vendetta*, read through Valerie adn Finch's experience, figures in a concrete manner a way of writing, and living, that is non-productive (homosexual), anti-binary (glove-like spatiality), and wasteful (shit and piss). Grounded in this space, V's "idea" is only "immortal" in scare quotes as this inch of integrity, this writing drenched in the fluids of mortality, grants each idea a diffident existence, absent and present, bordered and unbordered.

9. The Poles of Wantonness
Male Asexuality in Alan Moore's Film Adaptations
EVAN TORNER

At the July 25, 2009, San Diego Comic-Con, a member of the audience urgently asked Zack Snyder at the premiere of his uncut film adaptation of *Watchmen*: "Is Rorschach gay?" Snyder replied that he did not think so but tacitly admitted that the comic hero's sexuality is somehow a complicated issue. For if he is neither heterosexual, homosexual, or bisexual, but rather, against sexuality altogether, then he inhabits a grey area in humanity's social and perceptual taxonomy. I posit that Rorschach is asexual. Asexuality, an orientation describing those who do not experience sexual attraction, has the potential to upend implicit expectations for filmic desire and constructed sexual activity. Film studies has both *heterosexed* and *queered* the medium over the past three decades, but it makes me wonder if there could also be room for an *asexual* subjectivity in film? If so, how might film tropes and types encode and validate figures exhibiting asexual desire?

Few films let us both problematize and answer these questions as readily as the five adaptations of Alan Moore's comic books made over the course of the 00s: *From Hell* (2001), *The League of Extraordinary Gentlemen* (2003), *Constantine* (2005), *V for Vendetta* (2006), and *Watchmen* (2009). These films not only correlate with the conception and rise of David Jay's Asexuality Visibility and Education Network (AVEN) since 2001, but also demonstrate a shift from *unmarked* to *marked* asexuality in Hollywood figures, particularly at the level of the screenplay. Yet though Moore's comic work explicitly thematizes an imaginative playground of polyvalent sexual preferences — asexuality among them — the films noticeably struggle and fail to attain a similar level of nuance. Despite this, the male figures of these adaptations reveal both the discursive advance of asexuality into the popular consciousness and the ramifications it may have for the way we look at representations of desire in recent mainstream narrative cinema.

Examining Asexuality and Desire

As a sexual disposition that functionally does not produce "overt sociosexual activities" that would call attention to itself (Bogaert 284), asexuality remains a virtual non-identity for cinema among other visual arts. Asexual desire, though existent (Scherrer 630), must remain unmarked unless called forth by the screenplay, because only dialogue and elaborate audio-visual narration can supply the necessary cues that would contextualize it beyond sexual desire. Slavoj Žižek opens *A Pervert's Guide to Cinema* with the proposition that films "tell you how to desire" (Fiennes). And desire itself, as Bifo defines it, "is the psychic field in which imaginary fluxes, ideologies, and economic interests continuously clash" (23). In this metaphorical battle, films concern themselves with how to fight (i.e., express/repress, give in/stand firm) and against whom (i.e., homosexuality, fascist desire, etc.) within this field. The interrelated knowledge and fantasy constructions within the moving image strongly suggest certain readings and confer power on some identities over others. A viewer is taught they *lack* something external to themselves, and the film proposes a formula to overcome this lack. Because our sexual desire evolves unevenly throughout childhood — according to Freud[1] — symbols and narrative logic often inherit sexual undercurrents, and these undercurrents underwrite our everyday desires on their terms. Films play with this uneven development, usually posing simple narrative dilemmas about heterosexual desire. For example, in *From Hell*, will the good cop overcome his dark past to sleep with the hooker with the heart of gold? In *V for Vendetta*, will the kidnapped girl go so far as to bed her masked torturer? Is the person with whom we have the greatest sexual tension actually the "right" partner, as it normatively is in film? At what point does one decide a moving image of a man or woman is more attractive to watch than a real one sitting in the movie theater nearby? Such questions are only raised in retrospect after the film has released its grip on the viewers' sexual insecurities.

In practice, most films reward proceptive male desire — that of a man seeking a new female partner. Film viewers are often institutionally conditioned to consider such subjectivity "normal" and even come to expect it from their cinema experience. Yet asexuality's existence openly prompts discussion of the distance of some individuals' erotic perception from the norm. In fact, modern philosophers such as Jean-Paul Sartre, Maurice Merleau-Ponty, Emmanuel Levinas, and Luce Irigiray have grappled with the epistemic concerns raised by this norm for decades.[2]

As it turns out, Mina Harker and Alan Quatermain's initial sex scene in Moore's *The League of Extraordinary Gentleman* comic provides a useful means of exploring theories of erotic perception. Sartre's *choice* model considers all erotic desire a deliberate decision to pacify the Will by "absorbing the Other" (Sartre 210), or a body with the potential to reshape our own. Though masquerading as Mrs. Quatermain, Harker freely offers her body to Quatermain as well as a similar choice to desire: "It is entirely up to you where you sleep Mr. Quatermain, I am quite sure." Harker's naked body becomes a known quantity for the reader, yet Harker can choose to refrain from emotional commitment and having the desire transform her. Merleau-Ponty's *vision* model is predicated on the notion that no other vision is possible other than an obsessive, desiring, *embodied* look (Waddell 44), debunking the mind-body dichotomy of the Enlightenment and objectifying all bodies before the gaze. Once Harker propositions Quatermain, the reader attributes sexual desire to her eyes looking back at him, and a similar-albeit-repressed desire within his eyes, despite their obviously hesitant and anxious appearance. Much of the scene's reading pleasure is derived from this parallel attribution of absolute desire and conflicting emotions. Levinas' *simultaneity* model posits desire as a confrontation with the Infinite, an incoherent interruption of our passage through life, incorporating our bodies into their own spiritual transcendence. When Quatermain and Harker's relationship is consummated, the gaze dwells for several panels on their sexual activities as a pleasing interruption to the war against the Martians. When Harker climbs on top, they both close their eyes in desire for a vertiginous moment with transcendent desire. Finally, Irigiray's *possession* model acknowledges that desire exists only outside of the unequal discursive space shared by men and women, with true desire being that which subsumes the patriarchal domination of the female body: The dreamy, desiring look in Harker's eyes after coitus hardens when Quatermain's roaming eyes threaten to completely *know* her body and therefore possess it.

In films, comics, and other media, Sartre's erotic paradigm frames proceptive desire as a result of individual choice, whereas Merleau-Ponty relies on an embodied vision drawn in by attractive body types. Both rely on a presumed male subject and female object. Levinas avoids gender by conceiving of desire as a receptive longing for the Infinite in the Other, whereas Irigaray imagines a gender binary that involves the reclaiming of the gaze from its masculine, possessing quality. In effect, film figures are imbricated within the politics of the male gaze and typically corralled into one of these erotic epistemologies: they seek out sexual attraction, such as the innocently flirtatious looks between Nite Owl II and Silk Spectre II in *Watchmen*, are overcome by obsessive lust such as Hawley Griffin running amok in Rosa Coote's Academy in *The League of Extraordinary Gentlemen*, attempt transcendence through coveting another such as between Harker and Quatermain above, or take sides in a gender power struggle such as with Jack the Ripper's elegant seduction of women before slaughtering them.

Of course, asexuality fits imperfectly into these philosophies of perception, as well as representations of sexuality itself. To find out why, begin with David Jay's description of asexual attraction, which is the "desire to get to know someone, to get close to them in whatever way works best [...] [it has to do with being] attracted to a particular gender, and [identifying] as lesbian, gay, bi, or straight" (qtd. in Duenewald). As articulated here, asexual desire is hopelessly incorporeal: no acknowledgement, for example, of gender politics, the body, or even a distinction from other forms of sexual activity. It is instead a sexuality that seeks social intimacy with liminal physicality, a kind of desire to eliminate the complications of desire that they purport not to experience. Jay's statement constitutes part of his overall project to put a face on the "asexual" demographic. As with most young contemporary movements, idealism predominates within a social network premised on dispersed membership, few shared understandings, and some lively discussion boards. Be that as it may, the asexual subculture struggles to maintain a dialogue with the mainstream culture. Discourse about desire and sexuality remains embedded in the material processes of any given historical moment. Though Jay and a handful of others have legitimated the movement within the public sphere, they have not yet achieved their ideal discursive equilibrium. In a platonic discursive space, asexuals could openly identify as asexual *and* share this space with one of the other three sexualities: hetero, bi, or homo. In practice, however, the distinction between asexuality and returning to the closet and/or outright prudery is muddled with other religiously and politically charged behaviors. The inability to phenomenologically distinguish representative asexual behavior from its sexual or anti-sexual counterparts remains a primary obstacle to the recognition asexuals seek.

After all, once repression, celibacy, impotence and abstinence are introduced into the equation, the discursive field becomes crowded and turbulent. Impotence and abstinence both rely on the statement 'I would engage in intercourse, but...' and lie firmly under the sign of normative heterosexual desire. Celibacy would lie in the same space as well, but recent events concerning celibate homosexuals in the Catholic clergy have prompted thoughts to the contrary. Suddenly, sexual desire meets repressed desire, or a represented desire that a character markedly does not act upon, a typical means of suspense. Repression not only interrogates the three conventional sexualities, but is also deeply suspicious of a fourth that questions its very *raison d'etre*: how could one *not* want that which social conventions deny? Thus, asexuality does not enter into the discourse on its own terms, but via established representation systems already hostile or befuddled by its entry. Lack of desire becomes easily confused with repressed desire, denied desire, impotent desire, and platonic desire until the removal of restrictions. In fact, repression subsumes its entry into the sexual sphere entirely, or else non-asexual modes of perception project platonic desire for its own ends. Our global representation system simply expresses profound suspicion at the strange path asexuals follow, leading many in the movement to spend considerable time "trying to figure out where [they] fit" (Jay, qtd in Duenwald).

Tracking asexuality in film thus becomes a potential quagmire. Asexuality is *marked* when a figure verbally claims an asexual identity, openly disdains sexuality, or becomes an object of sexual tension so as to form a platonic relationship in the end, whereas it is *unmarked* when a human representation simply does not exhibit sexual desire in their gaze, dialogue, or gestures. Yet, while unmarked asexuality in the form of children, servants, mad inventors and racialized others is ubiquitous, marked asexuality in a protagonist becomes hard to distinguish from representations of sexual repression or celibacy. Asexual desire is coded within the diegesis as an abnormal aspect of a character's psychological profile: characters are too young, infantile, professionally disciplined, traumatized, hyper-violent or obsessive to contemplate sex. These plots and characters are not "desexualized" as in Mary Ann Doane's theory of women's separation from their own sexuality (Doane 18), but dramaturgically constituted to provide suspense while exploring alternate philosophical issues. That is to say: asexual subjectivity emerges from a film's *screenplay*— of chains of erotic events deliberately avoided and platonic relationships established — rather than from its system of gazes and montage.

Alan Moore and Marked Asexuality

Moore's comic work, well-identified as a veritable cabinet of curious sexualities, provides a multipolar view of wantonness and its discontents. From his exploration of healthy heterosexuality among superheroes in *Watchmen* to intrafamilial child rape in an off-issue of *Vigilante*,[3] from his sexualization of comic book heroes like Batman and Swamp Thing to *Lost Girls*' pornographic utopianism,[4] Moore explicitly deals with matters of sexual politics within supernatural, superhero, and metaliterary contexts. Some of his characters engage in sex, others refrain from it, and judgment is often withheld over either. Asexuality floats as an equal among its privileged peers, heterosexuality, homosexuality, and bisexuality.[5] Annalisa Di Liddo describes Moore's fiction as a scalpel that "he employs to deconstruct, manipulate and reassemble the forms of tradition and narrative" (15), and all aspects of human sexuality seem to go under the knife. Possibilities of sex are iterated but then boundaries are crossed and reconfigured to look as if they never existed.

But in Moore's comics, some characters draw clear boundaries against a society constantly inculcating desire, foregrounding asexuality as a distinct form of sexual agency. For example, "In Blackest Night"[6] features an alluring woman (Katma Tui) who finds a Green Lantern, Rot Lop Fan, that not only cannot see color, but is a male openly not interested in a woman who has been lauded for her attractiveness. A similar encounter turns up in the final issue of *Neonomicon*, in which the psychopath Aldo Sax stammeringly reveals to the attractive Merril Brears his asexual disposition: "I, I, I just never really liked the thought of, you know, dirty stuff ... I just ... I mean, genitals, all that." In *Top Ten*, a series highlighting the sexual underbelly[7] of a superhero city, Jeff Smax and the female cop Toybox discuss her having a drink with the aggressively bisexual Jack Phantom. "Since you ask, I'm not homosexual," Toybox claims. "To be perfectly honest, right now I'm not anything-sexual" (1.2). Sexual tension is simply removed from the central duo of the entire comic, replaced with a complex asexual relationship. The series also introduces us to Officer Joe Pi, a compassionate, communicative and utterly asexual robot in a world where even the robot "clickers" talk about sexual desire in their scrapper music. The artistic pornography that is *Lost Girls* even contains a character innocent of the bisexual antics at hand: Dorothy's dog Toto. Refusing to simply ignore sexual politics, Moore foregrounds the active complicity of characters' in their own desires, and accords due respect to those who genuinely lack them (as is his wont).

Unmarked Asexuality in From Hell *and* The League of Extraordinary Gentlemen

In due course of its demographic and financial logic, however, the movie industry has run roughshod over Moore's even-handed sensibilities. Moore has responded with well-documented dissatisfaction about his own movie adaptations, even humorously playing devil's advocate against modern cinema in general:

> [Film in its modern form] spoon-feeds us, which has the effect of watering down our collective cultural imagination. It is as if we are freshly hatched birds looking up with our mouths open waiting for Hollywood to feed us more regurgitated worms. ... Can't we get something else? Perhaps some take-out?[8]

At issue is the film industry's tyranny exercised over polysemy in film texts, in that a complex, elliptical drama like Darren Aronofsky's *Black Swan* is to be read as "smart" or "edgy," whereas an anxiously simplistic blockbuster such as Michael Bay's *Armageddon* is to be read as "entertainment." Demographic targeting outside the text affects the text itself, as fields of desire deemed appropriate for the target audience are shored up against contrary interpretations. Moore's multipolar equilibrium of desire and sexuality is collapsed to a bipolar, judgmental realm of good heteronormativity and forms of deviance.

Thus, adaptations of *From Hell*, Moore's graphic version of the Jack the Ripper murders, and *League of Extraordinary Gentlemen*, a kind of Justice League for Victorian England, represent the paucity of Hollywood imagination in light of Moore's depictions of sexual diversity. In the Hughes Brothers' *From Hell*, Detective Abberline (Johnny Depp) is transformed from a dour, married historical figure in the comic into a fictive, young widower who investigates the Ripper murders. His unmarked asexuality is clearly spawned from the trauma of losing his wife, and sealed by his inability to unite with his love interest Mary Kelly (Heather Graham) in the end.[9] He is unable to choose to desire (Sartre), instead letting arbitrary attraction (Merleau-Ponty) pull him into an unwanted relationship. His would-be sexual relationships are hermetically sealed in regret and narratively-enforced repression, clearly coded as such with his dreams of Kelly. Unmarked asexuality here signifies a cocktail of trauma, addiction, and self-sacrifice, evading a description of asexual desire as an everyday reality.

Jack the Ripper's assistant Netley (Jason Flemyng) meanwhile behaves as the infantile asexual, incessantly traumatized and castrated by his master's doings. His role as the silent *voyeur* in Moore's text, a role perhaps even more articulately represented in the cinema, is interrupted by ethical redundancy to prove a didactic point about enabling egregious crimes: he stammers and jitters throughout, the archetypal cowardly accomplice. The film itself falls into relatively predictable patterns of programming desire in the direction of a hopeful heterosexual union between Kelly and Abberline that then takes an unexpected dark turn. The Hughes Brothers' horror-thriller does the usual slasher genre work of transforming the "bad girls" (i.e., Kelly's prostitutes) into victims, with the heteronormative and morally upright Kelly and Abberline able to experience transcendent love due to several twists in the script.

The League of Extraordinary Gentlemen, on the other hand, dulls the sexual edge of its celebrity protagonists more for the sake of a younger target demographic than to mark asexuality as a concept with which to be reckoned. The original comic succeeds at entrenching sexual behaviors in the adventure characters that fit their personalities over the genre conventions. The young Mina Harker and older Alan Quatermain start a passionate affair as "man" and "wife," while the invisible Hawley Griffin is a serial rapist who is in turn sodomized to death by a vengeful Mr. Hyde. The Indian Captain Nemo (Naseeruddin Shah), the only one without a clear sexual identity, appears to bear an intimate relationship with his phallic sub, the Nautilus ("now, [his] only nation") and the sea itself ("Empire Dreams"). Platonic or generic sexuality cannot be found amongst them, contrasting with the generic heterosexual desire ascribed to all the characters save Nemo in the film. Without reference to his wife, the sea, or his pumping submarine, Nemo is cast adrift, othered even, an ill-fitting team member given neither the screen time nor the opportunity to flesh out his character. His combat capabilities and ownership of anachronistic technologies serve to stand in for his agency as one of the narrative's protagonists. Far from the obsessive asexual in the comics who serves as a counterpoint to Mr. Hyde's lust or Mina Murray and Alan Quatermain's relationship, Nemo becomes yet another filmic body in a crowded field of more desirous and attractive bodies — particularly those of the added characters, Dorian Gray (Stuart Townsend) and Tom Sawyer (Shane West).

Asexual Possibilities in Constantine

Moore did not provide the base plotline for Francis Lawrence's *Constantine* with Keanu Reeves and Rachel Weisz,[10] but his work on *Swamp Thing* produced the main character John Constantine: an allegedly bisexual and morally-ambiguous detective who has quite literally seen Hell and lived. This character took on a life of its own in the *Hellblazer* comics in no small part because of his unpredictable nature. Would he exorcise that demon, or would he sleep with it? Had he taken a side in the conflict between Heaven and Hell, or was he just biding his time to escape both their clutches into a third space? The *Hellblazer* series brought the Machiavellian divine/infernal politics of works such as Neil Gaiman's *The Sandman* and — like that series' *Lucifer* spin-off— explores them through a male whose sexual inclination is hard to pin down.

Constantine marks a turning point in Moore adaptations over the 2000s in the sense that, perhaps at the expense of the titular character's bisexuality, one major character is given the spotlight as a marked asexual: the angel Gabriel (Tilda Swinton). The film employs Gabriel's asexuality as a compromise for the removal of Constantine's comic-book promiscuity. Swinton's gender ambiguity as a woman in male drag actually heterosexualizes Constantine's desiring gaze at him/her exhibited in a shot-reverse-shot during their first meeting — and after s/he betrays him, s/he straddles him. The film furthers the straddling motif as a play on his excluded bisexuality when he straddles the demon Balthasar during a fight — a cold allusion to his otherwise healthy appetite in men. Angie (Weisz) takes on the acceptable role of Constantine/Reeves' developing love interest, but director Lawrence actually removed a post-coital scene with an attractive demon (Michelle Williams) to further accentuate Constantine/Reeves' sexual potency. In effect, the two near-kisses he shares with Angie/Weisz constitute a flirtatious mix of celibacy and asexuality designed to ennoble his character. After all, is he really attracted to her, or is he merely an asexual being misdirected by the Devil toward sexuality? No answers present themselves. The viewer must settle for numerous shots of a topless Reeves and Weisz in a wet t-shirt for their sexual voyeurism in this film. Here is a glimpse of what might be described as a more transcendent form of desire. The plot deters a heterosexual union to demonstrate his virtue, as with Abberline. Meanwhile, the asexual Gabriel has been unleashed on the world as an independent agent. Perhaps in this respect the film makes up for dulling Moore's sexual edge with an invitation to consider an asexual, alien being running among us.

Marked Asexuality in V for Vendetta *and* Watchmen

The film adaptations of *V for Vendetta* and *Watchmen*— if as imaginatively impoverished as the prior three films — at least remain closer to their Moore–authored source material. James McTeigue's *V for Vendetta* tells the tale of an asexual Guy Fawkes-styled hero V (Hugo Weaving) who takes on a dystopian British government along with his kidnappee Evey (Natalie Portman), whom he saved from a potential rape (Keller 191). As a subject of government test experiments, it can be contended that V is a "metaphorical invocation of the AIDS victim and/or the homosexual," though no homosexual desire is openly expressed. In the comic, V has at least symbolic heterosexual desire for the statue of Madame Justice when he says, "Please don't think it was merely physical. I know you're not that sort of girl. No, I loved you as a person. As an ideal." In the film, however, V's asexuality is rendered ambiguous: he expresses love, but no sexual desire, for Evey. She eventually kisses him on the mask. Evey's shaved head in turn ambiguates her gender identity and sexual availability, much like Gabriel's boyish appearance in *Constantine*. As with Abberline and Mary Kelly in *From Hell,* however, their love cannot be consummated beyond this due to plot exigencies. Asexuality between them leads to a higher cause, smacking of celibacy.

An independent asexuality can, however, be found in the character of Finch (Stephen Rea), the investigator tracking down the pair. A bachelor and obsessive asexual,[11] he nevertheless recognizes and lauds the Sartrean "choice" form of erotic perception. In one scene, Finch watches V kidnap Evey on a security camera and says, "At least some part of him's human, for better or worse." He sees V's platonic desire as evidence of human choice amidst political machinery. Later, this allegiance to desire allows him to transition to the revolution in the final sequence. V's masks — distributed by the thousands to the population — may mark a kind of asexual solidarity among the future British citizens, but it is the marked choice *not* to eroticize that makes Finch trustworthy and a role model.

The *Watchmen* film's commitment both to the aesthetic and sexual diversity of the original work redeems it somewhat from having allegorically "ripped the bones out" (Wolk 241) of Moore and Dave Gibbons' groundbreaking comic. In an alternative United States during the 1980s, an out-of-commission superhero team is confronted with the murder of one of their members, exposing larger geopolitical events. Team members have graphic sex scenes, there is an attempted rape among them, and at least one is more than ambiguously gay. Yet, again, the film's investigator, Rorschach (Jackie Earle Haley), assumes the role of the marked asexual.[12] His masked visage bears none of V's human features, however, resembling the DC hero The Question or the gender-ambiguous Blank character from *Dick Tracy* (1990). This lack-of-gaze constitutes an asexualizing trope, and is further exaggerated by his open hatred of sexual congress: he derides The Silhouette's death due to her "indecent (lesbian) lifestyle," kinky costume sex between two team members ("Nice pair of legs to motivate you"), and New York City in general ("Human cockroaches talking about their heroin and child pornography").

The viewer even identifies with Rorschach's marked asexuality via his interior-monologue-guided nightly ritual of scorning prostitutes and saving women from potential rapists. In one shot, he says in voice-over, "Even in the face of Armageddon, I will not compromise," as he walks right-to-left past the Dionysian temptations of a liquor store and a beckoning prostitute. After he leaves Moloch's apartment, a similar scene paralleling a panel series in the comic unfolds: a slow-motion tracking shot follows Rorschach as he walks down a rainy 42nd Street; two women in the background proposition an old man on the right, a sign advertises "Totally Naked Girls" on the left; and a prostitute solicits his business in the center (Moore and Gibbons 2.25). Thanks to the voice-over, the viewer is more preoccupied with the plot (or Rorschach's speculation on the plot anyway) than the copious sex trade being offered. The prostitute's proposition projects a pre-programmed system of desire and exchange onto him as a potential customer: "You want some of this? Fifty Bucks ... C'mon." Rorschach continues to walk. It cuts to a front tracking shot, the prostitute flips him the bird and adds: "Fuck you! I make more in a week than you do in a year, you fuckin' homo! So fuck you!" The viewer is asked to actively ally with his prudishness (he is, after all, our narrator), while also noting his confidence in being completely uninterested in the women there. The mildly homoerotic handshake he shares with Nite Owl II (Patrick Wilson), in which Rorschach holds his hand for two seconds longer than would be polite, expresses his platonic feelings for his friend without crossing a semantic boundary of implied sexual attraction. His unique combination of both infantile and hyper-violent asexuality serves to de-essentialize both modes, leaving a visible, complex character with whom the viewer can identify.

Conclusion

Returning to Di Liddo's metaphor of Moore's fiction as scalpel, we can roughly consider the films based on his work to be an *anesthesetic*, an interposition between his comic books' cutting edge position on sexuality and a young global cinema audience seeking tropes of the superhero film (e.g., *League, V, Constantine*) and the thriller (*Watchmen, From Hell*). Douglas Wolk describes Moore's art at its best as "a sort of inductive shock — carrying you along some place you don't want to go" (Wolk 255). Yet complex topics such as prostitution, child sexuality, rape, affirmative female desire and queer identity raised in his comic book writing are tamed and dramaturgically re-formulated in the film adaptations to mitigate this shock. If one wants the "true" Moore experience, the film adaptations seem to argue, one should first pay the comics publishing industry for the added cultural capital of reading his controversial, symbol-laden prose.

But as I have demonstrated, asexuality — as an aspect of human experience receiving increasing media exposure and cachet — has at least made its way through these films from a brute content control mechanism to an openly defined subject position jostling for discursive space amidst heterosexuality, homosexuality, and bisexuality. Netley's whimpering servitude and Captain Nemo's celibacy give way to Gabriel's confidence and Finch's upright, existential devotion to his work. Rorschach's dual embodiment of both infantile and hyper-masculine asexuality in *Watchmen* is exonerated by his unbreakable allegiance with the viewer and Kantian righteousness in a world of ambiguous values. It is but a mere peek at the dramaturgical potential of asexual desire.

In terms of the models of erotic perception, the ideal asexual desire aligns itself more with Levinas and Sartre, who focus on transcendent desire freely chosen, than Merleau-Ponty or Irigaray, who find desire only in terms of the body and power. Simply put: asexuality is couched in attraction that leads one within a safe distance of the Other, freely chosen and chaste to some degree. In turn, an affirmative film portrayal of marked asexuality is that which highlights agency over their erotic perception itself, as with Finch in *V for Vendetta*. And though Moore's polyvalent sexual imagination cannot yet achieve mainstream circulation in Hollywood superhero fiction, it at least highlights differing degrees of sexual attraction among adult male protagonists. The asexual female outside of law-and-order figures unfortunately still remains the domain of rare exceptions such as Hit Girl (Chloe Moretz) from *Kick-Ass* (2010), who has the advantage of being a child. Nevertheless, the absolute, dignified characterization of all four sexualities in feature cinema may indeed prove too rigorous an end-goal as the discourse about sexual subjectivity unfolds over time. As David Rodowick reminds us:

> Subjectivity is defined by social and historical processes that are irreducible to singular categories, and its forms and potentialities are always in flux. Only on this basis can we recognize and defend the multiple possibilities of identity and desire [Rodowick 140].

Thus the one percent of the populace identifying as asexuals may continue to advocate for fair media representation and the de-essentialization of sexualities in general, but their goals are perhaps best achieved only amidst cultural tectonics far greater than that of their movement, namely through the global language of demographics, purchasing power, and media access. Until then, asexuals, pained by a wanton culture, will have to endure a representation as nebulous and contingent as their own social movement.

Notes

1. See Sigmund Freud's "Three Essays on the Theory of Sexuality."
2. On this topic, James Waddell has outlined several notable models of im/proper erotic perception such as the *choice* model of Jean-Paul Sartre, the *vision* model of Maurice Merleau-Ponty, the *simultaneity* model of Emmanuel Levinas and the *possession* model of Luce Irigaray (Waddell, 96–98). Waddell's work substantially informs this article, though his summaries of erotic perception theory cannot be explored here.
3. "Father's Day Parts 1 & 2" (Vigilante Nos. 17–18, May-June 1985) in Moore, *DC Universe*.
4. As Noel Murray puts it in a review: "the *Lost Girls* narrative doesn't stop until everybody fucks everybody — even those they shouldn't."
5. The catch, of course, is that one can never presume *any* character's sexuality in an

Alan Moore comic book, as he consciously uses such notions as a suspense element. When Mina is berating Tom Carnacki in *League of Extraordinary Gentlemen Century: 1910*, for example, she yells at him: "Listen, you can have the double bed to yourselves tonight. I'm sleeping downstairs." After which Tom looks nervously askance toward the reader and says: "Mina! Don't tell the neighbourhood...." An asexual group image is replaced by one with a heterosexually independent woman in a polyamorous relationship with two men.

6. *Tales of the Green Lantern Corps Annual No. 3 1987* in Moore, *DC Universe*.

7. Included in this underbelly are not only frank discussions of AIDS via the S.T.O.R.M.S. subplot, but also moments where carnal knowledge becomes knowledge itself, such as Shockheaded Pete's viewing of pornography helping solve the case of M'rrgla Qualtz.

8. Moore, in a September 18, 2008, interview with the *Los Angeles Times*.

9. It is established that Abberline fleeing London would give away Kelly's position to the very conspiracy that dispatched Jack the Ripper to kill the girls in the first place.

10. That honor goes to the DC staff that produced the *Hellblazer* comic issues #71–75.

11. In the *V for Vendetta* comic, Finch has a wife named Delia who emasculates him by completely selling out to the Christian-fascist establishment (Moore 214), and he is also a homophobe. Comparisons between Depp's and Rea's characters in the films as suddenly wife-less male investigators would make an interesting study, particularly in terms of incarnating an unattached male workaholic ideal desired by neoliberalism.

12. Some have argued that Ozymandias is asexual as well, but the film's placement of the character amidst the Village People convinces at least this author that he is to be seen as homo- or bisexual.

10. Reflections on the Looking Glass
Adaptation as Sex and Psychosis in Lost Girls
Nico Dicecco

Alan Moore has famously lambasted filmic adaptation of his graphic novels. He has requested that his name be removed from many of these films and insisted that the money legally due to him be distributed amongst other artists involved in creating the comics (Moore, *Chain Reaction*). In a 2008 interview, Moore went so far as to declare, "I increasingly fear that nothing good can come of almost any adaptation, and obviously that's sweeping. There are a couple of adaptations that are perhaps as good or better than the original work. But the vast majority of them are pointless" (Gopalan). Yet, much of Moore's work is adaptive. I do not mean to say that his writing is merely overflowing with allusion; it is, of course, but that is not sufficient grounds to call his writing adaptive.[1] Rather, Moore uses extensive, connected patterns of intertextual reference to nuance his work. Accordingly, the meaning of his comics, at least in part, depends on the audience's familiarity with a prior text he adapts to his own fiction. Put differently, readers will get more out of his comics if they have read the precursor texts.

So why is Moore dismissive of others' adaptations? What does Moore do when he writes that makes his adaptive aesthetic valid where others fail? Even a cursory glance at Moore's adaptations suggests that faithfulness is not among his aesthetic goals, a sentiment that is echoed in the critical literature about adaptations. Since George Bluestone's 1957 *Novels into Film*, theorists have derided the sort of discourse that holds fidelity to a source text as an ideal. Yet, responses to a given adaptation outside of academia generally revolve around how closely the target text (often a film) reproduces the source text (often a book), as if the best adaptation would be a perfect replica of the original in a new medium. Theorists such as Robert Stam and Linda Hutcheon have pointed out the impossibility of such replication, and reject fidelity discourse because of its reductive logic. As theories of adaptation develop, however, it seems to me insufficient to merely reject fidelity discourse, considering its persistence in popular discourse. We need to better understand why audiences desire fidelity, a question that *Lost Girls* may begin to answer.

Lost Girls is an erotic comic book — or, to offer a neologism, a pornographic novel. As such, its adaptive aesthetic is tied up with its sexual aesthetic. Put another way, desire is among the narrative's central concerns, both as that desire relates to sexuality and to textuality. *Lost Girls* explores the relationship developed between Alice Fairchild (*Alice's Adventures in Wonderland* and *Through the Looking-Glass*), Dorothy Gale (*The Wizard of Oz*), and Wendy Potter (*Peter Pan*). The three women each recall and narrate to one another the complex, sometimes liberating, often traumatic, stories of their childhood sexual development. These stories-within-the-story are reinventions of the narratives written by Lewis Carroll, Frank L. Baum, and J.M. Barrie, respectively; in short, Moore's characters are adaptations of the original authors' work. In *A Theory of Adaptation*, Linda Hutcheon argues that the reception of an adaptation *as an adaptation* depends on a "knowing audience" (121). This phrase, *as an adaptation*, is key: you can read *Lost Girls* without knowing its precursor texts, but then it is effectively no different than a non-adaptive narrative. An adaptation experienced as an adaptation involves the audience revisiting the memory of a text while experiencing a new version of that text. Notably, the structure of *Lost Girls* recreates this attribute of adaptation in narrative terms. The childhood memories shared by Alice, Dorothy, and Wendy in *Lost Girls* provide a frame narrative for Moore's "retelling" of the stories by Caroll, Baum, and Barrie. In this way *Lost Girls* both is an adaptation and thematizes adaptation.

In line with the reflexivity of incorporating adaptation as a theme into an adaptive work, Moore uses reflection as a structural and a symbolic device. In the first sense, the narrative is structured in terms of characters reflecting on past sexual experiences. Accordingly, the adult frame narrator (whether Alice, Dorothy, or Wendy) functions like an adapted "version" of the "text" figured by her remembered childhood self. The age difference between the adult character and the remembered child mirrors the chronological separation between an adaptation and its adapted text. In the second sense, there is a literal mirror featured prominently throughout the narrative, most notably in the context of Alice's stories. This mirror plays a pivotal symbolic role, as the connection between Alice and her remembered childhood self is staged, not as a memory but as a present-tense interaction, via the intervening medium of the mirror. The mirror brings together sexuality and the comic book form to highlight the audience's role, as a desiring subject, in the text's adaptive non-reproductivity. In other words, the text reveals that its engagement with the original works of Caroll, Baum, and Barrie does not, and cannot, *exactly* reproduce those texts through adapting them in a comic, but the reader is in a position, if he or she desires, to conflate sustained intertextual engagement with reproduction. Moore critiques such a conflation of target and source text by framing Alice Fairchild's psychological trauma in terms of the logical violence implied by fidelity idealism. The particular attributes of the psychosis that Alice Fairchild in *Lost Girls* experiences after stepping through the looking glass parallel the metaphoric collapse needed to perceive an adaptation as aspiring to, or (worse) achieving faithfulness. *Lost Girls* suggests that such a goal would not only be "pointless" (Gopalan), but psychologically disturbed. At the same time, the desire to reconnect with the original text is the precondition for its function as an adaptation. As *Lost Girls* shows, the reconnection is positive as long as the integrity of the intervening medium, the mirror, remains. As it frames liberation and trauma, intercourse, and psychosis, the looking glass reflects *Lost Girls'* engagement with processes of desire in adaptation.

"Would you tell me please," said Alice, "what that means?"[2]

The link between metaphoric interaction or collapse and the knowing audience's role in constituting an adaptation qua adaptation forms the theoretical backbone of what follows. The premise is that the interpretation of adaptations as adaptations depends on a process similar to that used in the interpretation of metaphor. In *The Rule of Metaphor*, Paul Ricoeur describes the two processes involved in metaphorical reference, one destructive and one constructive. The first process is "semantic impertinence" (230). Ricoeur details the process: "the abolition of the reference by means of self-destruction of the meaning of metaphorical statements, the self-destruction being made manifest by an impossible literal interpretation" (230). The terms involved in a metaphorical statement are destroyed, rendered meaningless, because the copular verb "to be" which joins them suggests an impossible literal equation. In other words, the audience perceives that a term *is* what, in a literal sense, it *is not*. For example, the first line of the poem that begins *Alice's Adventures in Wonderland* is as follows: "All in the golden afternoon" (3). Though the statement lacks the copular verb "is" between the terms "golden" and "afternoon," which would be the traditional signal of metaphoric interaction, the immediate juxtaposition of the ideas nonetheless establishes their equation. A literal interpretation, however, is impossible; no afternoon is made of gold. The impossibility of literal meaning, however, instigates "semantic pertinence," the second process: "the self-destruction of meaning is merely the other side of an innovation in meaning at the level of the entire statement, an innovation obtained through the 'twist' of the literal meaning of the words" (Ricoeur 230). As the incongruous words interact, the reader is provoked to imagine various ways that an afternoon can be understood in terms of gold: for example, the color of sunshine or the vibrancy of youth.

The interaction of incongruous words is precisely what George Lakoff and Mark Johnson describe as the essence of metaphor: "understanding and experiencing one kind of thing in terms of another" (5). "Words" is even more restrictive than they would have it, with their inclusive "kind of thing." Accordingly, it is not outside the scope of their theory to treat adaptation as a metaphoric "kind of thing." For example, when the knowing audience reading *Lost Girls* encounters Bunny, with his white hair and anxious demeanor, the connection with "The White Rabbit" is clear. But, to use Ricoeur's terms in the context of adaptation, a literal interpretation of Bunny as *The* White Rabbit is impossible. The way that Bunny is illustrated (as human) and the narrative course that he follows (molesting Alice) destroy the possibility of his complete identification with The White Rabbit. No reader of *Alice's Adventures* puts the book down thinking, "That rabbit was such a monster!" the way he or she might with regard to Bunny. Yet, Bunny's divergence from the adapted character also instigates the new semantic pertinence. The literal meaning of Bunny as The White Rabbit is "twisted" in such a way that a productive interaction of the two figures is possible. In other words, those intertextually significant details (white hair, anxiousness about time, etc.) *make possible* a unique reading of *Lost Girls* conditioned by knowledge of the precursor text. The reader is provoked to imagine various ways that the one character can be understood in terms of the other: anxiousness about time as guilt, as fear of getting caught, and so on.

While examples like Bunny demonstrate the metaphoric possibilities inherent to some adaptations, because the difference between the adaptation and the adapted character is immediately evident, what needs more careful attention is the impossibility of literal meaning in *all* adaptations. It is much easier, for example, to see The White Rabbit in Disney's *Alice in Wonderland* as *The* White Rabbit from Lewis Carroll's *Alice's Adventures in Wonderland*, than it is to make the same identification for Bunny in *Lost Girls*. Nonetheless, the process of experiencing Disney's adaptation as an adaptation depends on understanding the chronologically latter character in terms of its precursor. Neither Bunny nor Disney's White Rabbit are literally Carroll's White Rabbit, and so our interpretations of the adapted characters *as* adapted characters is metaphoric, the interaction resultant from equating two unequal kinds of things. Accordingly, Disney's adaptation bears the same potential for its inevitable divergences to initiate new semantic pertinences as *Lost Girls*— both work *as* adaptations only insofar as the audience experiences the immediate text in terms of the adapted text. The differences between the adaptation and the adapted text do not need to be obvious; as Robert Stam points out, they are "automatic," necessitated by processes and media of production (56).

That said, the *desire* to interpret literally might remain strong. This is related to what Ricoeur calls the "ontological vehemence" of the metaphorical "is" (255). Whether the link is made explicit by a copular verb or implicit through juxtaposition, the force of the literal equation must be tenacious in order to instigate processes of metaphoric interaction. Put another way, though metaphor necessitates an impossible literal meaning, the semantic violence that the impossible linking incurs couples together with a copular *insistence*, a force that asserts — by virtue of terms being somehow fastened together — that "the afternoon *is* golden." As much as we recognize that the terms of a metaphoric juxtaposition are not equal, we must also, however unconsciously, treat them as if they were equal in order to make meaning out of their placement beside one another. What *Lost Girls* shows, through the image of the looking glass, is that adaptation is another method of metaphoric copulation.

The Looking Glass: Adaptation as Sex

Lost Girls begins with a chapter titled "The Mirror," in which adult Alice and her childhood self converse as though on either side of a looking glass. The mirror is a constant presence throughout this chapter, filling every comic panel, changing only in subtle ways as the scenes progress. Aside from the mirror frame, the first panel features only the words, spoken from some unknown spot in the room, stating: "Tell me a story" (1). The ambiguity here is key: Who is speaking and to whom? Without access to these narrative details, the audience is left only with the command. As the first sentence in *Lost Girls*, this command is in a position of thematic privilege, implying that what will follow is *about* storytelling.

What immediately follows, however, is actually a redirection from storytelling toward sex, which raises questions about what links these ideas. The second panel is a response to the command in the first panel: "Oh, I don't know any stories. Your little white breasts, they're so lovely. They'll never be as beautiful once you're grown. Will you touch them for me?" (1). The request is strange, in part because it is so explicitly sexual, but more so because it is evidently directed towards a child.[3] Panels that follow further the negotiation between the two characters in dialogue: the child demanding that a story be told, the other character — of whom we yet know nothing — bartering for sexual reciprocity. This other character says, "Well at least let me **see** you properly. Open your legs a little and I'll do the same" (emphasis in original, 1). The words "at least" here imply that the negotiation of sex for a story can be resolved with the compromise of reciprocal, visual access. Thus tensions in the link between sex and storytelling find relief in visual exchange. While this settlement establishes a non–physical sexual dynamic between the characters, we as readers have yet to confirm this implication with ocular proof: we have not seen their physical proximity to one another in the space of the bedroom or any precise identifying details — their names, ages, or appearances. The link between storytelling and sex being still ambiguous, this exchange further prompts the question of what the visual middle ground implies about the exchange between the reader and the text.

The mirror's status as a symbol of narrative self-reflection is reinforced when, later in the first chapter, we are introduced to Lady Fairchild. She discusses the purpose of fiction with Monsieur Rougeur, the manager of the Hotel Himmelgarten, where the bulk of *Lost Girls* is set. Their conversation about storytelling begins with Rougeur confirming that Fairchild is herself a writer of erotic fiction. To Rougeur, fiction is "the very *mirror* of reality [...] where memorable idealized characters reflect our *truest* selves" (6). Fairchild disagrees, suggesting that she favors "Plato's view ... the *ideal* is the thing; the world beyond fiction's mirror, *that* is the true world" (6). They foreground questions of narrative purpose: does fiction reproduce reality or reveal the world of experience as itself mediated?

Finally, the chapter comes to an end, resolving earlier ambiguities surrounding the conversation in the first panels by finally providing visual evidence. Fairchild, reflected in the mirror, naked on a bed, says to the looking glass, "Oh, I wish I could touch you," but she is told in response that the idea is "silly" (8). In turn, Fairchild says, "I know, I know. The barrier between doesn't melt anymore, does it, like silvery mist? It doesn't break. Dear child, I miss you terribly. Come and kiss me goodnight" (8). With those words, Alice Fairchild kisses her reflection. Finally, we as readers are given the visual access alluded to at the start of the chapter; the lipstick is ocular proof that the sexual interaction was masturbatory. There is no literal child and no physical contact, only memory, imagination, and hallucination. As the lipstick marks left on the looking glass attest, the mirror mediated any copulation. Alice's "true" self, her object of desire, was on the other side, physically inaccessible, firmly located in the world of ideals. Further, Fairchild's words are a direct allusion to specific language used in *Through the Looking-Glass*: "And certainly the glass *was* beginning to melt away, just like a bright silvery mist" (111). Prior allusions to Carroll's stories in *Lost Girls* were not so direct, so this moment allows the knowing reader the opportunity to confirm the intertextual engagement: Alice Fairchild is Alice.

    If the mirror is, or at least could be considered as, a meta-fictive symbol, its mediation of the sexual interaction between adult and child Alice comments on the sexual aesthetics of adaptation. The story that adult Alice attempts to tell throughout *Lost Girls* is her coming of age story — the story of the voice on the other side of the looking glass becoming the woman masturbating on the bed. It is the story of its *own* adaptation: of the childhood memory, the figurative stand-in for Carroll's original story, becoming the adult experience, the stand-in for *Lost Girls* as an adaptation. To be clear, the story is not exactly that of Carroll's Alice narratives, because the child-voice at the beginning of *Lost Girls* is herself an adaptation of Carroll's Alice. While the chronological difference between adult and child Alice figuratively constructs the child as the adapted text, that child figure is only Carroll's Alice insofar as the audience makes that adaptive identification. The mirror, then, is not *quite* a figurative reflection of the dynamic between the adaptation and the adapted text; rather, there is a layer of remove. The mirror reflects a remembered version of Carroll's Alice — not the text itself but the text filtered through the audience with which it converses. The attention to the visual nature of that exchange, the emphasis given to the verb "see," highlights both the medium and the genre through which the reader-text interaction occurs: the porno-graphic novel.

    The pornographic content here highlights the centrality of desire in the reading process. Significantly, sex in this chapter figures not as connection or reproduction, but as the *inability* to connect or reproduce. This inability never reduces or subverts the desire for interaction, or even the possibility of sexual fulfillment, though it does suggest that such fulfillment is masturbatory. Importantly, masturbation is celebrated, not derided. Considered as a self-reflexive commentary on its own nature as an adaptation, *Lost Girls* suggests that adaptation is a retrospective process. The experience of an adaptation does not involve actual interaction with an adapted text so much as the *desire* for interaction with that text, mediated by the lens of memory and imagination. Alice Fairchild *wishes* she could touch her childhood self, but ends up only touching herself *as if* she were touching that child. Similarly, an adaptation cannot be its source, but it can be treated *as if* it were its precursor text. As I mentioned earlier, the temptation to see Alice Fairchild as Alice is strong. The meaning of the adaptation as an adaptation is a creation singular to each audience member, but it can be a productive creation nonetheless; masturbation is not inherently narcissistic here. Accordingly, *Lost Girls* points to the nature of adaptations as autonomous texts, necessarily different from their ostensible sources, but mediated by the audience's desire to reproduce a remembered ideal. The reproduction is impossible, but the desire can produce a meaningful, satisfying experience.

The emphasis on sight in this chapter also draws attention to graphic novel form. As it were, the fantasy nature of the conversation between adult Fairchild and child Alice points more specifically to the porno-graphic novel form, where visual access and sexual desire are explicitly linked. Scott McCloud, in *Understanding Comics*, writes of a concept termed "closure" (63–67), which the frame mirror mediation of *Lost Girls* exploits to great effect. In a basic sense, closure refers to the fact that the panel borders of a comic necessarily cut off parts of the image. For example, in the first panels of *Lost Girls*, only portions of the bed and dresser are visible, the other parts implicitly existing just beyond the edge of the image. Accordingly, closure depends on the active imagination of the audience to account for the implicit content. What is particularly fascinating about the mirror in *Lost Girls* is that the frame-within-a-frame enacts a sort of closure-within-closure. In other words, we only see part of the dresser upon which the mirror rests, such that the panel border cuts off part of the mirror frame. Moreover, the bed is only visible *within* this partial mirror frame, as a reflection, so it is actually the mirror that cuts off our view. Effectively, our viewing system (the comic) includes a secondary viewing system (the mirror), such that the content of the comic is mediated twice over.

This parallel mediation, taken alongside the metafictive focus in the opening chapters, reflexively figures the limiting borders of the mirror frame as a synecdoche for the limiting borders of all comic panels. Further, since the mirror simultaneously represents adaptation as a process of reception, the closure of the mirror frame subtly points to the imaginative work required in adaptation. Just as the audience must imaginatively "fill in" the other half of Alice Fairchild's bed, so too must the audience "fill in" the difference between the allusive elements of *Lost Girls*, and the elements of the Alice narratives that they ostensibly "adapt." It takes a leap of imaginative thought to perceive an "adapted element" as such. A mirror may be just a mirror until the words "silvery mist" insist that the audience see it as *the* looking glass.

In line with this implication that the reader's imagination is crucial in the constitution of the adaptation qua adaption, the reader's reflection is actually figured, subtly, in the frame mirror of *Lost Girls*. The placement of the looking glass in the first panel is such that, were it really a mirror, the audience should be reflected. This phantom reflection opens up the possibility, in the first panel of the narrative, that the disembodied speech bubble beckoning,

"Tell me a story," addresses the audience. After all, it *is* the audience that must tell the story of an adaptation as an adaptation; the experience of intertextual interaction depends on the audience's imagination to fill in the implicit meanings, to see the adaptation *as if* it were the adapted text.

That the mirror also points to the scopophilic character of the pornographic novel form further implicates the reader in the dynamic of adaptive desire. Like adult Alice bargaining for visual access when physical contact is denied her, the reader can only interact with the text, and navigate its adaptive relations, through the representative medium that frames the interaction. As the graphic novel medium cannot literally reproduce a human body, the reader must make the metaphoric leap to identify the illustration with the idea it purports to represent. In the same vein, the desire for an impossible reproduction through adaptation motivates the leaps of metaphoric imagination that are required to experience Alice Fairchild *as if* she were Alice in *Through the Looking-Glass*. Though it is seductive to see the representative medium as reflective of reality, the interaction with the world on the other side of the mirror is imagined, and so solitary, masturbatory. The ideal — that other world one desires to reproduce, through representation or adaptation — may, as Miss Fairchild suggests, exist in the "world beyond fiction's mirror," but the reader cannot step through the "silvery mist." The mirror reflects the subject that looks into it: touching the text through the looking-glass means touching oneself, but doing so in a way that performatively constitutes a reflective fantasy *as if* it were mirroring reality.

Through the Silvery Mist: Adaptation as Psychosis

If the opening chapter of *Lost Girls* uses the frame mirror to highlight the boundary between a source-text and an adaptation, the ninth chapter, "Looking Glass House," uses the mirror to explore transgressions of that boundary. This chapter is littered with clues for the knowing audience to make connections to Carroll's Alice: the tumble down the rabbit-hole and the step through the looking-glass, the white rabbit, the size-altering potions, the pool of tears, and the caucus race. Notably, every adapted element is re-imagined within a child-molestation narrative. Most prominently, the white rabbit is figured as Bunny (Moore; 1.9). Learning that Alice is fourteen, Bunny suggests they share some wine, which makes Alice feel as though her body "had grown too large or too small" (4;1.9), just as the potion in *Alice's Adventures in Wonderland* changes the size of Alice's body (10–12); Bunny's fingers are figured as "strange birds in a deep salt pool" (5;1.2) like the animals in

Carroll's caucus race, which takes place in a pool of Alice's tears (21). The list goes on, but the most significant elements, for my purposes, are the tumble down the rabbit-hole and the step through the looking glass:

> The birds moved faster, caught up in a race with rules beyond my comprehension; purposeful and frantic. I imagined that I heard their cries, then knew them for my own. I fell, and from the hole's far end she fell towards me [...] his hand was hot between my thighs. I made pretence that it was hers.
> The mirror-glass was melting into silver, boiling into mist, and I reached out and felt young muscle in her shoulder, in her neck, the child-silk at her nape [Moore 5; 1.9].

The illustrations that accompany this text feature two Alices, reaching their hands toward one another, through the liquid glass of the same frame mirror that was so prominent in chapter one. This doubling figures a series of problematic collapses, erasures of significant boundary lines: imagination becomes indistinguishable from reality, the necessary difference between an adaptation and its adapted text melts into a silvery mist. The frame mirror that was earlier established to demarcate the non-reproductivity of the adaptive process is refigured to suggest what it means to identify an adaptation *as a reproduction*, rather than as an adaptation. In short, the melting mirror figures fidelity discourse as mental violence, psychosis.

In theoretical terms, stepping through the mirror is a failure to recognize the automatic difference of the adaptation from its source, which is necessitated by the difference in medium. Ultimately, the psychic violence resulting from Alice Fairchild's molestation demonstrates the danger inherent in a metaphoric collapse — that is, when the desire to interpret literally overpowers the recognition of necessary difference. Alice Fairchild's psychological trauma results in the literal rendering of metaphoric experiences — the inability to distinguish fantasy from reality, or adapted text from adaptation. It starts when she makes "pretence" that Bunny's hand is the hand of her double in the mirror (5; 1.9), and reaches an apex when later she is incarcerated in an insane asylum (5; 3.29). Notably, Alice Fairchild's failure to distinguish fantasy from reality is itself actually adapted from Carroll's narrative. For example, examine the discussion of the chess game at the end of *Through the Looking-Glass*. Alice asks her kitten to

> consider who it was that dreamed it all. This is a serious question, my dear, and you should not go on licking your paw like that [...] you see, Kitty, it must have been either me or the Red King. He was part of my dream, of course — but then I was part of his dream, too! Was it the Red King, Kitty? You were his wife, my dear, you ought to know [208].

Even after leaving the Looking-Glass world, Alice fails to distinguish between imagination and reality. The transformation of the kitten into the Red Queen is simultaneously treated as a dream and taken quite seriously — an excellent example of balance between the impossibility of literal equation with the "ontological vehemence" of the metaphorical "is" (Ricoeur 255). For Alice, the kitten *was* the Red Queen, even while remaining a kitten.

The strength of such "ontological" vehemence may begin to account for the strong identification audiences can make between an adaptation and its adapted text. But there is a danger in identifying to such a degree that necessary differences are obliterated. As Alice Fairchild reaches the end of her recollected narrative, her childhood self is committed to an asylum:

> That's where everything I'd done or imagined caught up with me, including my nightmares. I could barely communicate except in nonsense words, and every night my dream-horror rampaged closer. I pictured its veined neck, its swollen head and slitted eyes. It crashed through the turgid, bulgey ... **tulgey** undergrowth, making a slurred bubbling ... a burble ... as it ejaculated. It was a monstrous, quivering cock, and it wanted to **jab** me [Moore 5; 3.29].

The culmination of Alice's psychological collapse, foreshadowed by her touching her double through the frame mirror, is total consumption by all things she had "done or imagined." Significantly, the bolded words intertextualize with the jabberwocky poem in *Through the Looking-Glass* (116–18). The content of what "caught up" with Alice is both the character's diegetic memories and an intertextual engagement with Carroll's texts. In the comic panel, as a visual depiction of this psychological state and its intertextual nature, Alice is surrounded by images featured throughout her narrative, images which are also adapted from Carroll's stories. When she says that those things "caught up with her," she indicates her inability to distinguish the reality of her present moment (in the asylum) from an imagined reality or a memory. Effectively, the "ontological vehemence" of her intertextual experiences overpowers the impossibility of their literal meaning. Her remembered, hallucinated, or adapted versions of her childhood come to replace, in her mind, the reality she experiences in the present moment.

Conclusion: "Begin at the beginning and go on till you come to the end; then stop"[4]

The looking-glass as an intervening medium is central to the adaptive aesthetic of *Lost Girls*. The integrity of the mirror is the key difference between Alice Fairchild's conversation with her remembered "precursor" self in the first chapter, and her conflation with her memories in the asylum. In this way, the looking glass gets at how and why fidelity idealism is both persistent and problematic. Without allowing the adaptation to destroy its literal relationship to the adapted text, there is no possibility for producing new meanings via the metaphoric interaction of the current textual experience and memories of previous textual experiences. In more concrete terms, if our desire to see our own vision of the adapted text reproduced is too strong we lose out on the meaningful possibilities inherent to the adaptation's necessary difference from its source. Yet, our desire for reproduction is part of the interpretive process adaptations exploit to make meaning; our desire enables the "copular insistence," that force of the metaphorical "is" which encourages us to equate adaptations with their sources. Ricoeur writes that "it was and was not" distills all that can be said of metaphorical truth (224). In a similar fashion, an adaptation both is and is not its adapted text. It is a necessary paradox if adaptations are to be meaningful as such, but dangerous in the extent to which it flirts with our desires for fidelity.

As a comic, *Lost Girls* is automatically different from the novels it adapts. As a reflexive device, representing comic form, the mirror suggests that the recognition of automatic difference by an audience is not guaranteed, and that the interpretation of the text changes, for better or worse, in accordance with such recognition, or lack thereof. Recall the reader's phantom reflection, implied at the beginning of *Lost Girls*. This (lack of an) image suggests that the desire for replication reflects our commitment to our personal narratives. It asks us to recognize ourselves in what we read, even as it asks us to recognize the impossibility of seeing our own reflections faithfully reproduced.

Notes

1. See Hutcheon (9) for a useful definition of adaptation. She excludes allusions and brief echoes from the definition, reserving the term "adaptation" for works that involve an extended engagement with previous texts.
2. *Through the Looking-Glass* (163).
3. Unfortunately, I do not have the space to address the pedophiliac implications of this interaction. That said, further work might link *Lost Girls* with constructions of Victorian childhood sexuality, most thoroughly examined by James R. Kincaid.
4. *Alice's Adventures* (94).

PART III

Victorian Sexualities and the Écriture Féminine: **Women Writing and the Women of Writing**

11. "Avast, Land-Lubbers!"
Reading Lost Girls *as a Post-Sadeian Text*
K. A. LAITY

In *The Sadeian Woman,* Angela Carter wades into the sexual fray with as much verve as her inspiring muse, the Marquis de Sade, little knowing that some years later she would inspire one of the most revolutionary pieces of pornography of her own century, Alan Moore and Melinda Gebbie's *Lost Girls.* Carter found as much controversy as Sade, accused, for example, of "uncritically accepting the hierarchical thinking characteristic of the patriarchy" (Altevers 18). She pursued Sade because he does promote a kind of sexual freedom for women although it is tied to "his refusal to see female sexuality in relation to its reproductive function" as she notes in her introduction (i). Carter examines his works with a fearless eye and finds that the man who shocked the world with his sexual omnivorousness, "the prisoner who created freedom in the model of his prison [...] is as much afraid of freedom as the next man" (132). "He is," she argues, "on the point of becoming a revolutionary pornographer; but he, finally, lacks the courage" (132). He cannot conceive of a freedom that is not "defined by tyranny." However, Carter finds hope in his analysis because while "Sade remains a monstrous and daunting cultural edifice," she also believes he "put pornography in the service of women" (37). Sade may not have recognized the fact, but in so doing he paved the way for creators like Moore and Gebbie.

This tyranny is particularly true when it comes to his supposed freedom for women. Per Angela Carter, "The Sadeian woman [...] subverts only her own socially conditioned role in the world of god, the king and the law" (133). Woman can be free within her class, but she cannot be free from it — and from the scarce economy of pleasure that Sade holds inviolate. This guarantees that "a free woman in an unfree society will be a monster" (27). In *The Philosophy in the Boudoir,* Sade has the libertine Dolmancé express this zero-sum-game by declaring that "the idea of seeing another enjoy as he enjoys reduces him to a kind of equality with that other which impairs the unspeakable charm *despotism* inspires in him" (qtd. in Carter 143). This fear of loss is at the heart of the "holy terror of love" that Carter arrives at with some dismay by the end of the study, and which she identifies as "the source of all opposition to the emancipation of women" (150) and the source, too, of all immoral pornography. Considering this, where then to find the source of moral pornography like *Lost Girls*? It lies in freeing their characters from their traditional bonds and forging new ones based on moral connections that do not require women or men to conform to despotic structures.

Moore and Gebbie center their narrative on this freedom from Sade's immoral tyranny. Carter addresses Sade's shortcomings by including as a postscript a piece by Emma Goldman that suggests there is hope beyond the drawbacks of pornography dissected in the rest of the book and the dead end to which Sade brings her. Goldman writes that it is essential "to cut loose from the weight of prejudices, traditions and customs" and demand all equal rights, for "the most vital right is the right to love and be loved." This erotic economy of abundance flies in the face of Sade's economy of scarcity. Indeed, Goldman goes further, declaring that the "one great thing" is "to give of one's self boundlessly, in order to find one's self richer, deeper, better. That alone can fill the emptiness, and transform the tragedy of woman's emancipation into joy, limitless joy" (151). In allowing "Red Emma" to respond to the "Madman of Charenton" Carter knew how radical a proposal she was imagining in her search for the moral pornographer. Rather than Sade's despotic pleasure, Goldman offers unselfish, boundless abundance based on trust and respect: everything inimical to our history. To achieve this post–Sadeian pleasure, we need subversives, pornographers who are willing to overthrow not just the accumulated weight of gender roles over the centuries, but the materialist economic system that perpetuates this tyranny of desire.

Subversive Pornographers in the Making

I argue that we may have a pair of such subversives at work in the three-volume comic book *Lost Girls*. By using this particular medium, co-creators Moore and Gebbie have managed not only to exploit all the artistic possibilities of the juxtaposition of words and images, but in doing so have managed to create a subversive work that nonetheless avoids being recognized as the dangerous text it is, due to the denigration of the medium as a whole. "Comic book" remains shorthand for simplistic and dumb in popular culture, despite the existence of books of depth, intelligence, and great beauty like Moore's body of work. *Lost Girls* provides a kind of cultural time bomb, sneaking subversive sexual freedom and a new economy of pleasure into our lives by means of the format usually dismissed by academics and journalists as kids' stuff, the traditional home of adolescent male power fantasies — grounded in the materialist economic system — since the early part of the twentieth century, now familiar from superhero movie franchises crackling with special effects and explosions.

However, the verbal/visual mix of comics offers a perfect platform for moral pornography as it invites the participation of the reader in uniquely different ways than print or pictures alone do. Carter imagines that "the moral pornographer would be an artist who uses pornographic material as part of the acceptance of the logic of a world of absolute sexual license for all the genders and projects a model of the way such a world might work" (19). In addition, the moral pornographers must offer "a critique of current relations between the sexes" as well as a "total demystification of the flesh" for "such a pornographer would not be the enemy of women, perhaps because he might begin to penetrate to the heart of the contempt for women that distorts our culture" (19–20). In so doing, the moral pornographer must become "a terrorist of the imagination, a sexual guerrilla whose purpose is to overturn our most basic notions of these relations" (21), what Susan Sontag has called "a freelance explorer of spiritual dangers," one who "seeks to make his work repulsive, obscure, inaccessible; in short, to give what is, or seems to be, *not* wanted" (emphasis added; 45). We don't tend to consider the spiritual realm when we discuss pornography, but it is an essential element of this particular pair of moral pornographers, and indeed supplies an important element of their morality. The audience may initially resist, but they need what the artist offers.

Moore says that "most pornography is horrible, and not just from a woman's perspective [....] We felt we could reclaim and redefine what pornography was, and we deliberately chose to use that word. We didn't want to hide behind 'erotica' [....] *Pornos graphos*— drawings or writings of wantons — that will do" (Rose). *Lost Girls* realizes the possibility of moral pornography largely through the intimate juxtaposition of words and images where the visual lushness often helps soften the jangling horrors that the narrative offers (and the various traumas its three heroines have survived), its effects are deliberately disorienting, giving beauty to often ugly events. As Sontag argues,

> What makes a work of pornography part of the history of art rather than of trash is not distance, the superimposition of a consciousness more conformable to that of ordinary reality upon the "deranged consciousness" of the erotically obsessed. Rather, it is the originality, thoroughness, authenticity, and power of that deranged consciousness itself, as incarnated in a work. From the point of view of art, the exclusivity of the consciousness embodied in pornographic books is in itself neither anomalous nor anti-literary [47].

Lost Girls has that "originality, thoroughness, authenticity and power," from the passages that mimic the work of well-known artists like Beardsley and von Bayros to the ecstatic re-creation of the riot at the premiere of Stravinsky's *The Rite of Spring*. Sontag's "psychic dislocation" grows in the space between the lush beauty and the psychological horrors of this text, which include abuses as tragic as incest. The strength of the images is that they also help to convey a sensuality that the language only partially creates and to resolve traumatic narratives with powerful illustrations that reveal the capacity of the sexual imagination to triumph over past damages, as when a feisty Wendy stands up to the "Hook" who's been preying on the children in the park.

This authentic and collaborative work by a husband and wife team helps complicate the traditional male-centric nature of mainstream pornography and moves it beyond what Carter calls "the methodological defects of a manual of navigation written by and for land-lubbers" toward her "total demystification of the flesh" via its thorough sex-positive cornucopia of fantasies (15). This is, of course, no accident. When I interviewed Moore and Gebbie, they confirmed that Carter's study — as well as works by Simone de Beauvoir and other feminist writers — had inspired their project throughout the sixteen years of its composition, which began in the fifth installment of Steve Bissette's *Taboo* compendium in 1991. In the collection, the two call on a variety of techniques to create this elaborate sensual feast. As Moore explained, Carter "seemed to point to the possibility of a form of erotica that would be as inventive, as intelligent, as beautiful and as free of the kind of coercive, controlling elements that were to be found sometimes in other pornography and erotica." With *Lost Girls* the two wanted nothing less than a chance to change people's sexual imaginations, in keeping with Carter's assertion that "the more pornographic writing acquires the techniques of real literature, of real art, the more deeply subversive it is likely to be in that the more likely it is to affect the reader's perceptions of the world" (19). Moore and Gebbie made their artistic choices in order to achieve that ambition. Sontag seems to agree, writing, "Pornography that is serious literature aims to 'excite' in the same way that books which render an extreme form of religious experience aim to 'convert'" (48). Moore and Gebbie have every intention of converting readers to their "make love not war" philosophy embodied in *Lost Girls*.

Alice, Wendy, and Dorothy — Lost, Traumatized Girls

At the heart of the story are three resonant figures: Alice, better known in Wonderland; Wendy, mother to all the Lost Boys; and Dorothy, last seen in Oz. The three women — for they have all grown up by the time of these particular adventures — offer not only a link to these well-loved narratives, but also an opportunity to examine these iconic figures and reinterpret their stories as reflections of childhood sexual traumas that must be revealed in order to be healed: Alice's abuse, Dorothy's incest, and Wendy's prudish middle-class upbringing. In assuaging these traumas, Moore and Gebbie go a long way toward repairing the larger rifts within current sexual politics, such as those embodied by Wendy and her husband, each unaware of the secret yearnings the other possesses. The humorous shadowplay sequence between the two — where the shadows appear to be copulating while the husband and wife carry out mundane tasks — aids in producing that "critique of current relations between the sexes" and "total demystification of the flesh" that Carter imagined. Using these much-mythologized figures, Moore and Gebbie render them anew as specific and temporal women; given her mistrust of mythologizing, one can't help but hope that Carter would approve. Far from the "mythic abstractions" and the "collective, sexed being which cannot, by reason of its very nature, exist" (6), we have three women with the weight of mythology due to their literary histories, but the specificity of real individuals because of their artistic rendering.

Like a tripartite goddess, Alice, Wendy, and Dorothy are brought together as maiden, mother and crone, at a plausible time and location that allows them to experience the dramatic premiere of Stravinsky's *Rite of Spring* as well as the ominous dawn of the first World War in the wake of the assassination of Archduke Ferdinand and his wife. More to the point, they are brought together in the confines of a most unusual place, the auspiciously named Hotel Himmelgarten (literally "heaven-garden"), unlike the "model of hell" that Sade's characters create (24). By the end of the story, the hotel has been left nearly empty by the exodus in the face of the approaching war: Hell cannot be held at bay in a world that rejects the healing hand of sexuality. There they share the crippling tales of their childhood formulations of sexuality, each one maimed by Victorian or Puritan hypocrisy and even deliberate abuse. The tales associated with them turn out to be a twisted version of the true facts of their lives, a distorting prism of morality that hides ugly destruction behind a whimsical froth of invention. Alice disappears into her own reflection while a friend of the family molests her. Dorothy finds herself consumed by a 'tornado' of lust. Wendy finds sexual awakening and danger in Kensington Gardens. Immoral pornography would fetishize the harm by means of empty repetition; here they release the trauma in a kind of talking therapy instead, remembering the abuses they have never been able to speak about before. Dorothy reveals at last the affair with her father, Alice her insanity, and Wendy her frigidity. In so doing they each function as figures who refuse to become archetypes even as they offer genuine and healing relationships. They are at once so comfortably familiar and yet as vivaciously alive that they cannot be forced to submit to the mere fantasy of their stories.

In this re-imagining of the beloved children's book heroines, the reader finds them much changed — damaged women whose familiar tales mask real life ordeals that have stunted their sexual lives and kept them from achieving happiness. We first meet Alice, or rather, her reflection as the picture of the proper Victorian matriarch in the very first panel of the first page. The whole of chapter one (I.1.1–8) takes place through the lens of her looking glass. It is telling that we don't actually see Alice reflected until the fourth page, grimacing as a maid brushes her hair.

Things are not, of course, as they look. As we learn of her highly medicated state (I.1.3) and devotion to Sapphic pleasures (I.4.5), we also begin to understand the looking glass as a manifestation of her particular distress. When she reveals the story of her violation by a family friend, we see the girl dissociate from the trauma by retreating into reflections, and eventually the looking glass itself. All of Alice's remembrances reflect this theme and her stylistically rendered images keep the Looking Glass world intact. Alice proves as brittle as the glass into which she stares as a violated child and as a medicated adult. Her story has the vivid colors of a children's book, vibrant reds, playful blues, and cheery yellows (I.9.1–8). Her storytelling takes the same light: bustling along through tales of lurid abuse and servitude. Even the mirror, which she tells her maid in the final panel, "I couldn't bear to leave it, it's been in the family for so long now. Since I was a child, in fact" (I.1.4–6). The trauma the mirror contains has become inextricably bound to her own identity. While a treasure from childhood, the mirror's gilt border has a distinctly adult air, comprised of frankly sexual female figures. The object literally reflects her life and Alice often appears immobile before it.

We're introduced to Dorothy by her iconic silver shoes and her ready attitude toward sex, indulging in a quick liaison with new acquaintance Captain Rolf Bauer on the hotel grounds on her first night (I.2.4–7). While Dorothy seems initially to be the least inhibited of the three, we soon discover that her own tornado of promiscuity hides a more recent trauma of incest. As a young woman, Dorothy's prodigious libido found only surreptitious and guilty outlets on her remote farm, capped by her father's inability to control his own passion for her. Of the three, Dorothy makes the fewest strides forward toward a full sexual healing, yet her story fulfills Carter's moral purpose by exposing the violence and exploitation inherent in the sexual system of inequalities and its exploitation by those who share Sade's notion of tyranny (like Dorothy's father). Her flashbacks utilize the rich golden tones of a Kansas cornfield that Gebbie describes with film references, "Todd AO lights" and "Paris, Texas," as well as metaphorically render her life experiences as familiar characters from her travels to Oz.

Wendy is certainly the most repressed of the three. We see her arrive with her very proper husband as a tight bundle of denial (I.3.1). While her husband gives in to the ambience of the hotel very quickly — not only enjoying the erotic bedside reading offered by the hotel (I.3.3–6), but even indulging in a romp with Captain Rolf (II.13.3–8), much to his surprise and embarrassed delight — Wendy remains as rigidly self-contained as the black-bordered images in the boldly colorful flashbacks to her childhood games in the park with the real Peter Pan. Her tone is hesitant and full of shame, while hinting at the passion that lay beneath her fear and mortification, "Peter approached me, asking if I'd like to play. I couldn't speak, which he took as assent. Perhaps it was" (I.8.4). The unconscious sensuality that lies buried in her memory comes through in her close observation of the randy hotel employees and in a humorous sequence that juxtaposes the matter-of-fact actions of Wendy and Harold Potter, while their shadows seem to enact an erotic coupling behind them (I.7–8). Of the three, Wendy seems to recover the most by the end of their adventures, realizing what she had lost and restoring a lost verve and sexual excitement that she had thought departed forever. In our interview Moore described her as the most overtly heroic of the "girls"— facing the hook-handed molester on her own — but she has buried that triumph (III.27.5). Her Pan had awakened a sexuality that brought her out of a tightly-bound middle class existence, but this sensual nature frightened her with its passion and its wildness. Although the Darling children found a Neverland free of adult supervision in Kensington Park, they also discovered that this freedom left them vulnerable, such as when Peter's sister Annabella gets raped by the "Hook" figure (III.27.2). Wendy internalizes this lesson, swearing off the park and its games, marrying a much older man so his desire would be less and closing the nursery window at night so her own son wouldn't be "taken away by sex, by the wilderness, by the working class. By shadows. That will never happen, never. Never," she tells Alice and Dorothy, rewriting the force of Neverland (III.27.7).

Of Ritual, Healing, and Stories

These revelations are shaped by Moore's careful attention to form and Gebbie's luxurious artwork, which reflects the internal world of the three heroines. The form operates with ritual precision, a fact the *Rite of Spring* sequence brings into immediate relief as the women give way to wild passion while the audience around them erupts in the famous riots that accompanied Stravinsky's debut of the piece. Capping the first volume, this passionate explosion binds the three women together and makes possible their journey of confession and release. What had been surreptitious secrets revealed to strangers becomes a healing relationship of support. As they explore their sexuality together, the women slowly peel away the layers of pain and repression that obscure those long lost injuries that have prevented them from becoming fully integrated adults. They also begin the difficult process of rebuilding who they are.

Unlike Sade's closed sexual economy, the three women find that their shared experiences lead to an abundance. As Dorothy says, "I sure feel better all them secrets out in the open" (III.30.2). Instead of the authoritative hierarchies that tore their psyches apart, they have found equality, healing, and power in their communion. Their shared memories and sexual escapades even have a rejuvenating effect, as Alice mentions, "I can't speak for you two, but I feel positively girlish again" (III.30.2). Like a ritual immersion in the elements, they descend into memory by stages toward wholeness and renewal. As ritual theorist Viktor Turner argues, "the passage from one social status to another is often accompanied by a parallel passage in space, a geographical movement from one place to another" (25). The symbolic retelling of their traumatic developments within the hotel's carefully constructed liminal space allows for the heroines' re-entry into society changed and strengthened. As Wendy notes on their final day, "I feel full of possibility again, like when I was young" (30.3). The violence of the past and the threat of future violence by means of the approaching war for the moment remain at bay. Their grand ritual demands the high stakes of violence to avoid trivializing the importance of sex. As Richard Schechner argues in *The Future of Ritual*, "ritual violence is not a remembrance of things past [...] the present moment is a negotiation between a wished-for future and a rehearsable, therefore changeable, past" (259). These women have been telling one version of their past and living another. Only when they come together and perform an on-going ritual of celebration and healing are they able to move on both psychologically and geographically. They refuse to accept the limit of the encroaching Hell. "You don't think we ought've been gone sooner?" Dorothy asks. "Absolutely not. Sod the war. Finishing our stories was more important. More of a victory," Alice tells her (III.30.2). The ritual needed to be complete. They value for the first time their health and sanity above the normal concerns of the society in which they live. The women will not be beaten down by the dictates of war.

As harrowing as the back stories prove to be — and as *outré* as the women's fantasies prove to be — the luscious colors and nimble styles of Gebbie's artwork delight the eye on every page. The primary colors of Alice's world, the golden cornucopia of Dorothy's Kansas, and the pre–Raphaelite storybook hues of Wendy's memory charge every page with rich bounty. Carter might well warn that here we have a possible instance of that "liberal theory that art disinfects eroticism of its latent subversiveness" (19), but there is little in *Lost Girls* that can make the reader feel "safe." Moore and Gebbie's collection claims to assure its status as pornography even as it makes the reader admire its skill and beauty. Nonetheless, the images and often the text, too, self-consciously remind us of our artistic distance, the safety net removing us from the experience (we can observe incest without partaking or other practices that might make us blanch in life, because we are "only" reading), while the comics medium taunts us with its own *sub-rosa* status, still too marginal to take its place confidently as art, despite the many stellar practitioners whose work can be immediately recognized as art in any context.

In the end, Sade's potential objections come from his position as the incarcerated one: as Carter argues, "his solitude is the perpetual companion and daily horror of the prisoner, whose final place of confinement is the self" (33). His solitude reflects the zero-sum-game of his economic system: for one to win, others must lose. The three women, however, find much of their freedom in the shared experience, one which we vicariously get to share because it has an abundance. In the space between "the world" and "the wet dream" (19), we find our moral pornographers operating, bringing us both ecstasy and revivingly positive truths that can be shared.

Dancing on the Tightrope Between Art and Pornography

This tightrope between art and pornography is one that *Lost Girls* constantly dances along. You can see that in the reactions of many comics reviewers who found themselves put on the spot by the difficulty of assessing a comic that was both art and pornography, and most found it necessary to trumpet the art every time (if they did not dismiss the project out of hand). Even the normally erudite comics writer Neil Gaiman, while praising the myriad artistic qualities, found himself unable to acknowledge that there was anything alluring to be found between the covers, writing: "If it failed for me, it was only as smut; the book, at least in large black and white photocopy form, was not a one-handed read. It was too heady, dense and strange to appreciate or to experience on a visceral level. (Your mileage may vary; porn is, after all, personal.)" (Gaiman). For comics readers, whose beloved medium has been all too often dismissed as pornographic, the chance to cling to art proved too attractive to allow many to admit that *Lost Girls* could be pornography as well, despite its creators insistence on that tag, one which they knew would be problematic. In part this has to do with the unique capabilities of the comics form. Rather than the simple mimesis of video or film, comics offers an interpretive level of distance which allows art like Gebbie's to render often troubling images with exquisite beauty: as Sontag argues, this appropriation of art allows us a cognitive distance between the beauty of the rendering and the horrors rendered (47).

In making the case against pornography, Robert Stoller has written that "its moment of greatest thrill can be traced back to the moment of greatest trauma in the author's or reader's life" (qtd. in Gubar 737), and certainly within *Lost Girls,* that is often the case, but far from harming the reader, *Lost Girls* offers a wonderful opportunity for healing and reconciliation. Revelations of childhood horrors are often capped with full-page illustrations that at once capture the trauma, yet also defuse it while once again anchoring the women's narratives to the better known original stories. In our interview, Moore mentioned that "in the illustrations we depicted in a grotesquely exaggerated form each gender's most ridiculous fears concerning the other." For example when Wendy realizes that the predator who provides the real life model of Captain Hook is terrified of her now-womanly body, her power explodes in a *vagina dentata* image that's both grisly and hilarious, making ridiculous that which had been feared (III.27.6). Rendered as the wily crocodile that has got a taste of Hook and cannot resist him, the vaginal image swallows an alarmed-looking Captain, who ejaculates as he is consumed, holding onto Wendy's knickers as if for dear life. There's even an alarm clock tied to the crocodile's tail. Likewise, the trauma of Alice's childhood abuse gets writ large as a marauding cock and balls, chasing her through the tulgey woods, burbling, ejaculating — "it wanted to jab me!" Alice cries (III.29.6). In a formal sense, we quickly get accustomed to reading the single panel pages as moments to pause and reflect upon their revelations; in a visual sense, we have the narrative episode tied together in a metaphorical image that reconciles the discomfort and the horror to make possible a renewed wholeness for the reader as well as the heroines. They are often exaggerations that also remove much of the discomfort with humor, making those innate fears so ridiculous that they lose all power.

Comics, of course, also offer words. Unlike prose novels, however, in a graphic novel the words alone do not bear the responsibility for rendering the images — or, should I say, the reader's own imagination does not bear the full responsibility for creating the tableaux, which lets her off the hook for depicting some of the more scandalous scenes, a fact which the dialogue occasionally highlights. For example in Book III the hotelier M. Rougeur reads aloud a story of incestuous love from his infamous "white book"—a collection of erotic stories penned and illustrated by many an illustrious guest—while fucking a thirteen-year-old chambermaid. The tale in question, allegedly penned by Pierre Loüys and illustrated by Baron von Bayros, appears across the top panels of the page, while Rougeur's commentary on the tale runs across the bottom. He reminds his audience that the images offer only "the idea of incest" and that the young children cavorting "are fictions, as old as the page they appear upon, no less, no more" (III.22.4). In a perhaps too didactic moment, Moore has Rougeur reiterate "if this were real, it would be horrible," which while true enough, certainly need not be spelled out quite so directly. However, he recovers with the humorously ironic declaration from Rougeur, "I, of course, am real, and since Helena, who I just fucked is only thirteen, I am very guilty" (III.22.5). This insistence on plunging the reader into taboo territory of the most transgressive kind is precisely meant to accomplish that lesson: that for the erotic imagination, Moore and Gebbie clearly believe, *everything* must be possible. If we are to be truly free, we must be able to imagine with impunity things we would not actually wish to do without feeling fear or inhibition. What carries a weight of abuse and damage in the real world must be allowed to exist in the boundless abundance of the erotic imagination.

As Joanna Russ writes in her study of the power of women's slash fiction, "sexual fantasy can't be taken at face value[....] What excites in fantasy is both far more exaggerated than real life and not the same as in real life" (88). We cannot control what sexually excites us: we can only control what we decide to do about it. Russ argues that "what seems to be happening in sexual fantasy is that any condition imposed on or learned with sexuality is capable of becoming sexualized, either as sex or a substitute for sex or as an indispensable condition of it" (89). The randomness of our sexual sparks can be channeled through fantasy without repercussion. Despite assorted panics about pornography leading to either child molesting or serial killing sprees, imagining the forbidden does not automatically lead to crime. Rape-survivor, former prostitute, novelist and director Virginie Despentes writes in *King Kong Theory* that "our sexual fantasies say a lot about us in the same indirect way as dreams. They don't reveal anything about what we want to happen in real life[....] What arouses us, or fails to, comes from dark, uncontrollable places in ourselves, and rarely fits who we consciously like to be" (80). The systematic denigration of pornography comes from a fear of giving shape to those unconscious desires. However, as Despentes suggests, "it is actually censorship that has shaped, created and defined the history of X-rated films. Whatever is forbidden to be shown will soon turn up in porn cinemas, which makes for an interesting exercise in transgression" (82). We can either accept the darkness of our libidos or we can continue to fund their underground existence and sneak off to shameful locations.

Moore and Gebbie know this and try to lead us back with the Lost Girls to a location where we can accept our wildest imaginings and learn, in their words, to "make love, not war" (Rose). At heart it's a realization that we find it easier to declare enemies than to admit to the truth of our lust, particularly for women. Our Puritan heritage assures that most women will be raised to think their natural sexual instincts to be shameful. Texts like *Lost Girls* offer another avenue to embrace and celebrate those feelings, to trumpet them to the world at large. Like the female writers of slash fiction that Joanna Russ explores, Moore and Gebbie also want a "sexual intensity, sexual enjoyment, the freedom to choose, a love that is entirely free of the culture's whole discourse of gender and sex roles, and a situation in which it is safe to let go and allow oneself to become emotionally and sexually vulnerable" (89). Between the covers of this gorgeous collection, where every liaison is allowed and illustrations as luscious as sweet cakes abound, they have created a place for this, one which readers might use to take back to the "real" world. For as Carter reminds us, "History tells us that every oppressed class gained true liberation from its masters through its own efforts" (151). Moore and Gebbie point the way to true erotic liberation, but it is we who have to choose to be free.

12. The Undying Fire
Erotic Love as Divine Grace in Promethea

CHRISTINE HOFF KRAEMER

Promethea disappointed many of its early readers. After an action-packed opening, the series quickly veers into didacticism as the comic becomes a primer in Alan Moore's metaphysical belief system, the Western mystical tradition. Also called Western esotericism, this spiritual tradition includes aspects of natural philosophy, mystical Christianity, Judaism, and ancient pagan religions, and it was part of the Renaissance intellectual culture that gave birth to modern scientific thinking. Practitioners of Western esotericism engage in meditative and ritual practices to refine the individual self and bring it into harmony with the totality of Being. Moore denies, however, that his exploration of Western esotericism in *Promethea* has "religious" intentions (Robinson). He believes his philosophical system can operate alongside a variety of religious perspectives and specifies his total disinterest in officiating rituals and building churches. Instead, the magical world view of *Promethea* is "simply a new way of seeing the ordinary universe that surrounds us, and ourselves as creatures in that universe" (Robinson). This new perspective, he believes, will help to combat destructive political tendencies that he sensed arising after 9/11 (Babcock 30). Despite Moore's distancing himself from "religion," however, it is a religious audience (consisting primarily of contemporary Pagans) that has most embraced *Promethea* in trade paperback form (Kraemer and Winslade 288). Though Moore thinks of himself as teaching religiously neutral tools for thought, *Promethea* has a distinctive and coherent theology that resonates with both contemporary Paganism and new movements in liberal Christianity. Against the traditional Christian doctrine of original sin, from which so much body-denying and sex-negative theology has come, *Promethea*'s vision of the divine asserts the cosmological centrality of erotic love.

Moore and artist J.H. Williams created the kabbalistic issues of *Promethea* less as narratives than as environments into which the reader would be drawn. As Moore put it, "What you were seeing in the comic is not the report of the magical experience. It *was* the magical experience" (Cooke and Koury 31). Expository writing lacks the tools to communicate an experience of magical attitudes and perceptions, so Moore harnesses the visual and intertextual possibilities of comics to his purpose. Through techniques such as breaking the fourth wall (having the characters address the reader), calling attention to the non-linearity of time suggested by the comics form, and expressing in images that which cannot be expressed in words, *Promethea* seeks to blur the boundary between fiction and reality and trigger a transformation of consciousness in the reader.[1]

Though Moore may have intended the comic as an introductory magical primer, *Promethea* appears to work best for prepared readers. Contemporary Pagans, with their emphasis on the experiential, already have a context for the idea of a magical or devotional comic: it is meant to be meditated on, not merely read. Those who come to the comic without a context for Moore's theology may appreciate the formal experimentation, but find the comic as a whole to be either preachy or merely incomprehensible. If a reader is struggling just to decode the exposition, the subtleties of *Promethea* may be lost amongst text boxes of unfamiliar words. The necessary context is missing.

This essay, therefore, focuses on providing context. *Promethea* uses the comics form in inventive new ways, and this innovation will provide a rich vein for future criticism — but only if readers are not terminally confused by the plot. Rather than providing a close reading of *Promethea* or focusing on its formal elements, I will situate it within two different theological traditions, then broadly trace the theme of love through the narrative. Although I acknowledge the limitations of expository writing, I hope this essay will still "point a finger at the moon," as the Buddhist saying goes — that it will successfully gesture toward concepts that are beyond words. If these theological aspects are ignored in the text, Moore's mysticism is reduced to mere politics: sexual libertarianism, body-positivity, or some other more familiar, secular philosophy. Though *Promethea* can be read politically as a queer and sex-positive text, its ultimate vision is one of spiritual liberation through knowledge of divine love.

"The Erotic" as a Theological Category

In both queer Christian theology and contemporary Pagan theology, the erotic is understood as a fundamental quality of God/dess's love. Queer Christian and Pagan theologians share similar concerns when they attack traditional Christian notions of the sinful and tainted human body. The doctrine of original sin, which frames the body's desires as untrustworthy, is discarded, as are prohibitions against homosexuality and the free expression of sexual desire. Moore makes no claim to writing formal theology, but he acknowledges two different artists as major influences: Christian mystic William Blake (1757–1827) and Western occultist Aleister Crowley (1875–1947). Blake's erotic mysticism has resurfaced in recent Christian and post–Christian theology. Much of the poet's work, such as *The Marriage of Heaven and Hell,* celebrates the body and affirms the holiness of desire while implicitly condemning the restrictive practices of the Christian church.[2] The impact of Blake on Moore's spiritual practice is clear in *Angel Passage,* the piece of ritual theater that Moore wrote, performed, and recorded in the poet's honor.[3] Blake's understanding of carnal desire as divine also clearly informs Moore's notion of divine energy in *Promethea.*

Although Moore prefers to refer to himself as a magician rather than as a Pagan, his understanding of his spiritual practice as "magic" and his seemingly only half-ironic worship of the "sock-puppet" snake god Glycon have much in common with the syncretic polytheism and creative rituals of contemporary Pagans (Kraemer and Winslade 288). Like Moore, Aleister Crowley would have considered himself to be a magician, not a Pagan. However, Western esotericism in general, and Crowley's work in particular, has had a major influence on the burgeoning Pagan movement.[4] Moore's understanding of kabbalah and Western esotericism in *Promethea* draws directly on Crowley's writing: Jack Faust lends books by Crowley to Sophie when she asks him to tutor her in magic (*Promethea* #10), and Crowley himself appears as a character throughout the series, with *Promethea* #12 using images of Crowley on nearly every page (Kraemer and Winslade, 280–1). This theological debt to Crowley and Western esotericism is a large part of why Pagans have claimed Moore as their own (Pitzl-Waters "Importance of Alan Moore"; Kraemer and Winslade 288).

Crowley's theology entered contemporary Paganism through the work of Gerald Gardner and Doreen Valiente, who publicized the supposed rediscovery of an ancient form of British Paganism called Wicca in the mid–1950s. In the Wiccan ritual of the Great Rite, celebrants participate in the creation of the universe through one of two symbolic acts: inserting a blade into a cup, or engaging in heterosexual intercourse (usually in private). Both acts represent a primal, erotic union of active and receptive forces that Wiccans generally conceptualize as the God and the Goddess (Hutton 236). The image of a blade or wand being inserted into a cup appears explicitly in *Promethea* #10, where it represents both the union of divine energies and the sexual intercourse in which Jack and Promethea are engaging. Later, in *Promethea* #28, the act of a "wand"—in this case, a stirring stick for a drink—being inserted into a cup recalls this same union of energies and sets the apocalypse in motion. In both cases, events on the human level resonate with the movement of cosmic forces. Because the divine infuses all of Being, even the most ordinary wand and cup can represent the original union of active and receptive energies: primal Force flowing into primal Form.

The idea that the universe is created, sustained, and transformed by the erotic interaction of energies is not limited to British Wicca or to Moore's work. In the 1970s, Starhawk, an American Pagan and ecofeminist theologian, advocated for a less heterosexually-inflected vision of creation than that in British Wicca: she conceptualizes life force as the movement of energy between many beings rather than just two (20, 234, 267). Calling this connective web *the erotic,* she defines it as something deeper and also broader than sexuality. Contemporary to Starhawk's writing, black lesbian feminist poet Audre Lorde described the erotic as the impulse to flourish, a desire for pleasure that drives one to resist oppression and strive toward joy. For Lorde, the erotic can be expressed sexually in the bedroom, but it is also present in every moment of intense engagement with the world (54–9). In the 1980s and 1990s, queer Christian theologians such as Carter Heyward and Marvin Ellison also defined the term in Lorde's sense, with Heyward declaring in *Touching Our Strength* that "My eroticism is my participation in the universe" (25). Such expansive definitions hearken back to the work of early twentieth-century psychologist C.G. Jung, who famously spoke of eros as "the great binder and loosener" within the psyche, between people, and between the individual and the world — in other words, as a cosmic relational principle (254).

Not all contemporary Pagans share this theology of the erotic; some are focused on reconstructing ancient Paganisms from other parts of the world and have not been influenced by its centrality in Wicca and religious witchcraft (Strmiska 18–22). Because Wicca has been extensively popularized, however — so much so that, in many people's minds, "Wicca" is synonymous with contemporary Paganism — many Pagans do affirm the sacredness of the sexual body and the erotic character of nature and the divine. Doreen Valiente's "Charge of the Goddess" is a widely known piece of Wiccan liturgy that serves as an ethical proof text for many practitioners. Written in the voice of the Goddess, it declares,

> And ye shall be free from slavery; and as a sign that ye be really free, ye shall be naked in your rites; and ye shall dance, sing, feast, make music and love, all in my praise.
>
> For mine is the ecstasy of the spirit, and mine also is joy on earth; for my Law is Love unto all Beings. [...] Let my worship be within the heart that rejoiceth; for behold, all acts of love and pleasure are my rituals [Valiente *Charge* 54–5].

Among other allusions, Valiente's Charge echoes Crowley's declaration that "Love is the Law, Love under Will" (I. 57) and draws on imagery from the first chapter of his Book of the Law (Serith).[5] In this text, eroticism and spirituality are fused; Valiente stands in good company with Rumi, John Donne, and other devotional poets who have couched God's love or their love for God in erotic or romantic terms.

Moore shares Valiente's association of freedom and erotic expression with both Pagans and liberal Christians. For many Pagans, spiritual and sexual liberation are not only intertwined, but inseparable (Urban 15–20). Moore implicitly affirms this belief in *25,000 Years of Erotic Freedom*, where he argues that freedom of sexual expression is and has always been the cornerstone of a flourishing culture. His persistent advocacy for gay, lesbian, bisexual, and transgender rights is explicit in *The Mirror of Love* (2004), an illustrated work with José Villarrubia celebrating same-sex love throughout history, and mourning the persecution of same-sex relationships. In an appendix, Moore provides contact information for several gay rights organizations and cheers the 2003 repeal of Section 28, a law that labeled gay family relationships as "pretend" and prohibited authorities in England and Wales from "promoting" homosexuality (111–12). The theological underpinning of this political commitment—in other words, the belief in the erotic nature of divine love—is the central theme of *Promethea*.

While Moore's theology is more closely related to contemporary Paganism than to queer Christian liberation theology, queer Christian theologians' commitment to erotic liberation and social justice situates them as Moore's allies in the cultural struggle over sexuality. Marvin Ellison's *Erotic Justice*, for example, explores erotic love as a moral and political force. Ellison claims that the failure to value erotic pleasure is one of the cornerstones of social and economic injustice in Western society. He writes, "Every oppression involves violence toward the devalued body," whether that oppression involves domestic abuse or sexual assault, mandatory unpaid overtime, sweatshop working conditions, laws criminalizing consensual sex acts between adults, or hate crimes committed against minorities (15). To affirm the human right to pleasure, in Ellison's view, strikes directly at society's tendency to eroticize power inequalities, as well as the propensity to uncritically accept that those in power have the right to control the behaviors and exploit the bodies of the politically disenfranchised (41). Other Christian and post–Christian theologies, such as those explored in Marcella Althaus-Reid's *The Queer God* and the collection *Toward a Theology of Eros*,[6] focus specifically on the nature of God's love for creation and for humanity. For these theologians, the belief that God incarnates (in the person of Christ, or in the perpetual creation of Being, as in process theology) is evidence for the eroticism of God's love. The presence of an embodied God is offered as proof of the divine desire for flesh (Burrus xxi).

Connecting the Human with the Divine in Promethea

Divine eros drives the apocalyptic plot of *Promethea*, not divine wrath. In contrast to the plagues, wars, and ultimate annihilation imagined in mainstream apocalyptic literature, *Promethea*'s apocalypse recaptures the original Greek meaning of the term: *revelation* (Boyer 23). Here, the end of the world involves not its physical destruction, but a global spiritual awakening to the nature of divine love.

At the climax of this shift in consciousness, science heroine/demigoddess Promethea speaks to the reader directly. Encouraging the reader to come close and hold her hand, Promethea addresses the audience as part of a universal divine self that is eternally in the process of becoming: "All is one, and all is deity, this beautiful undying fire of being that is everywhere about us, that we are. [...] Know you are everything, forever. Know I love you" (*Promethea* #31). For Moore, love is more than right relationship between human beings; it is the universe reaching out compassionately and erotically to every being within it. Although such love is not necessarily sexual in a physical sense, in *Promethea* sexuality often operates as a metaphor for the passionate, intimate, and embodied qualities of divine love. The understanding that human love is an aspect of divine love helps to support a positive theology of human sexuality.

Promethea begins and ends with human love. The story opens with the child Promethea's father allowing himself to be murdered so that his daughter can safely flee (*Promethea* #1), and closes on Sophie as she kisses her boyfriend and chooses an ordinary life free from superheroic adventures (*Promethea* #31). Between these moments of loving self-sacrifice and domestic contentment, however, is a great deal of struggle, pain, and suffering. After the lost child Promethea is taken into the realm of the gods, she becomes a demi-goddess herself (*Promethea* #1). Although she no longer has a body of her own, she becomes able to manifest physically by possessing the bodies of willing human beings. Many of the human vessels of Promethea prior to Sophie die gruesome deaths, most related to romantic or emotional involvements: Anna perishes giving birth to her lover's child (*Promethea* #4); Margaret kills herself in the aftermath of World War I, unable to bear the weight of human suffering that she has witnessed (*Promethea* #31, epilogue); Bill is murdered after his lover discovers that when not possessed by Promethea, Bill is male (*Promethea* #7).

Part of the impact of divine love, as it is experienced by all those who survive the apocalypse, is that it redeems these human loves by putting them in a larger context. Promethea's revelation is panentheistic — in other words, all is in and of the divine (*Promethea* #31). In this paradigm, separation and loss are part of a useful illusion, not fundamental realities. This perspective contradicts the human/divine and body/spirit dualities that characterize many traditional Christian theologies.[7] Here, God/dess is not solely transcendent and beyond the human world, but is also fully immanent and present in all of Being.

Yet one duality remains relevant: the apparent separation of Self and Other. The ability to maintain a separate identity and personality is part of the ongoing self-exploration of the divine. As Burrus puts it, God desires the flesh and so incarnates into it, including into the bodies of human beings (xxi). This incarnation into separate, differentiated selves makes relationship possible. Without such manifestation, God is all undifferentiated, unitary potential — there is no Other, and therefore no relationship. Having manifested Herself in the diversity and multiplicity of the universe, however, God becomes capable of a near-infinite variety of flavors of love and connection. As Crowley's Book of the Law states in the voice of the Goddess Nuit, "I am divided for love's sake, for the chance of union" (I: 29). The glory of communion, reunion, and erotic connection are not possible without separateness and division — though separation and division also open the possibility of violence, to which even *Promethea*'s post-apocalyptic utopia is not immune.

In *Promethea*, to know the nature of divine love is also to know the nature of the self and the universe. Separation is temporary and, in some ways, very much a frame of mind. In the aftermath of the apocalypse, people acknowledge their dead loved ones in their daily lives, speaking to them as though they might hear, and sometimes feeling that they receive answers. Loves that have crossed over into death are no longer considered lost, but instead a sense of their continuing presence is woven into everyday life. Post-apocalypse, one FBI agent remarks to Sophie that he has begun to talk to his father in his imagination, and finds himself simultaneously drawn to the Baptist religion of his childhood and to the worship of a Greek goddess. She replies:

> Yeah, well, that's okay. It's okay to worship everything. I mean, it's not like there weren't going to still be questions and choices after the apocalypse. What, did we think we'd all just go to Heaven and there'd be no more problems, or diseases, or earthquakes?
>
> No, we all woke up, the day after the world ended, and we still had to feed ourselves and keep a roof over our heads. Life goes on, you know? [*Promethea* #31].

Much of *Promethea*'s theology is summarized here. Divine love recontextualizes the lives of individuals, giving them access to a consciousness that is not bound by linear time.[8] The dead, rather than appearing to be lost, seem close and accessible in a way that allows the living to focus joyfully on the present. Knowing that the divine is manifest in all things, anything can become a focus of devotion to the whole; as Sophie says, "It's okay to worship everything." Yet moral and ethical choices remain, as well as the hard work of living — not unlike the Buddhist saying that both before and after enlightenment, one must "chop wood, carry water."

Much of *Promethea* plays with the notion of microcosm and macrocosm, the idea that patterns in the human realm reflect the patterns of the universe as a whole. In the comic's conclusion, Sophie settles comfortably into relationships with her friends and her lover and embraces the simple beauty of domesticity (*Promethea* #31). The narrative closes on Sophie kissing her boyfriend Carl — a kiss, he implies, that will last forever, part of the endless story being told in the many-dimensional mind of God. This ordinary human love is a microcosm of divine love: erotic, intimate, and deeply personal. Their kiss is God/dess reunited with Herself: a cosmic truth captured in the most quotidian of moments, and no less holy for its lack of metaphysical fanfare.

Sophie's journey as Promethea compels her to experience and then embody the eroticism, tenderness, exhilaration, and terror of divine love. As the facilitator of the apocalypse, Sophie-as-Promethea plays the role of both universal Mother, the mother for whom so many characters cry out at the moment of their deaths,[9] and the Great Whore, the destroyer of illusion who ends the world. Interposed with the various Prometheas' more straightforward superheroic adventures, this preparation — much of which is narrated as an explicit journey up the kabbalistic Tree of Life — is the context in which Moore develops *Promethea*'s theology of love.

Erotic Love as the Ground of Being

Sophie's first major experience with the eroticism of Being comes as a result of her bargain with the magician Jack Faust. In return for his tutoring her in magic, Sophie agrees to allow Jack to have sex with Promethea. In Sophie's initial encounters with him, Jack is portrayed as a villain: lecherous, hostile, and manipulative (*Promethea* #4, #9). The sexual encounter with Promethea, however, brings out Jack's humility and tenderness and becomes an important lesson for Sophie in the nature of magic and the universe

(*Promethea* #10). Explaining the sacred symbolism of the body as he goes, Jack leads Promethea through a "sacred strip-tease" that narrates the descent of the goddess Inanna to the underworld. As they undress, Jack describes the breasts as symbols of both physical and spiritual nourishment, the vagina as the Holy Grail and cup of divine compassion, and the womb and phallus as ways to represent the fundamental creative energies of the universe.

Rather than sliding into dry didacticism, however, the conversation between Jack and Promethea is infused with flirtation, blushing embarrassment, and frank desire. The sex act is tastefully and tenderly portrayed as Jack's seedy bedroom begins to resonate with images of caves, temples, and gardens, all places where human beings have made love throughout history. Seemingly opposed forces melt into each other and become paradoxically one as the characters join together in pleasure, and time slips as Sophie-as-Promethea hears her own voice, a short while in the future, coming from the street outside. Entwined, the two move into an altered state of consciousness, feeling life force, conceptualized here as the snake-like Hindu kundalini, rising through their bodies and triggering a variety of emotions and sensations. As the energy current reaches the level of the heart, Jack whispers, "This is the sun. This is the gold in us. And you are almost. Me. And I am. Almost You." Someone — and from the layout, it is deliberately unclear who — responds, "OH, LOVE ... LOVE" (*Promethea* #10). The scene climaxes — literally — in an ego-shattering orgasm that reveals the selves within: Sophie within Promethea, the young man that Jack once was within him, and a variety of gods and other spiritual forces. Through a spiritually-intentioned act of sex, Jack and Promethea win a taste of the divine love that is present in all things, as well as participation in the primal creative forces that can be symbolized by the wand and cup or by the phallus and womb.

In the aftermath, Sophie and Jack awake to find that Promethea has departed, and they share a few awkward but tender moments together. The experience has transformed their relationship and removed their contempt and dislike for each other. Jack sends Sophie home with a chaste kiss on the forehead, an armload of books, and an embarrassed admonition to be careful. Sophie does not have the vocabulary to explain what happened to her friend Stacia, however, nor does Stacia have the ears to hear: she is simultaneously horrified and perversely fascinated by Sophie's having "humped the hippy" and portrays the event as a delightfully kinky human-goddess-human threesome (*Promethea* #10). Sophie cannot explain to her that, in having sex in this way, she and Jack became representatives of the divine uniting with itself in love and pleasure, nor that the experience was both holy and transformative.

Later in the narrative, human love sets Sophie on a journey into Heaven and up the Tree of Life, where she hopes to help the recently deceased Barbara find her long-dead husband, Steve. Originally derived from the system of Jewish mysticism called Kabbalah, the Tree diagram is understood by contemporary occultists as a map of Being that describes the stages of the divine creative process that ultimately produced the physical world. At the top of the Tree is God in a state of potential, utterly ungraspable by the human mind; at the bottom is physical manifestation. In between are a series of sfirot,[10] or emanations of divine energy. Moore portrays the sefirot as heavenly realms populated by spirits, gods, and other beings; every realm has its own rules and aesthetic and, in many cases, its own physics. In their search for Steve, Sophie and Barbara explore the sefirot systematically. Each kabbalistic issue uses a different color palette and artistic style to capture the mood of the sfira it explores, with some issues making homage to famous artists such as M.C. Escher or Vincent Van Gogh.

In the sfira of Netzach, which takes place at the blue-green bottom of an ocean, Sophie and Barbara are pushed and pulled by the powerful currents of their human loves and experience the pain of relationships gone awry. Only when they surrender to the current do they experience "Victory," the bliss of knowing that love is "the principle the entire universe is founded on," as Sophie says (*Promethea* #16). Barbara and Sophie speak of the rough currents that result from fighting love out of fear of its loss, a reactive process that frequently obscures the tenderness of love relationships. Using much the same terms as the theologians described above do about "the erotic," Sophie describes love as an attractive force: "Particles, organisms, planets and suns.... It's all about attraction. It's how everything holds together." Not just an emotion, love is also a kind of physical principle that characterizes all the relationships of the universe, not just those between people or deities.

As Sophie and Barbara climb higher, they enter Tiferet ("Beauty"), the realm of the human self raised to its most ideal. There, they encounter another model of divine love, that of the dying and rising gods, including Jesus Christ, who is portrayed reverently as an example of the divine willingness to incarnate in flesh and submit to earthly suffering. Boo-Boo, Barbara's guardian angel and own highest self, guides the two travelers through this sfira and remarks of the crucifixion tableau, "But even [...] at the lowest Auschwitz-end of what humans are, and what humans do ... our highest point is still with us" (*Promethea* #17). Divine love is infinitely humble, willing to touch all parts of being, even at the cost of experiencing torture or being treated as a criminal or a dog.

This characterization of divine love as holy even in situations traditionally considered profane is also relevant to the sfira of Binah, where Barbara and

Sophie encounter the feminine divine. Moore characterizes Binah ("Understanding") using images of the divine as both Virgin and Whore, although, against the mainstream conventions of Western religion, the two images are equally venerated. Rendered with heavy black lines reminiscent of medieval or Renaissance woodcuts, the Whore of Babylon appears jeweled and voluptuous, riding a beast as she does in the biblical book of Revelation. Moore follows magician Aleister Crowley in seeing this image, held up as the personification of carnal sin in many Christian traditions, as pointing to a truth about the nature of humanity's relationship with the universe. "When men KNOW her, she is then called REVELATION, for she lewdly shews herself," explains the Elizabethan magician in Moore's text (*Promethea* #21). The mystical unveiling of the divine nature of Being is compared to a prostitute shamelessly exposing herself, inviting all to come and experience her intimately. Then the Whore speaks for herself: "About the markets of the world I am sent bare, until the worst of creatures may lie down with me. Though wretched and with sores, they shall not be refused. [...] I am She no earthly Man or Woman may embrace, that yet is Whore to ALL." No one, no matter how poor of body or spirit, no matter how dirty, diseased, or broken, is refused the erotic love of the Goddess, who is the face of Being itself. Understanding — a deep understanding that does not shy away from hard truths, but reveals each person exactly as he or she is — is portrayed as a whore, because such understanding holds nothing back.

Framing divine love in human metaphors emphasizes its continuity with human love. In Chesed ("Mercy"), for example, Sophie and Barbara experience divine love as a fierce, fatherly protectiveness (*Promethea* #19). This love is grounded in personal terms when Sophie meets Juan, the human father she never knew. Near the top of the Tree, Sophie and Barbara enter Chokhmah ("Wisdom"), the sfira where God's life force first bursts forth into creation. Caught up in the sfira's energy, Sophie and Barbara once again experience human sexuality as a metaphor for the overwhelming intimacy of divine love, which they have come to feel for each other:

> BARBARA: [Everything here] is alive, and fertile, and ... I keep wanting to say sexy, but that's not it. Or if it is, it's not physical sex. Not human sex. It's Godsex or something. [...] Sophie, you were right! This is where the stars spurt into being!
> SOPHIE: *(gazing at Barbara surrounded by tiny stars)* Barbara, you look so good. This will sound wrong, but I wish we'd had sex while you were alive.
> BARBARA: Yeah. I know what you mean. And I feel we can just say that here, honestly, without any misunderstanding. It isn't sex, exactly...
> SOPHIE: I know. It's whispering afterwards. Soul touching soul. Oh, Barbara.

BARBARA: I know. Love. We love each other. Oh, Sophie. We're at the source [*Promethea* #22].

Here, as in Promethea's sexual encounter with Jack Faust, the intimate touch of divine, erotic love produces a softening between the characters, a tenderness and desire that did not exist between them before. The pages that follow, however, explore a different tenor of divine eroticism: primal forces coming together in a kind of lustful ravishment, a metaphor for the joyful violence of creation that is simultaneously sacred and profane—"taboo," as Sophie puts it.

Although Moore represents the mythological rape of Selene by Pan in this issue, he makes it clear that this is not a rape in the human sense of forced sex. Here, divine love as ravishment emphasizes the paradoxical wantonness and glory of the universe's birth. Divine love is compassionate, unconditional, protective, and self-sacrificing, yes, but it is also forceful, wild, shameless, and hungry—dangerous, though utterly without malice. This is a love that could drive an apocalypse, a love that could end the world. Sophie and Barbara's trip ends at the top of the Tree, where Barbara finds her husband Steve waiting, unwilling to dissolve back into God without her (*Promethea* #23). Joining hands, the reunited couple and Sophie leap back down into manifest existence, where Sophie becomes herself again and Barbara and Steve incarnate as a pair of newborn twins. Having experienced the divine at its least human, at the moment where Being and Nothingness meet, the characters tumble back down into the human world, carrying divine love with them.

Conclusion

Although *Promethea* uses a variety of metaphors to represent divine love, sexuality is among the most prominent, highlighting its intensity, its desire for the flesh, and its tenderness, rawness, and intimacy. Divine love is not specifically about genital acts, but the use of this imagery nevertheless reflects Moore's affirmation of a fierce and loving human sexuality. Despite the problems caused by human limitations, human beings are shown to participate in and embody the love of the divine for the universe. The microcosm reflects the macrocosm; in loving each other, *Promethea* suggests, human beings allow God/dess to love Herself. As in both contemporary Pagan and queer Christian theology, this panentheistic perspective affirms the world and the human body and lays the theological groundwork for an ethic that understands pleasure as a basic human right.

Notes

1. For an examination of these formal elements, see Kraemer and Winslade.
2. Moore notes in *25,000 Years of Erotic Freedom* that many of Blake's explicitly sexual artworks and doodles were altered or destroyed after his death by admirers concerned about the poet's legacy (17–18). In addition to their shared focus on spirituality and sexuality, Moore and Blake also share a medium; Blake's writing was frequently paired with juxtaposed illustrations in a fashion that anticipates the comics form.
3. Released on CD as *Angel Passage* in 2002.
4. Contemporary Paganism claims as many as 1.2 million adherents in the United States alone (Pitzl-Waters, "Parsing the Pew Numbers"). Although contemporary Pagans represent less than 1 percent of the U.S. population, the wider influence of the movement is suggested by a Barnes & Noble executive's estimate that the Pagan book buying audience numbers 10 million (Lewis 19).
5. See Valiente *Rebirth* 54–61 for a discussion of Valiente's efforts to revise liturgical materials derived from Crowley's work, as well as discussions of her other sources, such as Charles Leland's *Aradia*.
6. Edited by Virginia Burrus and Catherine Keller.
7. The subject of dualism in Christianity is a complex one, both because some Christian theologies reject such dualisms, and also because dualistic ideas in Christianity often originate historically with non–Christian theological sources. The work of biblical scholar Elaine Pagels (including *The Gnostic Gospels* [1979], *The Origin of Satan* [1988], and *Adam, Eve, and the Serpent* [1995]) is recommended as a nuanced introduction to the topic.
8. For an explanation of Moore's beliefs on the nature of time in divine consciousness, as well as the comic book medium's special ability to present information nonlinearly, see Kraemer and Winslade, 294–5. See also *Promethea* #28 for Moore and Williams' attempt to represent this timeless perspective by representing the flow of time as a comic strip, out of which the blond FBI agent Karen temporarily falls.
9. For examples, see Margaret's remark in *Promethea* #5 and the Painted Doll's in *Promethea* #21. Several individuals also mistake Promethea for their own, human mothers in *Promethea* #27.
10. Or sephiroth, to use the more traditional but less accurate transliteration of the Hebrew.

13. "It came out of nothing except our love"
Queer Desire and Transcendental Love in Promethea

PAUL PETROVIC

Many of *Promethea*'s (1999–2005) early critical readings divorce the queerness from the text and extract only the apocalyptic aspect of the comic, focusing on Book 5, the last of the books (Rosen 35 and Lioi 150). Critics have often fallen into the authorial fallacy by singling out Alan Moore's interviews where he jokes that *Promethea*'s first 12 issues, books 1 and 2, were meant to establish a comfortable narrative space with a "superhero conceit" that he and artist J.H. Williams III could then subvert for their exploration of magic (Kraemer and Winslade 274). These readings are too quick to emulate Moore's tone and neglect any importance in the early books of the series. By confining their scholarly focus to this narrow element, they effectively reduce the early issues to lesser artifacts when, in reality, they include key juxtapositions that cannot be understood if the last book is considered in isolation. This essay, then, offers a corrective to the existing scholarship in that it both assesses the whole of the text's themes, and, furthermore, reintegrates the queer aspects of the narrative back into the frame, ultimately assessing how this queerness directly informs *Promethea*'s call toward transcendent love. As a result, Moore and Williams's *Promethea* problematizes traditional theories of love and desire by deconstructing the heteronormative quality of sexual love, reinscribing instead a queer and matriarchal love.

A secondary intention is to devote more attention to the stylistics of the art woven throughout *Promethea*, grounding transcendence in all of its multivalent forms, especially in its gendered designs, where panels and borders are gendered as normative and heterosexual, while the foregrounding of gaps acts to queer and liberate that conventional sensibility. As such, this essay traces the visual element which comics theoretician Thierry Groensteen suggests is "essential to the production of the meaning that is made through it" (8). That is to say, since so much of *Promethea* is situated around paying homage to earlier illustrators and art styles, these citations deserve greater focus. In many ways, Annalisa Di Liddo's monograph study on Moore's fiction still offers the fullest analysis on the art design employed by Williams throughout the series, detailing how both authors pay "ironic, affectionate homage to such [pulp] magazines by drawing on both their iconography — especially in issue covers — and their emphatic, often verbose language" (87). Di Liddo likewise notes how José Villarrubia contributes digital art in an early section of book 2, but this notation does not lead to any extensive evaluation of Moore and Williams's collective goals (92). Such critical neglect is ill-timed since this is one of only two instances where Williams does not contribute to the interior art of *Promethea*.[1] Villarrubia's contribution is more than mere postmodern play; he returns for the close of the series and collaborates with Williams, synchronizing the idea of an artistic, digitized "hyper-real" revelation for the characters and readers alike (2, 15).[2] However, Villarrubia, a gay painter, is also able to interrogate the historical homophobia that plagued, and still plagues, much of America's heteronormative society.

Certainly Moore and his artistic collaborators have long advocated the normalization of queer identity in his works. *Watchmen* (with Dave Gibbons), *V for Vendetta* (with David Lloyd), and *Top 10* (with Gene Ha), among others, feature queer characters who are often marginalized or punished by the restrictive societies that they belong to for their identification with same-sex desire. Similarly, Williams's later, Eisner award-winning work on *Batwoman* suggests the same dedication to and valorization of queer identity. To read this advocacy of queerness in *Promethea* as apolitical or unimportant to the text's meaning is to divest the political potential from it. Julia Erhart offers a comprehensive definition for the usage of this loaded term.

> To begin with, "queer" was intended as a productively disruptive alternative to what was seen as the assimilationist and conservative aims of post-liberation movement majority gay culture. If liberal gay rights advocates located homosexuality within the separate-but-equal discourse of difference, "queer" was impatiently oppositional in its stance, celebrating and drawing attention to rather than minimizing its difference from the hegemonic (hetero)sexual norm [173].

As a result, both Moore and Williams offer a latent subtext, breaking free of restrictive binaries and symbolizing how queerness can lead to an embrace and celebration of all forms of human culture, identity, and sexuality. Yet the text likewise engages these issues of opposition, initially employing binary oppositions in the form of characters' strict acceptance of gay culture (e.g., Bill Woolcott, Sophie Bangs) and others' adamant refutation of the same (e.g., Dennis Drucker), before ultimately denaturalizing these issues to such an extent that the binary is itself shattered, leaving in its stead a polyvocal perspective on sexual and gender identity. In other words, the text breaks down the essentialist notions of ideology, borders, and socialization that predicate normative American society, regenerating in its stead a counter-perspective that offers queered transcendence as a "productively disruptive alternative" for recovery. In this way, *Promethea* repudiates the construction of heterosexual ideology as normative and reverses such hegemonic principles. Because of this focus, *Promethea* dialogues with and needs to be considered as part of the emerging Lesbian, Bisexual, Gay, and Transgendered (LBGT) literary canon.

Complicating Queer Sexuality

Moore experiments with several interpretations of queer sexuality in *Promethea*. For example, in the very first issue, Stacia, Sophie's friend and later human shell for Promethea, pejoratively refers to Sophie as "totally gay" for caring enough to research the history of Promethea (1, 7). Stacia levels this form of derogatory rhetoric at Sophie again as they part: "Aah, you want my body, you homo. Admit it" (1, 8). Such a critique, however flippant and ironic, is wholly in keeping with Stacia's consumption of lowbrow culture, such as the unintelligible, vacuous Weeping Gorilla media that surrounds her. She finds nothing offensive in this slur and recycles its iterations. Sophie herself does not appear much more mature in her handling of queer desire at this early stage. When the two are later confronted by latent queer desire, having slept off a night of battle in the same bed, both respond through repression and transference, channeling an infantile "Eugghh!" on the realization that they slept together (1, 93). Neither respond with a considerate reflection on the constructedness of sexual desire; instead, each harnesses the same kind of linguistic and psychological response. It is with little surprise, then, that part of Moore and Williams's agenda is to denaturalize this response, to reveal how it is socialized and thus able to be unconstructed.

Moore is strategic in the text's exposure of homophobia, often casting an accusatory lens toward the essentialism of heterosexuality. Furthermore, in the text's scenes leading up to Bill Woolcott's murder, he decenters the idea of an essentialist queer identity. Although Bill slips easily into a feminine identity because of his self-identification as gay, he is equally quick to complicate the gender work, noting how "Bill hadn't necessarily ever wanted to be a woman, but I guess he'd always wanted to be a goddess" (2, 17). Within this dialogue, Bill dismisses Promethea's biological sex as motivating factor and celebrates instead her status as a female icon, subscribing to transgendered desire. This act is magnified both by the presence of the female Bill escorting Sophie through Bill's material "earthly memories," and through his symbolic doubling with the female Roger of the Five Swell Guys, who is continually questioned about her sexuality and whether the "the old Roger [is] ever coming back?" in a male form again (2, 17; 1, 158). Significantly, the questioner of this second statement is Stacia, still ever judgmental about queer gender. Yet even though the uneasy slippage between genders is challenged socially by Stacia, reinstituting the desire for clearly codified gender roles, Sophie begins to accept this normalization of queer identity.

Both women experience conversions that challenge their simplistic assessment of queer identity and sexuality. As Sophie interacts with the other Prometheas, for instance, such an adolescent approach is shed in favor of a mature understanding and working through of identity, whether heterosexual or queer. Indeed, her encounter with Bill Woolcott, a writer and illustrator of the comic *Promethea* who self-professes to be "as gay as a spring lamb," enables her vision of queer sexuality to expand beyond pop culture stereotypes and helps her consider the culture through a personal lens, even if Bill at first only offers a facile and orthodox impression of gays (2, 7). The banality of Bill's metaphor is itself later challenged as the entirety of this seventh issue, collected in the beginning of book 2, offers a postmodern deconstruction of the 1950s romance comics that DC and Marvel Comics pedaled to a female readership. The cover itself metatextually alludes to an another comic, Bill Woolcott's *Promethea*, which shows Bill in his Promethea guise tearfully leaning into FBI agent Dirk Dangerfield, a comics surrogate for his real liaison with FBI agent Dennis Drucker. Moore deliberately queers this pandering to the female gender, which featured endless reiterations of the patriarchal man protecting the submissive woman, having Bill-as–Promethea think, "How can I tell Dirk that I'm not the woman he thinks I am?" (2, 2). By appropriating these genre conventions, Moore and Williams suggest that this issue will offer little other than a moment of subversive and parodic gender play. This homage, that is, exposes the gender performativity of women's comics, a genre wherein women were typically constructed, thought up, and drawn by men, but it simultaneously introduces a degree of postmodern pastiche, such that this caricature seems unlikely to confront the horrors of reality for gay individuals.

Borders, Gaps, and Butler

Moore and Williams undercut this homage of women's comics by focusing so specifically on the brutal homophobia of mid-century America. Initially absent in Williams's first playful images, this historicity becomes more and more pronounced, and as Villarrubia's art becomes integrated, the reality of Bill's gender transgressiveness is understood. The queerness of the affair between Dennis and Bill becomes realized, and with it Moore orchestrates one of the most extreme of all the images present in the text. Because Bill merely offers a perfunctory and seemingly inconsequential phrase, the extremity of the fact that "Dennis found out" is highlighted (2, 19). Few, if any, readers are prepared for the graphic and photo-realistic execution that follows: the bullet Dennis fires is captured in midair, eternally frozen, as it explodes through Bill's skull. Bill's pencil, the means through which he finds entry into artistic creation and imagination, is reduced to an empty and useless object. Such emptiness of future creation is echoed by the physical repetition of the murder in the second panel, which Groensteen contends allows for "a dialogue *in praesentia*, a direct exchange between images that are in a situation of co-presence under the gaze of a reader" (148). Although the second historical and material representation of Bill's death is braided to the first, the addition of Sophie and Bill's movement away from the scene uncovers a secondary meaning and extends beyond the first reality of brutal homophobia. They are not bound by the historical and temporal past, but are free to traverse the Immateria and enter a boundless space beyond this site — that is to say, the imagination (2, 19). Contained within the imagination for Moore and Williams are the comics that allow for imaginative movement, transcending the constancy of homophobic oppression harbored in mid-twentieth century reality. In this respect, art acts to denaturalize essentialist assumptions about death and the transcendence thereof.

This mediation between essentialist reality and a liminal space is key for *Promethea*. To draw from Judith Butler's theories of sexuality, normative systems of heterosexuality are built around borders, around the absence of gaps. Likewise, queer freedom comes from the "gaps opened up in regulatory norms" (Butler "Critically Queer" 22). Here, the formal particularities of comics design that Groensteen identifies, wherein panels have borders but nonetheless have between them gaps, fosters the Butlerian stutter. At stake in reality is Bill's identity and a lack of future artistic creation; similarly, Dennis's identity is frozen in this eternal rejection of Bill, but he is also suspended in the liminality between his avowed heterosexuality and his suppressed gay identity. Yet the dialogue, the gaps between, of concurrent panels within the Immateria allows Bill to move beyond his static death, a fact that Dennis cannot replicate since he has no access to this realm. Dennis is immobile in the first two panels, bound by a regulatory, bordered existence; Williams and Villarrubia visually argue here that Dennis permits nothing in his identity to cross gaps or thresholds (2, 19). In contrast, Bill-as–Promethea moves in the gaps between panels and iterations. This formal engagement with comics structure undermines human tendency to think in terms of the monadic individual and opens up interpretation to the world, denaturalizing assumptions about ontology and moving Sophie toward an awareness of humanity's dynamic connection to reality. If Dennis's tears during the murder offer a discursive reprisal of the cover's themes about gender work and fear, they nonetheless acknowledge that such open transgressiveness will be resisted at this historical moment. At the same time, Moore and Williams certify that American society, in all its heteronormative veneer, is implicated for inculcating such contempt and homophobia.

This internalized homophobia also mirrors the public trepidation over the foreign other as *Promethea* becomes more active and conversant within its post–9/11 context. During the following scene Bill's own dismissal of Dennis's violent reaction is itself interesting, as it ostensibly borders on acquitting Dennis's homophobic purging: Bill asserts that "what's most awful is that it came out of nothing except our love" (2, 19). Beyond the macabre pun on coming out, Moore establishes a symbolic link between love and fear, one that Moore and Williams echo in book 4 and the religious crusade between a Muslim and Christian Promethea (4, 140–160). Scholar Björn Quiring critiques *Promethea* formally for offering only a "pretty univocal" approach to salvation, but this appraisal misses the fact that for Moore and Williams, especially in post–9/11 America, a polyvocal consciousness is what is advocated and necessary to thrive internationally. For example, Christine Hoff Kraemer and J. Lawton Winslade were the first critics to cogently identify how *Promethea* operates within a post–9/11 context (276). It is worth noting that although much of the early run of *Promethea* takes place in an imaginary New York City, divorced from any real administrative political or governmental engagement. After the terrorist attack on 9/11 and as the series progresses, Moore and Williams move the milieu of the text more and more into a wholly recognizable and contemporary America, complete with then–President Bush and a rising U.S. conflict with Iraq. This socio-historical shift in environment is predicated by the escalating tensions of a post–9/11 need for a polyvocal consciousness. Such an idea becomes apparent as Williams illustrates, amidst a series of bubbles encapsulating the key historical moments of the twentieth and twenty-first century, the second plane attack on the World Trade Center moments before impact (4, 119). Later, during a flashback to the warring Muslim and Christian Prometheas, the narrative — significantly contained in a blue and yellow balloon — notes how "the planes hit the buildings. And the smartbomb hits the mosque" (4, 158). References also abound during a section parodying John's revelation, "We all looked up to blinding spectacle, said holy this and holy that, so it was like the terrible blue day again, but night now, with two towering absences more visible" (5, 55). The Five Swell Guys, Moore's jesting at the Fantastic Four throughout the series, finds a secondary context as the series closes. Although there have been visual intimations that the group has lost one of their own, such context finds a payoff when Kenneth reminisces about how "we lost Bob at the WTC" because of a stock meeting (5, 59). Because of these echoes toward a traumatized post–9/11 society, the need to identify with a maternal polyvocality becomes more and more pronounced. Separatism is what has led to such wanton destruction; Moore and Williams petition that a movement away from separatism and an embrace of the interconnectedness, of the one voice linking all of humanity, would lead toward cultural understanding and harmony.

Indeed, *Promethea*'s ultimate reality privileges a polyvocal consciousness, albeit one framed around matriarchal rather than patriarchal concerns so as to counter the cycle of hegemonic violence and oppression. As Moore's narration in this later spiritual battle suggests, "At last, locked in their death-grip, two religions looked into each other's eyes and recognized themselves. Knew then that both were halves of what had been one holy, undivided source. Thus, drowning in their blood with realization mirrored in stunned eyes, they tried to kiss, but died before they did" (4, 159). The connection extends to lesser analyzed sections of the comics medium, including letter design. Although such an idea likely originates from Moore's textual notes, letterer Todd Klein positions the opening narration of this issue within a yellow and blue text balloon, suggesting a unified narration to the idea of Promethea (4, 141). However, the following panel by Williams has text balloons divided in half, with each side refusing to acknowledge or extend the coloration into the other. It is certainly intentional that in this simultaneous execution of the Prometheas, too late to bear witness to their holiness, the lettering again becomes linked. As such, the ultimate fate of that battle is reflected in the first failure between Bill and Dennis to recognize how difference and faction rises from an originary love: "it came out of nothing except our love" (2, 19). Dennis merely surrenders to his sociocultural doctrine and executes its endgame. Throughout the series, *Promethea* argues for polyvocality to be found and understood within the gaps and imagination of regulatory discourse.

At this early stage of the narrative, though, Sophie still seeks to implement a binary attribution of guilt and innocence to Dennis and Bill, but this notion is one which Moore quickly denaturalizes. Sophie witnesses the present fate of Dennis, housed decades later at The Laing Clinic and seemingly rehabilitated, and exhibits a yearning that things could be different. As she says, trailing off, "if he hadn't been so bigoted about..." but Bill silences such a wish, reminding her, "don't blame Dennis. I'd never told him about Bill. I was being dishonest and I knew it" (2, 20). Bill shoulders the blame, absolving Dennis of his violent act even as he chronicles for Sophie the complications he enacted to satisfy his queer desire. In Moore and Villarrubia's collaboration, designed with Williams's approval, they interrogate the sacrificial offering of life needed in order to maintain a heteronormative social order. Although Bill is materially dead, he remains a goddess in this non-material state, and he and Sophie continue her education, leaving behind the catatonic and tortured Dennis Drucker.

When Moore and Williams return to Dennis Drucker in book 4, he is bitter and shrill, exhibiting the same voluble attitude toward queer sexuality that Stacia reveals. When his doctor asks him whether he would mind if FBI Agents Karen Breughel and Lucille Ball ask him questions about Promethea, Dennis preemptively retorts, "Why wouldn't I? You think I'm a fag?" (4, 5). Dennis, having had decades to dwell on his fatal action, spews forth only pejoratives and a denunciation of his queer desire which he unwittingly acted out with Bill. Dennis, then, adopts an obstinately heteronormative veneer as his shield. As Judith Butler explains, construction of one's sex

> not only takes place *in* time, but is itself a temporal process which operates through the reiteration of norms; sex is both produced and destabilized in the course of this reiteration. As a sedimented effect of a reiterative or ritual practice, sex acquires its naturalized effect, and, yet, it is also by virtue of this reiteration that gaps and fissures are opened up as the constitutive instabilities in such constructions [emphasis added; 10].

In other words, precisely because Dennis projects such a vehemently heterosexual pose, the "gaps and fissures" of sex that Butler discusses become exposed. His fervent denial of any queer undercurrent recursively challenges his identification with heteronormativity. Moore and Williams offer another symbolic double, however, as Dennis's overly malicious language toward gays becomes mirrored in Stacia's queer awakening that transpires in this same issue. This doubling is more aggressively shown ten issues later when Moore and Williams literally mirror these two storylines in a double-page spread (5, 92–93). As Sophie has asked Grace Brannagh (the 1920s Promethea) to help Stacia fill in on earth and harness Promethea while she explores the Immateria, Grace confronts Stacia, caressing her face, "I'm rather enjoying our little partnership ... just like you are" (4, 3). Stacia, threatened by the unconscious sublimity of her desire, can only respond with a stunned "Oh golly." Under such provocation, Stacia realizes that her construction of heteronormativity is imperiled, but capitulates to both Grace and her own wish. The iteration of pejoratives was not enough to destabilize her queer identity.

Transcendence and Apocalypse

When Sophie returns and propagates the apocalypse in New York City, although her revelatory change is felt the world over, Moore and Williams cede the payoff to Dennis's garrulous heteronormativity. In a rejoinder to his earlier machismo, Dennis surrenders and finds himself repeating, "I'm sorry. I'm sorry for what I've done" (5, 56). His earlier inflexibility shifts to penitent guilt over his homophobia. As Agent Hansard states, Promethea is causing "religious visions," and so Dennis's apology is demarcated as speaking directly to Bill, even though Williams does not depict Bill in the panel (5, 57). This vision, then, allows Dennis's coordinates of reality to be reordered and for his apology, endlessly reiterated just as his shooting eternally looped in the Immateria during Sophie's education, to reconstitute his gay desire. At this moment Dennis joins Bill in the recursive gaps offered by the Immateria, where imagination offers an out beyond the restrictions of normative genders or socialization.

The religious vision is followed by Dennis's material confrontation with the past, with Villarrubia additionally returning to the series to digitally color Williams's work as the two offer a synthesis of photorealistic hyper-reality. Dennis stumbles into a room in the Immateria which duplicates the shooting in all its detail, though faded with age, an uncanny echo given that the initial appearance of Villarrubia's digital art appeared in 2000, and three years have passed since *Promethea* last presented this image. However, revisiting Groensteen, this braiding "is precisely the operation that, from the point of creation, programs and carries out this sort of bridging," so that the "reprise of the same panel at two locations in a comic, contiguous or distant, does not constitute a perfect duplication. The second occurrence of the panel is already different from the first by the sole fact of the citation effect that is attached. The repetition raises the memory of the first occurrence" (146, 148). Groensteen's idea of panel citation firstly offers an interesting echo of Butler's theory of gender as iterative and as citationality; moreover, this reoccurrence does more than raise the memory. In fact, rather than this recitation leading to stolid reinforcement of a self-regulating homophobia, Williams and Villarrubia engineer the moment graphically as a way to denaturalize repetition when Dennis confronts his past. Amidst this simulacra of Dennis murdering Bill, Dennis's present self registers a new emotion — guilt rather than homophobia — which in turn constitutes a gap between the original act and reaction. Dennis's reaction, despite the braiding of synchronous panels singular to the comics form, frees him from the heteronormativity that plagued him and caused him to execute his lover. As with Sophie and Bill, Dennis, although initially stunned into silence and tears at the reminder of his (self-)hatred, finds release from the iterative apology that he again voices. Bill, in his goddess guise, comforts Dennis and offers a revelation that releases him from his guilt, saying, "Dennis, honey, it's all right. Everything's all right now. Now we can be together. Now everyone can be together" (5, 93). Promethea's act of revelation enables the lovers to co-exist on a spiritual and material plane. These crimes over non-conformist and oppositional gender roles are revealed to be, at least momentarily, wiped clean, so that all departed lovers can be brought together in those individuals willing to "stay awake" and on a high level of consciousness (5, 146).

The epochal moment arrives for Dennis Drucker through Agent Hansard's conversation with Sophie, after Promethea's revelation has been delivered to the people of the world. Hansard notes how Drucker has returned to the FBI, confiding how "it's like the apocalypse drove him sane. He's a terrific agent, and he has this happy relationship in his head with ... well, one of the Prometheas, I suppose" (5, 148). Despite the pause and qualifier, in this post-apocalyptic setting, Hansard does not come off as judgmental. Rather, his tone adopts a calm matter-of-factness that is made all the more prominent through its rhetorical juxtaposition between sanity and the imagination, concepts that *Promethea* celebrates as foundationally linked. As Promethea muses at one point, in a moment that could easily summarize the queer relationship between Dennis and Bill, "Surrender to love ... because in love ... surrender ... is ... victory" (3, 97).

Moore and Williams likewise connect this queer aspect to other couples, including, as mentioned earlier, Stacia and Grace. Stacia's refusal to relinquish Promethea back to Sophie after the latter returns from the Immateria reverberates with elements of Dennis and Bill's arc, although the central conflict is inverted. Stacia, rather than executing Sophie because she cannot accept the gay ideology she herself manifested while controlling the Promethea idea, is willing to execute Sophie precisely because she does accept, and wants to stay with, Grace, stating, "We love each other" (4, 145). Sophie lashes out, derisively challenging Stacia and the gender politics of her affair by recycling Stacia's old pejoratives back at her: "You think just because you've got your dykey little crush on Grace, all that changes" (4, 146). What Moore and Williams stage in the gutter in these two double-spread pages (4, 144–147), though, draws from an earlier visual about a symbolic tower, where a pontificating Austin Spare, walking with Sophie and Barbara Shelley in the Immateria, states that "the lightning is what teaches us humility" (3, 75). In this later issue, it is Sophie and Stacia who fall from the tower because neither is willing to offer the other humility. Instead, Stacia responds to Sophie's insult by striking out with violence, echoing the historical precedent of the religious feud between Muslim and Christian Prometheas. The subversive twist in this context is that the feud is not a long-lasting religious crusade, but limited by queer sexual desire and a refusal to reconcile humbly.

The college students surrounding Sophie and Stacia respond to the growing feud with stereotypical apathy, justifying their disinterest by marginalizing the conflict and invoking a heteronormative iteration of difference. They dismiss the violence outright, proclaiming that "they're just a couple o' lezzes" (4, 146). This utterance seeks to reclaim the right to define queerness for interests of the public orthodoxy. Further, it wants to position Sophie and Stacia's feud as something subhuman, divested of importance, and thus able to be simultaneously eroticized and rejected as other. The students' insulting rhetoric provides a hegemonic, heteronormative overtone to the scenario and situates how transgressive it is to publicly come out, even on a likely liberal college campus. Part of Stacia's animosity certainly transpires from the fact that Sophie has, in a moment of conceit and arrogance, just outed her in public. This moment, however, has much greater personal and political resonance for her than for the listless student body.

Although Stacia and Grace are separated from harnessing Promethea together, decreed by a "shade" of King Solomon in an ironic wink to Biblical history, she declares her hatred against Sophie, but Stacia and Grace are united again when Sophie stages her revelatory baptism to the far corners of the world (4, 170). The symbolic echo between Bill and Dennis and Stacia and Grace finds overt synthesis when Williams illustrates Dennis and Bill's reconciliation after the women's reconciliation in the double-spread page, with the gutter linking the two scenes through blooming flowers and proclaiming them to both be "the lovers" (5, 92–93). After Stacia says, "Oh, Grace. Grace, I love you so much…," in delirious excitement over their meeting, Grace responds by acknowledging, "I know. I know you do" (5, 93). Similar to the gay fantasia that transpires between Bill and Dennis post-revelation, where Dennis finds Bill omnipresent within his imagination, Stacia and Grace become irrevocably linked. Her disgust with Sophie collapses and she finds release in her queer desire. Because of the temporal breach revealed to society, these couples find a way toward queer renewal and reconnection that has been forcibly denied them by heteronormative reality. Yet Stacia takes this idea of queering further than any other through her later confession to Sophie after the revelation.

Despite the spiritual reunion with Grace, Stacia still harbors a need for material sexual desire, and so she ends up with the FBI agent Lucille Ball. However, in a further queering of this lesbian affair, Stacia admits to Sophie that "sometimes, in bed with Lucille, it's kind of a threesome" with Grace, even though Lucille "doesn't know" (5, 150). Despite the ostensible innocence of this scene, the addition of partners, while deconstructing another layer of normative concepts about individual's commitment to another, suggests how even a queer relationship may become hegemonic if trust is obfuscated. Further, Lucille offers Moore and Williams access to an agent who is first so loveless and divested of an emotional core that she is rhetorically shrill and naïve in her political orthodoxy. Her aggressiveness best shows through when she fascistically defends their governmental need to arrest Promethea to Tom Strong, the Superman surrogate and defender of Millennium City, where Sophie has hidden in the beginning of book 5, contending that "we know she's a terrorist," because "she's of Middle Eastern origin" (5, 8). This simplistic discourse flattens any notion of a polyvocal togetherness, spreading instead faction and strident separatism. Although the counternarrative espoused by *Promethea* that Lucille merely needs a revolutionary queer experience to shake her out of her regressive politics can be written off as Moore's wish-fulfillment, the fullness of sexual experimentation proffered by the preceding narratives offers a route beyond such parochial readings.

Finally, although Sophie herself does not engage physically in queer sexual intimacy, nor does she feel a need to be confined by heteronormative desires. For example, she co-opts the Promethea guise so that magician Jack Faust can have an affair with the perfect idea of Promethea; she exchanges that act for teachings about greater harnessing and control of the magic she wields as Promethea. Yet this aspect is neither harmful nor destructive, as presented by Moore and Williams throughout the 10th issue. Sophie exists instead as a perfect bisexual pluralism. Later, while in the Immateria with Barbara Shelley, the two come upon the realm of Chokmah (wisdom). Sophie exclaims to Barbara, "This will sound wrong, but I wish we'd had sex while you were alive," stating how this act would be like "soul touching soul" (4, 93). Such an expression of queer desire seems less out of character than a natural exploration of the fluidity, and iterative nature of sex as citationality, afforded in this non-material environment. Lest the series have no normative relationship to serve as a foil, Sophie returns to Carl, a lover she met while in Millennium City, who she had partnered with during a three year disappearance from her duty as harbinger of the apocalypse. Despite the often radical agenda of *Promethea*'s sexual design, Sophie confesses to Stacia that she "kinda wanted a Catholic wedding, with everything" (5, 151). Such a gesture is not meant, it should be noted, as a damnation of the regressive nature of mainstream Christian religion. Sophie's wish, rather, is to embrace "the symbol. That's true. That's real" in an environment now polyvocal about such spiritual endeavors (3, 129). This movement is constituted by a reciprocity now established between Sophie and Carl; whereas volume 5 of *Promethea* opens with Sophie sublimating her powers and hiding her true identity from Carl, there is now no such division or demand from either party. Instead, each is blessed by the other; the same promises to be true with Bill and Dennis.

Such concerns are situated by a new economy of love placed on society, borne out by this matriarchal transcendent love offered by Promethea. This new economy offers to bring it out from the margins of consciousness and to suggest instead that "war and murders and rape" become the liminal economy (5, 149). Williams's artistic employment of religious polyvocalism throughout this page definitively repudiates any notion of a univocal failing on the text. Moore and Williams finally express what Calvin O. Schrag, synthesizing Kierkegaardian philosophy, calls a command "that one love unconditionally, without recompense or expectation in return, [that] is indeed a markedly transcendent love, surpassing all teleological, deontological, and utilitarian economies whilst, nonetheless, providing them with a transcendent content and measure" (35). This love, woven throughout *Promethea*, is to achieve a higher transcendence and appeal to higher consciousness. Returning to visual design and symbolism, Sophie's emergence from the apocalypse leaves her changed; she is shaded and colored as an ethnic other. She is now, in brief, the Muslim and Christian Promethea united as one, suggesting how inconsequential race and ethnicity are in a larger community attentive to the political stability offered by peace and transcendent love.

To close, then, through Moore and Williams's imagining of a society now blessed to experiment generously with sexual freedom, *Promethea*'s ending echoes another classic of gay literature similarly predicated on revelation and transcendence, Tony Kushner's 1993 *Angels in America*. Although Sophie states the euphoria offered by Promethea is only temporary, and that wars, rapes, and murders may continue to be invoked by those hegemonic forces unwilling to respond to her call, this assertion in many ways offers a link to another revelation, especially Prior Walter's closing statement to the audience, "The Great Work Begins" (148). Moore and Williams similarly implicate *Promethea*'s readership to steer their societies toward a social and cultural environment where such (queer, transcendent) desire may be understood as normative, away from the strictures of homophobia. Moore and Williams examine the ways in which love is represented in the various Promethea figures and their respective lovers, analyzing the heteronormative, spiritual, and transcendental epistemologies of love, and this triangulation, visual as well as narrative, represents *Promethea*'s queer design. The use of narrative braiding and queer desire support the text's ultimate urge for the individual reader to adopt a polyvocal sensibility, one that oppositionally resists the violence endemic of both patriarchal and hegemonic interests, and in this way mirror Moore and Williams's plea for us all to surrender to love.

Notes

1. Charles Vess's classical artwork in book 1, issue #4, being the other example (1, 97–104).

2. Because of Moore and Williams's inclusion of chapter summaries, these pages are also counted in any page count for citation purposes. Thus, the Alex Ross variant cover to Promethea #1 is actually listed as (1, 2), since the chapter summary page appears before it, etc.

14. Self-Conscious Sexuality in *Promethea*
Orion Ussner Kidder

Alan Moore has spent most of his career as a comic-book creator exploring a specific set of themes, and two of the biggest are sexuality and reflexivity. He explores sexual politics largely by including both straight and queer sexuality as a presence in his work rather than eliding it, as is traditional in popular entertainment. He has employed some form of reflexivity — references to the text from within the text — in almost all of his work since the early eighties, and he often uses it to focus attention on some element of storytelling itself that he then scrutinizes: the superhero in *Marvelman* and *Watchmen*, Victorian science fiction in *The League of Extraordinary Gentlemen*, the insidiousness of propaganda in *Tom Strong*. These two seemingly unrelated themes, sexuality and reflexivity, come together almost seamlessly in *Promethea*. I say "almost" because the combination is not flawless. Unfortunately, while the series has a fiercely pro-feminist and queer-positive agenda, it occasionally falls back into precisely the objectification of women and homophobic clichés that it fights against. That combination of success and failure is what this chapter investigates.

The investigation takes the form of an analysis of two sets of linked subplots: one feminist and largely successful, and one queer-themed and seriously flawed. The feminist subplots comment on the practice in which a male artist projects an idealized identity onto a female muse. The queer-oriented subplots depict two romances — one lesbian and one transgendered — that ostensibly end happily but are dysfunctional in the mean time. While the feminist commentary works by exposing the process of objectification and offering a way to avoid it, the queer sub-plots depict lesbian and transgendered relationships as prone to violence and doomed to tragedy, respectively. Furthermore, these commentaries, successful or otherwise, are still contained within a relatively narrow set of acceptable narrative and visual possibilities as offered by the mainstream comic-book culture. When they succeed, it is because they offer a solution that that culture is willing to accept, and when they fail, it is because they brush up against what that culture is not willing to accept. To explain how these subplots work and why they succeed or fail, I want to first talk about a few theories of sexuality and reflexivity.

Matthew T. Jones' "Reflexivity in Comic Art" argues that self-reflexivity is especially appropriate to erotica, specifically comic-book erotica, because both modes inspire intimacy. Metacomics, he says, "contextualize the narrative act and experience an approximation of intimacy or closeness by making clear the link between the comic text and the outside world in which it was born, and of which it is a part" (284). Instead of ruining the suspension of disbelief, he argues that metacomics draw the audience into the world of the comic book, specifically, in the case of erotic metacomics, when the object of the sexual gaze begins to gaze back (Jones 277). Jones borrows the concept of the *gaze* from film studies, citing several texts on the subject (Stam, Beggan, Recchia). The notion of the gaze traces back to Laura Mulvey's "Visual Pleasure in Narrative Cinema" in which she refers to the male, scopophilic *look* created by production and consumption practices in the film industry. Jones uses the concept somewhat against the grain as he argues that self-reflexive erotica can ethically retain the gaze because self-conscious characters imply the consent that Mulvey's look specifically lacks.

Mulvey's "look" is scopophilic by virtue of being covert. Hollywood cinema creates "the illusion of looking in on a private world" even though cinema itself is "there to be seen" (835). Hollywood film achieves this effect through such conventions as invisible editing, unselfconscious characters, and the practical realities of exhibition, a darkened theatre in which the audience members cannot see each other, and therefore, forget that they are in public (835). The contradiction, then, is between explicit exhibition and covert viewing. To create the proper, scopophilic effect, the film itself has to recreate the conditions of a Peeping Tom. One of those conditions, an important one, is that the object of view cannot have the power to refuse the look. Indeed, she cannot even know she is being looked at even though her function in that moment, on the screen, is quite precisely to be looked at. Mulvey makes quite clear that the purpose of her argument is to analyze this pleasure in order to destroy it (835). Jones' self-reflexive gaze inverts Mulvey's look by altering a key element: consent. A self-conscious fictional character ostensibly knows that he or she is being looked at and, in Jones' examples, agrees to it. In the context of erotica, he or she even gains sexual gratification from it.

There are, of course, many subgenres of erotica and pornography that do not involve the characters' consent, but Jones is talking specifically about self-reflexive erotica in which the characters do invite the audience's gaze and enter into an active dialogue with that audience. The defining feature, then, is consent, not self-consciousness. Self-consciousness is just an efficient way of achieving consent. Since Jones does not look at any queer metacomic erotica, a study of queer erotic comics and whether their look/gaze differs from that of straight/male-oriented material would be helpful. Jones goes on to name five metacomic techniques, but that granular element of his argument is not pertinent to my discussion. There is one gap in Jones' argument that is pertinent, however; he does not address the problem that fictional characters — as not real people — cannot actually consent because their creators control them. *Promethea*, however, overcomes this problem by depicting the entire scenario, both looking and being looked at, making the spectator and the spectacle equally fictional. Furthermore, the series depicts both a positive and a negative example of the looking/looked-at dynamic and functions as straightforward social commentary that uses self-reflexivity. The ethics of self-reflexivity is central to my discussion, which is why I use Linda Hutcheon's notion of "complicit critique," developed as part of her theory of historiographic metafiction.

Historiographic metafiction is an element of the whole postmodern mode that "depends upon and draws its power from that which it contests" (*Poetics* 120); postmodernism, for that reason, is preoccupied with satire and metafiction, modes which construct something — the subject of the satire, the sanctity of the fictional world — in order to then deconstruct it. Hutcheon argues that "[f]iction and history are narratives distinguished by their frames [...] which historiographic metafiction first establishes and then crosses" (109–110) using devices such as breaking the fourth wall, explicit intertextual references, and the like. Although Hutcheon does champion the political possibilities of postmodernism in both *A Poetics of Postmodernism* and *The Politics of Postmodernism*, she also takes great pains to point out that "this is a strange kind of critique, one bound up [...] with its own *complicity*" (Hutcheon, *Politics* 4). For this reason, it is "not truly radical; nor is it truly oppositional. But this does not mean it has no critical clout" (Hutcheon *Poetics* 120). The notion of "complicit critique" traces back to Jacques Derrida, who in "Structure, Sign and Play," argues that "we cannot give up [...] complicity without also giving up the critique we are directing against this complicity" (355). Complicit critique is not just a strategy, according to both Derrida and Hutcheon, but a necessity. A critique necessitates a perpetuating description, placing the critic in an inevitable position of complicity. Metafiction, for example, does so by building an immersive, fictional world, complete with frames that mark the boundaries between itself and reality as well as between itself and other fictional worlds, and then violating those frames. Patricia Waugh, on the other hand, argues in *Metafiction* that violating those frames does not necessarily involve obliterating them. She describes the "two poles of metafiction" (53) as the *structural* and the *radical*. The first tests its frames but ultimately leaves them intact, and the second either "delights or despairs" in shattering the frames. In either case, Hutcheon would argue that the frame has to be there first, so that it can then be removed.

When Porn Gazes Back: Look vs. Gaze

True to form, *Promethea*'s feminist subplots depict, first, a dysfunctional and sexist version of the poet/muse relationship in order to, second, present a functional and healthy version of it. Promethea, the title character, is the essence of a girl from Ancient Egypt who was granted immortality by being transformed into a story (1, 21). Throughout history, then, anyone who became particularly interested and immersed in the Promethea story could become a version of her that combines the host's personality with Promethea's iconography. These many and various Prometheas gradually build not just a single story of her but a cycle of stories. In several instances, though, the summoner does not become Promethea but rather projects her onto someone else, hence the theme of artists and their muses.

Promethea #4, "A Faerie Romance," relates the story of a fictional American poet, Charlton Sennet, who writes an epic poem set in "some Arcadian backwater" (1, 34) as a tribute to *A Midsummer Night's Dream* and its depiction of fairyland, although it also resembles *The Faerie Queene*. The poem comes to focus on a minor character called "Promethea" who appears in Sennet's dreams and strongly resembles his maid, Anna (4, 10). The dream sequence itself implies that he had sexual feelings for Anna already and that the coincidence of those feelings and Sennet's use of the name "Promethea" in his poem was enough to call up the Promethea spirit. Sennet accidentally transforms Anna into Promethea by reciting his poetry to her, they subsequently becomes lovers, and Anna becomes pregnant and dies in childbirth, delivering only a cloud of mystical symbols (4, 14). Anna never asks for Sennet to transform her, and they have no relationship prior to the transformation. This example differs sharply from Steve Shelly, who writes a Promethea comic book within the *Promethea* universe. Both Sennet's *Faerie Romance* and Shelly's *Promethea* comic book display the frames within frames that are typical of metacomics and metafiction in general. Unlike Sennet, though, Steve projects Promethea onto his wife, Barbara, but does so with her willing participation, and she even carries on acting as Promethea after Steve dies, even though she is less and less able to distinguish between "Barbara" and "Promethea" without his strong vision of her. She appears, then, as a heavy-set, middle-aged woman dressed in a classical-themed superhero costume (1, 23) rather than as a conventionally attractive comic-book superheroine.

Sennet and Anna represent the widespread poetic practice of singing the praises of a woman's virtues in the practical absence of any knowledge of the woman in question. Dante's Beatrice, in his *Divine Comedy*, exemplifies this practice, for example, and Cervantes' Dulcinea del Toboso, from *Don Quixote*, parodies it. Sennet barely knows Anna when he projects his lusts at her, and his mystical projection becomes synonymous with an objectifying scopophilic look. At the moment of her death, however, she wonders if he knew her at all: "Did you love me?" (4, 13). This "me" is separate from the Promethea spirit whom Sennet had sex with. Anna is a fantasy example of Mulvey's *look*: born of a power disparity — they are literally master and servant — and a desire to make the object of the look conform to a set of straight-male expectations. For a brief moment, though, the spectacle looks at the spectator, creating enough of a hint of Jones' self-reflexive gaze to imply a potentially ethical and healthy artist/muse relationship, a possibility that *Promethea* explores through Barbara and Steve.

Barbara willingly receives Steve's projection of strength and beauty, and she possesses a great deal of personal agency, the likes of which Anna never has. She consents to be looked at and plays along with her husband's vision of her. She is still an object of an erotic look, but she also gazes back and enjoys it, marrying Steve's scopophilia with her own exhibitionism and dispelling the power dynamic that Mulvey describes. Steve does not project someone else's identity onto Barbara, as Sennet does with Anna. Instead, he sincerely sees her as a demi-goddess, and she accepts his vision of her. Barbara becomes a heroine and an able fighter before she dies (1, 17), and she journeys through the Tree of Life in order to rescue Steve's dead spirit. To do so, she enters what is in effect the godhead of Promethea's universe, a place where individual identity is lost in communion with the ultimate divine presence, but her sense of self— unlike Anna's self which dies both symbolically and literally — is so strong that she can enter that godhead, find her dead husband, and leave again of her own free will (23, 1). Williams depicts the total disillusion of identity, interestingly enough, through a self-referential sequence of panels that model the traditional production of American comic books: from rough stick-figures with placeholders for word balloons, to pencil sketches, and finally to inked panels with lettered balloons (23, 1). This art reveals the hand of the artist and, following Jones, creates a moment of intimacy between the audience and the creators that highlights the intimacy that Barbara and Steve share.

True to Hutcheon's characterization of metafiction, *Promethea* recreates the literary practice of projecting invented identities onto women, and it does so in order to mount a commentary on it—the positive, alternative possibility of gazing with consent—which demonstrates the efficacy of Jones' concept of a self-reflexive gaze. Anna only confronts Sennet on her death bed when it is too late to either reject his projection or volunteer to take part in it, but Barbara and Steve collaborate to create a mutually fulfilling fantasy. *Promethea* uses fundamentally self-reflexive effects—complicit critique and the self-reflexive gaze—to mount a feminist analysis of the artist/muse relationship.

Crying Games: Lesbian and Transgender Romance

The queer subplots in *Promethea* do not, however, present as coherent a commentary and fall back on less self-conscious depictions of traditional homophobic and transphobic clichés even as they employ metacomic conceits. The queer subplot involves a former version of Promethea, Grace, who initiates a sexual relationship with the until-then-homophobic supporting character, Stacia. The trans-subplot involves William "Bill" Woolcott, a male illustrator who transforms himself into Promethea while he draws his own *Promethea* comic book; Bill preceded Steve on the same series of comics, a sequence that obliquely reflects upon the American comic-book industry itself in which the same character is potentially created by hundreds of different people.

Stacia is the lead's best friend and, for the first half of the series, is consistently, if playfully, homophobic. She refers to Sophie, the lead, as "totally gay" (1, 5–6) for doing her homework, and claims, "Aah, you want my *body*, you homo. *Admit it*" (emphasis added, 5–6) when Sophie expresses a desire to spend time with her. Stacia's homophobia turns out to be a predictable cover for her own homosexuality. Mid-way through the series, she temporarily takes on the Promethea spirit by merging with Grace, a former host and a warrior. Grace seduces Stacia (19, 1) while Sophie/Promethea explores the cosmos with Barbara. Upon Sophie/Promethea's return, Stacia/Grace refuse to step down because they are in love and not being Promethea any more would separate them. The two Prometheas' battle is paralleled with the Crusades, the last time that two Prometheas fought each other (#24). One Christian and one Muslim incarnation of Promethea meet on the battlefield, just as Sophie/Promethea and Stacia/Grace do, and a dramatic two-page spread depicts both fights with the face of the original Egyptian girl, Promethea, screaming in pain (24, 20). The Christian and Muslim Prometheas occupy opposite positions on the page, each fighting on the opposing sides of wars between Christianity and Islam (24, 14–15). The Christian is in blue, the color of Virgin Mary, while the Muslim is in gold (24, 1). However, the color coding and page positions constantly switch, implying that the two are not polar opposites but rather two aspects of the same basic idea: monotheism. The issue therefore characterizes the wars between the two faiths as tragic, pointless, and ultimately self-destructive. This historical commentary is blunt but effective. The relationship between Stacia and Grace, however, does not resolve until the end of the series because Stacia is kidnapped and kept drugged by the United States government until issue #30. After she recovers, she comes out of the closet and strikes up a relationship with a minor character named Lucille. Stacia carries on her relationship with Grace in the afterlife, though, and does not tell Lucile about it (31, 18). In the process of creating an allegory for religious conflict, then, lesbian love is left with two options, violence or infidelity.

Promethea provides an even more damning example, however, one that rehearses a set of transphobic clichés even while ostensibly presenting a pro-trans narrative. The comic-book artist who drew Promethea before Steve, Bill Woolcott, died in the sixties, but his spirit lives on in the form of his Promethea persona, a sixties "Silver Age" superheroine. Bill/Promethea describes his male self as "gay as a spring lamb" (7, 4–5, 5) and explains that he "hadn't necessarily wanted to be a woman, but [...] always wanted to be a goddess" (7, 15, 1). Bill, in life, therefore has a flexibility of gender. He can occupy either of two genders more or less at will: gay man or goddess. This flexibility is unlike what Judith Halberstam identifies as the ironic rigidity of most trans characters in mainstream film, such as Dil in *The Crying Game*, who cannot "flow back and forth between male and female" and instead "insists on being recognized as female" (Halberstam 81). However, after Bill's death, Bill/Promethea does indeed insist that she and Bill are two different people, even speaking of him in the third person and the past tense, declaring: "I'm not a guy. William *Woolcott* was a guy. If anything, I'm his *imagination*" (7, 2–3). In death, then, Bill ends up occupying the fixed gender, female, that he managed to avoid in life, recreating the rigidity that Halberstam identifies as a stereotype of transgender identity. Rather than ascending to a kind of Heaven, which would arguably be the fit reward for a superheroine, Bill/Promethea is symbolically punished by being locked forever into a single gender, the exact opposite of the fluidity that he experienced in life.

Bill's full name and his queer/trans identity also obliquely references William Moulton Marston. Marston, a public intellectual and a psychologist who promoted dom/sub relationships with women in the dominant position as a way to tame masculine violence, created Wonder Woman as a vehicle for those very ideas (Daniels, *Wonder Woman* 28, 30). Marston was also a member of a polyamorous triad that consisted of himself, his wife, and their mutual lover, a young woman. Marston's original *Wonder Woman* comics do indeed carry all of these themes, but they are hidden in plain sight as superhero conceits in what Freya Johnson, speaking about the homoerotic themes in Batman, calls a "supratext," something so obvious that it "goes right over the head of the mainstream viewing audience" (Johnson). Bill/Promethea's costume, with its high boots and prominent scarab symbol on the chest representing Ancient Egypt (7, 13), does strongly resemble Wonder Woman's dress. Bill/Promethea directly addresses the silliness that she experienced as a 1960s, comic-book superheroine *and* as the creator of one such comic book: "I didn't think it was silly. I thought it was *playful*. It was meant for *children*..." (7, 6–7, 1). This line of thinking is consistent with one of Moore's career-long motifs, the reconciliation of contemporary American comics with the silliness that Bill/Promethea refers to. Sometimes, Moore has condemned that mode as politically misguided and even tacitly fascist (e.g., *Marvelman* and *Watchmen*) but by the mid–nineties, when he was writing for America's Best Comics, he began celebrating it. Bill/Promethea's description very much matches his output during that time: playful, child-like, ostensibly aimed at children. This remark stands out as a defense of the playful comics of the 1960s. It asserts that its playfulness is what makes it fun, but also that the young age of its audience justifies that playfulness.

However, Bill's queerness also indirectly references a tendency to read superhero comics retroactively as thinly-veiled homoerotica, which Moore himself does repeatedly throughout his career: Silk Spectre in *Watchmen* and Glory in *Supreme*, for example. The two elements come together as queer camp: the performance of homoerotic scenarios such that they are infused with sexuality that is both innocent and experienced at the same time. This queerness, of which Bill/Promethea is a blindingly obvious example, contradicts her own assertions about the innocent, child-like nature of those comics and undermines Moore's over-arching argument. Indeed, all of his seemingly playful America's Best titles contain within them glimmers of the political and sexual implications of the superhero, most explicitly *Tom Strong*'s hints of fascism and *Promethea*'s sexuality. Bill/Promethea's assertion about the playfulness of 1960s superhero comic books eventually rings false. In fact, her naiveté leads her down the path to her own tragic end.

As Promethea, she meets and falls in love with an FBI agent, Dennis Drucker, and as Bill, he writes a version of Dennis into his *Promethea* comics. Halberstam describes the traditional transphobic narrative that follows from this familiar premise, using *The Crying Game* as her example. The trans character "fail[s] to pass and threaten[s] to expose a rupture" (Halberstam 77), and the relationship is "now coded as homosexual" (82) in order to place it into a category that heteronormative values can contain. But those values also code the relationship as monstrous, conveniently leading to the conclusion that the trans character "must be punished" for his, her, or hir "treacherous deceptions." True to form, the romance between Bill/Promethea and Dennis ends violently when Dennis learns that the iconically female Promethea is also the very male Bill. Bill/Promethea's dialogue implies this whole narrative scenario through a haunting, single line: "Dennis found out" (7, 17). These three words encapsulate the pattern that Halberstam identifies. They imply the duplicity, the shock, and the impending danger of the situation, as heteronormative stories tend to present it, even when those stories overtly sympathize with the trans characters as in both *Boys Don't Cry* and *Promethea*. Indeed, Dennis finds out and then shoots Bill through the head (7, 17) in a panel rendered even more dramatic and gory because that section of the series takes the form of a photonovella: photographs arranged as comic panels rather than colored line drawings. The straight male character transforms into the victim and takes revenge on the trans character who has, likewise, transformed into the villain. *Promethea* mitigates this typical transphobic narrative a little, though. Dennis is so traumatized by his own actions — killing a demi-goddess whom he loved — that he ends up in a straightjacket and a padded cell, forever stuck in the moment when he killed Bill. Indeed, the photographic stillness of Dennis' insanity — the photographic panel appears frozen as other characters move through it (7, 17, 1–3) — makes it function like a cinematic freeze-frame, an eternal murder that Dennis is stuck in for decades.

Halberstam also speaks of a motif of weeping in trans-themed films. This theme is foregrounded in the titles of *The Crying Game* and *Boys Don't Cry*, in which "The tragic transgender, indeed, weeps because happiness and satisfaction, according to transphobic narratives, is always just out of reach" (82); both lovers do, indeed, literally weep in *Promethea* in the above photographic panel. Bill/Promethea weeps at the memory, and Dennis weeps as he shoots his lover in the head. The larger point of Halberstam's observation, though, is that transgendered love stories are almost always stuck in the mode of tragedy, that tears are the only allowable result of a trans romance. *Promethea*'s fantastic premise does allow for something of a happy ending, however. After the revelatory apocalypse that ends the series, living people have access to the afterlife, and so Dennis and Bill/Promethea take up their romantic relationship once again, across dimensions (31, 16). This ending is explained second-hand, though, and not prominently displayed, as opposed to Bill's graphic and gory murder, and it is safely heterosexual now: Dennis is a man and Bill/Promethea is quite emphatically "not a guy" (7, 2–3).

Although the series does grant happiness and romantic satisfaction to the trans character eventually, it comes only after punishing *hir* for deceiving the straight man and fixing *her* gender such that the relationship is recoded as heterosexual once again.

Moore and Queerness

These feminist and queer/trans narratives have a particular presence in Moore's corpus. He has been including queer themes in his comics at least since *V for Vendetta* (1982–1988); he specifically created *AARGH* (*Artists Against Rampant Government Homophobia*; 1988) to protest anti-queer legislation leveled by Thatcher's government; and he co-created *The Mirror of Love*, an illustrated poem that praises the cultural contributions of queer artists, scientists, and thinkers throughout history. Although Moore is not gay himself, he was for several years part of a polyamorous triad, much like William Moulton Marston, and clearly has a personal stake in queer rights and the social recognition of alternative sexualities (Moore *Blather.net*). Like many straight male writers who support queer rights, though, he has almost exclusively written female queerness into his work. Bill/Promethea is a rare exception and only a nominal case because her relationship with Dennis is effectively heterosexual, both before and after Bill's death; and although there are several scenes of gay male sex in *Lost Girls*, the overwhelming majority of sex in that book is lesbian or heterosexual, and far more often the former than the latter. This preoccupation hints at precisely the kind of scopophilia that Mulvey discusses at length, and it's related to another of Moore's motifs.

Moore often links female bisexuality with enlightenment, reducing that bisexuality to a product of a certain kind of knowledge and experience rather than an innate sexual orientation. For example, *Promethea* consistently portrays Sophie as heterosexual, but she expresses a desire to make love to Barbara when they both enter the heavenly sphere of wisdom (22, 13). Mina Murray, in *The League of Extraordinary Gentlemen*, starts out as cold and even prudish, but by the end of *Black Dossier*, she is bisexual and polyamorous, presumably as a result of the time she spends in the Blazing World, even though Allan Quatermain spends just as much time there and implies that he is interested only in women (18, 17). Alternatively, *Lost Girls* consistently portrays Alice as a lesbian but after the climactic storytelling session/orgy in which the three protagonists work through their respective traumatic experiences, she suddenly expresses a desire to pursue Monsieur Rougeur, stating, "Frankly, *anything* seems possible now. / Who knows? We could take turns being the lady" (30, 2).

The implication seems to be that enlightened women automatically become bisexual and that attraction to both sexes is the product of an expanded, open mind rather than just being an orientation unto itself. In this way, Moore undercuts many of his feminist and queer-positive story elements by fetishizing female bisexuality to the point of objectification.

This fetishization points to an explanation for both the successes and failures that I have discussed. The common factor is, to put it bluntly, the audience's own scopophilia. The desire to sexualize and objectify female sexuality — including lesbian or bisexual imagery — is the consistent factor here. The muse narratives offer one negative and one positive version of a situation in which a man projects a sexual fantasy onto a woman, but even in the positive example, the projection still happens. The book still fulfills the viewer's desire to look. That is not to say that there is something morally unacceptable about *Promethea*'s solution to the problem — consent *is* the difference between morally acceptable and unacceptable sexual behavior. It is merely to suggest that this solution is acceptable within a mainstream comic book partly because it allows the projection to continue. This solution can function within the somewhat narrow set of requirements of an entertainment industry that is based in no small part on the spectacle of improbably beautiful bodies in violent and/or sexual situations. A solution that involved not looking at all would fall flat within that industry.

By contrast, the queer narratives do not quite work because they contain imagery and elements that still make the mainstream audience uncomfortable: butch lesbians and transgendered lovers. The Stacia/Grace version of Promethea is still an idealized female body in many ways, but she is just masculine enough that she contrasts with the other Prometheas, whom Williams draws as more traditional feminine archetypes: the innocent little girl (Little Margie), the superheroine (Bill), the fantasy warrior-woman (Grace without Stacia), and the angel of mercy (Margaret). Stacia/Grace is a soft-butch lesbian, and so the romance between Stacia and Grace is only a stone's throw away from the traditional, male fantasy of lipstick lesbians who, in essence, perform for the enjoyment of a straight male viewer. Similarly, the trans love story must, as Halberstam succinctly explains, end in tragedy or some form of heterosexuality in order to fall into an acceptable span of heteronormative values. The fantasy elements of *Promethea* — actual transformation from gay man to goddess, the ability to carry on relationships with people who have died — allow for both tragedy and heteronormativity; Bill is punished for deceiving Dennis, but they strike up a conveniently heterosexual relationship by the end of the series. Moore's nearest cousin character to Bill/Promethea, the transgendered and eternally randy Orlando in *The League of Extraordinary Gentlemen: Black*

Dossier, retains the ability to float between male and female. However, once again, Orlando is conveniently female at the end of the narrative so that she can form a three-way relationship consisting of two women and a man—conveniently absent of any male homosexuality it can serve as fantasy fuel for a straight male viewer. *Promethea*'s commentaries on gender and sexuality succeed or fail because they exist within the constraints of mainstream comic-book publishing in which only certain fantasies are acceptable. This is not to say that its successes do not count, but it does grant us a glimpse at the narrowness of the range of acceptable forms of "success."

15. I Remain Your Own
Epistolamory in "The New Adventures of Fanny Hill"
LLOYD ISAAC VAYO

Included among the documents in Alan Moore and Kevin O'Neill's *The League of Extraordinary Gentlemen: Black Dossier*, on a coarse stock befitting its purported vintage, is a slim pornographic volume entitled "The New Adventures of Fanny Hill: Or, The Further Memoirs of a Woman of Pleasure, as recounted to Mr. John Cleland." With a given publication date of 1912, the novella is positioned as a sequel to the notorious *Memoirs of a Woman of Pleasure*, acknowledged as the first pornographic novel and subject to obscenity trials in England. Written as a follow-up letter to Cleland, the novella continues Moore's artful recontextualization of literary figures,[1] and is complimented by O'Neill's images, yielding a portmanteau, an epistolamory, a love developed through and primarily contained within letters, which stands as a unique contribution to the constellation of affections in the *Dossier* and the series as a whole.

Though other instances of correspondence do appear throughout the *League* volumes, it is only in "New Adventures" that epistolamory fully takes shape, coalescing around notions of paradoxical disconnection. Previously stable relations between writer and reader, woman and man, text and image, and language and meaning are problematized in the course of Hill's narrative. Hill maintains a virile motility akin to the mails themselves through which her correspondence is to travel, journeying through many hands and to sundry destinations. In the course of these movements, Hill consistently practices a form of love characterized by these paradoxical disconnections, utilizing the porno-, the covertly and overtly sexual content of her narrative, as a means of giving the -graphy, the letter itself and its own subtle and delicate theoretical formulations, space to articulate this new amorousness.

The recipient Cleland, original destination of Hill's letter, is pushed aside for the reader-as-proxy recipient, who reads the letter in his stead/instead, enacting less a receipt than an intercept. The protagonist Hill moves from failed heterosexual monogamy in her relations with beau Charles to emotionless casual encounters in the aftermath of their fractured relationship, finally arriving at a more successful matriarchal self-sufficiency marked by lesbian practices in one of the locales to which she travels. The images within "New Adventures" are doubly graphic in their hyperbolic literalization of the double entendres larded in the text, offering a basic visual rendering of events that reflects the logical conclusion of the innuendos contained in the narrative. Finally, those double entendres deftly tongue around more delicate subjects, language being manipulated to spare both readers and censors the trials of limited imagination.

As a means of addressing these complex movements, the following analysis will begin with an understanding of Moore's selection of Fanny Hill for recontextualization, one that also pays heed to the dense history surrounding the original volume. Next, attention will be devoted to a look at past epistolarities so as to grasp the vocabulary within which and against which Moore's epistolamory does its work. Finally, the discussion will arrive at a clear formulation of that epistolamory through an examination of the tensions outlined in brief in the plot summary above (the relations between writer and reader, woman and man, text and image, and language and meaning).

Adventures Old and New: Moore's Fanny

Before undertaking an analysis of the unique epistolamory present in "New Adventures," one must first identify the elements at play in the *Black Dossier* novella and the logic of Moore's decision to include a continuation of Hill's narrative within his own, as well as its rooting in the original *Memoirs of a Woman of Pleasure* and the mind of its author, all of which, in combination, provide the foundation from which that epistolamory may arise. Beginning with the basic elements of "New Adventures," the novella (such as it is, spanning only sixteen pages, yet presenting a various and coherent closed narrative within that meager breadth) consists of pages dominated by large images which take up nearly two-thirds of the available space, the balance belonging to text. The images, printed upon the rough off-white paper, resemble either intricate woodcuts, or perhaps engravings, bearing at once a significant degree of detail within their otherwise chunky graphics, and maintaining an air of high drama throughout. As for the subjects of those images, Moore elects to depict scenes contemporaneous to Hill's narrative, albeit with a more distant correspondence than one might expect from their prominent placement, with prolific nudity and sexual escapades dominating, often within the strange cultures and locales explored by Hill in her Gulliver-esque travels, some of which do indeed take place with/in the footsteps of Lemuel himself.

The text relates an extravagant tale in a decidedly matter-of-fact, nearly conversational manner and tone. Though engaged in an encyclopedic description of Hill's hedonistic pursuits,[2] the language and, to a lesser degree, the content of the text is reserved, demure, as if making concessions to an unprepared audience, though its accompanying images belie the true content of Hill's doings. The most remarkable, or most often marked, of the aspects particular to this text is its frequent and deft use of double entendres, veiling sexual content beneath benign language, leaving it to Cleland-as-primary reader and/or the audience as secondary reader to reconstruct the full meaning of Hill's deconstructed prose.

Moore's interest in Cleland's original novel demonstrates its consonance with his own thematic preoccupations, his acute critical facility, and his personal experiences with the problem of censorship. Perhaps best known for his iconic *Watchmen*, Moore is also the author (and collaborator with various illustrators, including Dave Gibbons, David Lloyd, Eddie Campbell, and Kevin O'Neill) of *V for Vendetta*, *From Hell* and, most importantly for this analysis, *The League of Extraordinary Gentleman* series, a three volume set (at present) that includes the *Black Dossier*. Across his entire body of work, Moore produces what Annalisa Di Liddo calls "a thickly stratified basis of archetypes and genres that results in a dense narrative landscape [...] the amount [of allusions] is overwhelming, and their nature is re-elaborated and reshuffled to such an extent that an estranging, almost whirling effect of polysemy is guaranteed" (41). Based in references drawn from a broad selection of Victorian literature, including main characters Mina Harker/Murray (from Bram Stoker's *Dracula*), Captain Nemo (from Jules Verne's *Twenty Thousand Leagues Under the Sea*), Allan Quatermain (from H. Rider Haggard's *King Solomon's Mines*), Dr. Jekyll/Mr. Hyde (from Robert Louis Stevenson's *The Strange Case of Dr. Jekyll and Mr. Hyde*), and Hawley Griffin (from H.G. Wells' *The Invisible Man*), the *League* volumes exemplify this hyper-referential intertextuality, with the inclusion of "The New Adventures of Fanny Hill" standing as one of the lengthier literary references in the series.

Within this thematic concern with referentiality, Moore has three primary aims, all of which are achieved to a greater or lesser extent in "New Adventures": imperial critique, expanded literacy, and transgressive anti-censorship. Di Liddo notes Moore's overarching "embrace [of] a critical perspective in which the crisis of English values leads to the acknowledgment of a wider, more vibrant and variegated notion of identity" (102), giving particular attention to "Victorian culture as the fullest representative of the imperial mind, its ideals of dominance and oppression, and its systematic repression of otherness" in the *League* volumes (102). As part of that critique and its basis in hyper-referentiality, Moore also endeavors to encourage readers to follow those references to their origins, relishing "the idea that you can use a comic to make people interested in books again" (181), as stated in George Khoury et al.'s *The Extraordinary Works of Alan Moore: Indispensible Edition*.

As presented in *Black Dossier*, Moore's/Hill's text does not exist in a vacuum, itself admitting the existence of the preceding *Memoirs*, necessitating a closer look at the novella's original locus in that infamous novel and its author. At first, John Cleland eluded identification as the author of the novel, *Memoirs* remaining "for long an underground book," as noted in Peter Sabor's introduction to the text (vii), in part due to the obscenity trials that plagued the novel in both un- and expurgated variations. Cleland produced the text "[d]uring a detention of over a year in the Fleet prison" (ix), a novel of such ill repute itself arising from within a den of likeminded souls, though Cleland himself was there for more banal reasons related to outstanding debts. Though his later work would gain attention on the basis of its infamy, and his legacy is directly indebted to *Memoirs*' varied reception, Cleland did his best to refute any efforts at attribution, assigning the novel and its attendant guilt to "a prominent writer of bawdy literature" (xiii) in one moment, and to "a young gentleman of the greatest hopes that I ever knew" (quoted in Sabor xiii), in both cases distancing himself from authors of the bawdy persuasion, while gesturing towards his own aspirations as an author as well as the upward mobility of his protagonist, Fanny Hill.

Moving from the author to his produce, *Memoirs of a Woman of Pleasure* appears in its first edition in 1748–9, and is subject to numerous reprintings in a wide array of formats and languages. Centered around Fanny Hill, a jilted lover who turns to prostitution during a hiatus in her relationship with Charles (though the two eventually reconcile and marry), the novel takes on the epistolary form, existing primarily as two long letters from Fanny to an unnamed "Madam," recounting her experiences with her time-honored (though not always honorable) profession. The novel concerns itself with thematic notions common to novels of the era, with William H. Epstein observing numerous parallels to Daniel Defoe's *Moll Flanders* and Fanny's common "habit of settling her accounts at each stage of her career, of balancing, as does Moll, her financial gain against her spiritual loss" (Epstein 93); it also reflects common social situations, chief among them being "an essential problem which most eighteenth-century women were unable or unwilling to confront: how, in a man's world, were they to find peace and freedom?" (97). Fanny herself struggles with that very question throughout the novel, using florid, euphemistic language to describe the visceral pursuits of her vocation (in part due to Cleland's pretense as a writer, and in part due to concerns of censorship), though not euphemistic enough to satisfy the moralizers of the time. Recipient of a reputation exceeding its purported offense, the novel is censored for much of its existence, only coming to wide (legal) distribution in 1963 in the U.S., and 1970 in England.

Letter Never Sent: Past Epistolaries

With the background of Moore's "New Adventures" and Cleland's original *Memoirs* in place, it is necessary to examine epistolary precedents so as to gain a sense of the literary lettering of the past and its treatment in the *Black Dossier*. Looking not so much at the mechanics of the epistolary as to the qualitative currents within the genre, the epistolary exists primarily as a genre of fiction, though also as a real world phenomenon chronicled in the mid–to-late-eighteenth century. Within this generic context, three primary relations appear: that between the epistolary and history; that between the letter writer (often a fictional character) and her/his recipient(s); and that between the letter writer and notions of spatiality. A brief glance at each of these relations will do much to ground the forthcoming expounding of epistolamory in Moore.

An epistory (or epi-history) hovers on, around, near, but is not itself historical in the strictest terms; Rebecca Earle asserts that "[m]ined for quotations, read for content, analyzed for meaning, letters form the hidden underpinnings of much historical research" (Earle 1), establishing a documentary reliance on these "fictions of the self" (2). Of the numerous historical moments of interest within the century-spanning demarcation of Earle's *Epistolary Selves: Letters and Letter-Writers, 1600–1945*, one in particular proves of special value to the height of the epistolary form (the mid–to-late–eighteenth century in most renderings): the negotiation of the public and private, both prior to and in the act of epistolary composition, and also subsequently in the act of reception, especially as mediated through the novel. During this period, "[t]he belief that the familiar letter represented the truest, least affected form of written expression fuelled the custom of presenting fictional letter collections as genuine correspondence that had inadvertently fallen into the hands of an editor" (5), with authenticity arising from the perception that such eavesdropping was unauthorized, illicit, and therefore an act of intrigue. For women, assumed authors of the bulk of epistolary writings due to the gendering and sexualization of the semi-consenting provision of letters to a rapacious public, this tension manifested as a debate over whether "reading and writing encourage[d] temporary isolation, and thereby, introspection [or whether that opinion ignored] the companionate, communal nature of family reading" (6). Rooted in the particulars of its apex, epistolarity in this case is subject to both a historicization and feminization, in both cases ascribing a delicate dynamic between the introspective letter writer and the specular reader.

Delving further into the conjunction of public and private spheres within the realm of the epistolary, the unique interaction between the letter writer and recipient, taking place within the literary frame of the epistolary novel, is founded in a complex chain of trust outlined by Janet Gurkin Altman in her *Epistolarity: Approaches to a Form*: "In order to make a *confidence*, as epistolary characters so often do, one must have *confiance* in the *confident*" (Altman 48), suggesting the potential for a closer bond between letter writer and reader than a simple sender-receiver configuration. This confidant (usually male), in whom the letter writer places her/his confidence, may be passive, "fulfill[ing] his [sic] minimal, passive, twofold function: he listens to confessions, he listens to stories" (50), or active, the latter being more common via inclusion of the confidant's voice in quotation/paraphrase/absentia. The confidant "derives additional power and perhaps his most essential role from the mere fact of receiving letters [and] is most fundamentally an archivist" (53), gaining most power from the act of passive reception and presentation of the collected letters to a broader audience. On the rare occasions that a letter writer changes confidants, that shift "can often signal an important moment in the epistolary hero's development" (54), development *within* a confidant transferring into a development *between* confidants, an elision of the private into the public of an at first marginally, then significantly larger audience.

Beyond the movement within and between confidants, the letter writer demonstrates an auto-mobility, as unfolded by Donna Landry in her "Love Me, Love My Turkey Book: Letters and Turkish Travelogues in Early Modern England." Landry contends that the letter writer is in perpetual motion:

> If we explore the spatial dimensions of the letter, the letter writer is always in some sense a traveler. An epistle documents what has happened to the writer since the last epistle. And so the letter writer is always traveling, explicitly through time, and either explicitly or implicitly across space [Landry 51].

Though couched within her larger analysis of literal (and literary) narratives of travel in Turkey, Landry gestures towards what she calls "the irritation of influence" (56), not only within travels taken in the footsteps of previous epistolary writers, but within the epistolary itself, Samuel Richardson's 1740

Pamela: Or, Virtue Rewarded casting a long shadow over others taking on the epistolary form. Still, followers in the Pamelan path, "subsequent travelers[,] have often prided themselves upon correcting the reports and views of previous travelers" (52), each iteration of the epistolary exercising a drift, continental or otherwise, from its predecessors. Overall, the epistolary strikes a balance between the public and the private, springing from and supporting historical loci, appealing to the confidant within and outside of the novel, and maintaining a dialogue with likeminded mailings, all qualities present in and contributing to the unique epistolamory of "New Adventures."

Pushing the Envelope: The Epistles of Moore

Having located "New Adventures" in relation to its author (Moore), its elder (Cleland's *Memoirs*), and its sender (the epistolary precedent), one may now examine its unique rendering of the epistolary such that, in the peregrinations of Fanny Hill, a new love is formed, a broadening of both the sender and receiver that yields an epistolamory. This love arises from a quartet of tensions present in the neo-narrative which, in combination, produce an obscurity, an ungraspability that makes the reader, be it the "Mr. Cleland" to whom the single epistle of "New Adventures" is addressed or the audience at large, want to hold the text that much closer: tensions between writer and reader, woman and man, text and image, and language and meaning. Each in turn will demonstrate one facet of the new amorousness posited by Hill (and, by proxy, by Moore) in "New Adventures," culminating in a fuller understanding of epistolamory as a phenomenon.

In terms of the tension between writer and reader, in its first line, "New Adventures" sets out its specific reader, the letter being addressed to "My Dearest Mr. Cleland,"[3] appealing to him variously throughout the text, and making reference to "your own account" in one moment, suggesting that one of the individuals, Captain Clegg, that Hill encounters has read *Memoirs*. Hill self-identifies shortly after the opening invocation to Cleland, assuring her specific reader that she is "still your own sweet, young Fanny," situating herself in relation to Cleland and implying a certain degree of ownership (if not full-on creation) of at least her narrative self, if not her entire person. At this point, there is but a single writer (Hill) and a single reader (Cleland) evident, at least within the narrative frame of the novella, though both categories expand by implication.

Behind the apparent pen of Hill, devoted to relating her own experiences in the period following that captured in *Memoirs*, lies the meta-letter writer,

Alan Moore, who creates and/or ventriloquizes Hill in much the same manner as her original penman, Cleland; this is a layered authorship that expands that positionality while simultaneously varying its gender. Moore inhabits Hill in the manner of Cleland. Similarly, behind the devouring eye of the apparent reader, Cleland himself, identified as the recipient of the epistle with a specificity lacking from the original *Memoirs* and their indistinct address to a "Madam" (gender being varied again in this case), is the reader of "New Adventures" more specifically and the *Black Dossier* more generally. As a product of these expansions, more are taken in, drawn into Hill's narrative, held rapt by the sheer force and scope of her address, imperfectly privy to the private, and most like what they find there.

Including the aforementioned gender variations present in the shift in address from "Madam" to Cleland and the writerly inhabitation of Hill by dual personages Cleland and Moore, "New Adventures" makes a passing mention of "the changeable, immortal warrior Orlando, who was female at the time of [Lemuel] Gulliver's demise," referencing a central figure in the overall *Dossier*, one whose mutable gender identification and facility for passing is derived from Virginia Woolf's *Orlando: A Biography*. If Orlando's own indistinct and inscrutable gender identification contributes to the tension between woman and man within "New Adventures," so too does Hill's own fluid sexuality. Examples of this fluidity include Hill's encounter with Moll Flanders, involving "sweet Molly's hand below my petticoats and all our raiment lost," as well as her visit to Micromona, "a peculiar country that is ruled by women and where men are kept only as slaves," and another to Tryphême, where "women are encouraged to go naked save for silver sandals and a yellow scarf upon their heads," amongst a number of heterosexual encounters. These examples at once place Hill's sexual identification in question, while suggesting a differing valuation of female and male gender identity.

Where Orlando frustrates gender binaries through physical transformation and an accompanying fluctuation of affections, Hill produces a similar frustration through praxis only, her polymorphous sexuality generating additional interest in the reader already hailed by the multiple address. Though herself of relatively stable gender, Hill's favor for Micromona and Tryphême, societies either ruled by or dominated by women, the former possessing a clear leadership dynamic, and the latter suggesting greater freedom (at least in aesthetic terms) in relation to "[m]en, less pleasing to the eye" (Moore and O'Neill), implies a greater valuation of femininity and female gender identification. This pseudo-partisan alignment appeals doubly to the broadened reader, either affirming female identification and its attendant value, or subtly denying male identification through an exercise of participatory denial (maintaining sexual contact while implying inferiority), in either case inflaming that reader further with each passing page.

Such a difference between text and image, between gender subtext and visual referents, extends to the novella as a whole. O'Neill, following in the footsteps of *Memoirs* and its "host of artists intrigued by the novel's visual riches" (Sabor viii), creates a profound disjunction between Hill's deft wordplay and indirectly pornographic prose and the uncompromisingly visceral, albeit always artistic and not altogether graphic, imagery that accompanies it. As an illustrator, O'Neill's work is characterized by Moore as "meticulous, but there is an exaggerated and cartoony quality [an] almost cartoony flexibility" to his art (Khoury et al. 181), what Di Liddo alternately terms "the grotesque, hyperbolic trait" (Di Liddo 104), suggesting the very sort of hyperbolic divergence that exists between Hill/Moore's nearly polite (if innuendo-laden) descriptions and O'Neill's depictions. For example, as a complement to Hill/Moore's relatively benign description, "[d]uring a fierce tempest ... [Clegg] insisted that I be lashed to the wheel for my own safety" (Moore and O'Neill), O'Neill offers a nearly nude Hill being penetrated from behind by Captain Clegg, a more abrupt version of the scenario provided by Hill/Moore that is characteristic of other such divergences throughout the novella.

This divergence between word and image, between description and depiction, creates a tension, one that problematizes the believability of either the narrative, the images, or both, with the truth of Hill's experience lying perhaps somewhere in the interstice between the two. The text dissembles, while the images chronicle that disassembly, that removal of garments allowing for the pornography of the text to emerge, a disrobing that simultaneously forecloses the reader's imagination (Cleland or otherwise), directing the reader to a specific and limited understanding of the text, while the totality and truth of the text eludes that reader's grasp. By rendering Hill's descriptions in such a fashion, O'Neill threatens the lure of Hill's text, its requirement for audience participation and, within that participatory reading, a fantastic possibility of real participation in likeminded scenarios. When, for example, O'Neill translates Hill's evaluation of Gulliver as "stimulating company" into an image of a bare Hill stretched across Gulliver's lap, writhing ecstatically as he tweaks her nipple, no small amount of imagination seems forestalled. Yet, the very volume of such scenarios cannot be stanched by the limited number of images, leaving much for the reader to construct, and much for Hill to instruct in her pedagogical role as letterer/lecturer.

Where the discord between word and image potentially threatens the power of Hill's narrative, Hill/Moore's numerous puns, euphemisms, and double (if not triple) entendres at once manifest a tension between language and meaning, while also involving the reader in the proceedings, suggesting an amorous mutuality that meets at the linguistic level, be it that of the word, the tongue, or their jointure in the cunning linguist. In its first iteration, at Cleland's hand, that original author values a light linguistic touch, criticizing Laurence Sterne's prose, with a "bawdy too plain" (quoted in Sabor xii), a coarse simplicity of language that Cleland rectifies in his own novel and that Moore recaptures in his novella. Epstein notes how Hill "borrows, and then exaggerates outrageously, the euphemistic diction and metaphorical construction of the most refined and cultivated contemporary prose styles" (Epstein 106), a methodology that Hill/Moore revisits in "New Adventures" not only as a gesture toward authentic mimicry, but also as a comment on Moore's own experiences with censorship and its potential evasions.

"New Adventures" swells with such euphemisms, and the glancing blows that they produce encourage the reader to greater heights of investment in her amorous advances through her narrative and, it is hoped by some, outside of it, to a different form of address that directly reaches the reader without any necessary "Mr. Cleland." In Moll Flanders' words to Hill, "[d]iscussing love, your warmest treasure ... is your euphemism" (Moore and O'Neill), and Hill generously shares that treasure with all and sundry. To name just a few of these euphemisms: when speaking of Gulliver, she pronounces him to be "stimulating company"; while aboard Clegg's ship, he suggests "that he take me up the southeast passage"; and when traveling with Queen Venus, "ventured alone down that pellucid passageway under the hill, the very mound of Venus" (Moore and O'Neill). In each instance, the text provides an orality, a rendering in words of the deeds depicted in O'Neill's images, an orality that demonstrates a deft use of language, while giving a very vaginal rendering of that doubled tongue, consistent both with the flickering ministrations of language and the lesbian undertones of Hill's gender and sexual identifications.

What, then, is this epistolamory that is birthed from the tensions between writer and reader, woman and man, word and image, and language and meaning? It is, at base, a salutary difference, one of many on offer in Moore's updating of Cleland's text. Often published under erroneous titles in its various un-and expurgated versions (as *Fanny Hill* or *Memoirs of Fanny Hill* [Sabor vii]), the novel-turned-sequel novella is once more in error, its title beginning by naming the Hill unnamed in Cleland's original. Additionally, where *Memoirs* ends with Hill "able to retire from her career as a prostitute happily married" (xviii), "New Adventures" finds Hill back in a version of the trade, albeit one geared towards safe passage rather than fee-based entry. Where Cleland's Hill finds lesbian advances "at once alarming and enticing [though] she disapproves of lesbianism" (xxiv), Moore's Hill shows less trepidation.

Yet, it is not this difference, but rather a diffidence, that enthralls, that produces epistolamory, a love not occurring within the epistle and its pages, but in the liminal space between letter writer and reader, in the referential void of implication, where what the reader brings to and hopes to derive from the text is of signal importance. The above analysis demonstrates the various liminalities present in Hill/Moore's narrative: the multiple writer(s) and reader(s), the multiple and multiply genders and gendered, the variant images and their muted textual bases, and the lingual lightness of euphemism. It is from these liminalities, from the liminal writ large, that epistolamory arises and, ultimately, from the reader's portion. Hill is coquettish, is hard to get, to comprehend, the aforementioned multiplicities providing for as many readings as there are readers. As such, reading her narrative, as provided by Cleland or Moore, demands an investment, necessitates a pursuit, requires a level of commitment beyond that of simple letter writer and reader, beyond the threshold of audience to that of Altman's confidant, one possessing a fidelity to and a related faith in the letter writer.

However, Hill does not succumb to the reader so willingly, so easily, proving to be less reliant on the reader for salvation (or, indeed, less reliant on salvation, either being beyond the dire circumstances of her first iteration in *Memoirs* or being free from want of rescue in her control of her own circumstances in "New Adventures"), playing something of a game of hard to get, though not wanting to be gotten, either perceptually or sexually (her lesbian leanings refuting the male readership, and her fleeting affections dismissing the female readers). Hers is a relationship of rupture, a relationship founded on what happens between the letters, within the measured words and between their containing lines, of implication, literalized in part by O'Neill's images, but only ever partially, indirectly, the distance between word and deed being foreshortened, but never foresworn. Hill is elusive, allusive, evading narrative fixity in either *Memoirs* or "New Adventures," constantly on the move, a traveler within and between texts looking for a fellow traveler. Her letters are paradoxically intimate, yet shared with others, Cleland and the larger reader engaging her actively, though with greater energy on their side of the equation. The epistolamory that results is fragmentary, is fickle, taking place in the bounce between letter (writer) and reader, reliant on implication, imposition (of the reader on the letter writer), and an impolite attention to that which remains unwritten, due either to its pornographic or personal content (or perhaps both). Where other locations within the *League* series manifest an intra- or intertextuality within the larger frame of the series itself, "New Adventures" expands its love to the realm of intersectionality, to the meeting of (letter) writer and reader, an interactivity unique to its scarce pages. Moore and O'Neill's "New Adventures" is therefore less novella than novel, providing a new form of affection through its consultation with an aged articulation.

Notes

1. These recontextualizations are many, drawing characters from authors such as Bram Stoker, Jules Verne, and H.G. Wells, among others, and transplanting them into alternate contexts in which the overlapping references to their original texts create a rich interplay. Moore practices this recontextualization not only in the *League* novels, but elsewhere throughout his corpus, including most notably in *Lost Girls*, where Alice from Lewis Carroll's *Alice's Adventures in Wonderland*, Dorothy from L. Frank Baum's *The Wizard of Oz*, and Wendy from J.M. Barrie's *Peter Pan* all find a new home in Moore's narrative.

2. Numbered among Hill's pleasure-minded undertakings are an encounter with the aforementioned Gulliver, a tumultuous and storm-tossed voyage with Captain Clegg (of Russell Thorndike's *Doctor Syn* novels), and travels with a group whose members included Natty Bumppo (of James Fenimore Cooper's *Leatherstocking Tales*), each of which bear the mark of Hill's singular focus on the amorous.

3. It is worth noting here, in passing, that the pages of "New Adventures" are themselves unnumbered, unpaginated, making Hill's on-location dispatches, both concerned with loci and, in that sense, locative, that much harder to locate.

Afterword
Disgust with the Revolution
ANNALISA DI LIDDO

Finding the words to conclude such a comprehensive survey about love and sex in Alan Moore's work is no easy task indeed. To be honest, when it comes to Moore, drawing conclusions is never easy — the encyclopedic and often intricate nature of his creations makes it impossible to single out univocal or unambiguous interpretations. This author's comics and prose writings (and poetry, and performance, and records, and underground magazines, to be more specific as to the wide span of his output) feature a complexity of content and structure that joyfully caters to different angles and perspectives. As the editors of this book remind us of in their introduction, the element that triggered the birth of this collection was exactly the realization that love and sex can be seen as one of the key impulses lying at the core of much of Moore's work. Especially in light of many of his latest pieces, Moore can very much be seen as the creator of a pansexual narrative universe: the sexual instinct permeates every interest and urge for expression, and every experience is consequently suffused with erotic feeling. This pansexuality is closely connected to the notion of anarchy that Moore has openly embraced since the early days of his career as an artist, and it remains consistent with the views he has expressed through his comics and other creative works.

One of Moore's latest projects, *Unearthing*, is quite illustrative of this pansexual tendency. Originally a short story to be published in Iain Sinclair's *London: City of Disappearances* anthology, the text then evolved into a spoken word performance to be accompanied by music and by Mitch Jenkins' photographs. When opening the box set in which the work was released in 2010, the viewer is immediately confronted by an image of Selene, the moon goddess, eyes inviting and legs wide open to fully reveal her exposed sex. *Unearthing*, a work of "human excavation" (Doran, "Hipster Priest"), is an evocative psychogeographical account of the life of Steve Moore (no relation), a colleague, fellow occultist, and close friend of our author's-actually "one of the most influential figures in [his] life, (Gieben, "Alan Moore") — and the painter of the above — mentioned Selene portrait. The history of Shooter's Hill, where Steve Moore has lived since his birth, is recounted together with the history of British comics in which he played a key role. Through these histories, indivisible from them, runs the line of his biography: a life characterized by isolation and disappointing love stories counterbalanced by Steve's erotic relationship with Selene, his "moon-wife" (Moore, *Unearthing*), his "imaginary love, compensatory delusion" (*Unearthing*). Her hallucinatory presence is first only faintly perceived, but it later becomes so intense that it absorbs Steve's whole existence, so that the author himself claims to have seen her during one of his friend's sporadic visits to Northampton. Selene thus becomes Steve Moore's obsession and guide in life, and above all in occult practice. The carnal experience, then, appears as the core of magical practice and as the crucial means to reach enlightenment and wisdom, as in *Promethea*.

This kind of pervasive pansexualism, however, is not devoid of complications. Representations of love and sex in Moore's work are indeed as manifold as the explosion of faces and identities caused by the orgasm of porn star Mayor Uvula Cascade and her dysfunctional predecessor Sonny Baskerville (plus his multiple personalities) in *Promethea* (5, 122–24), and they can look just as troubling. The many faces of sex are neither all beautiful, nor always successfully rendered; as some of the essays in this book point out, Moore's portrayals can be seen as failing to comply with the feminist or queer agendas he otherwise frankly supports (see Kidder, for instance), or to exhibit reticence toward sexuality in general (see Candelaria and Flynn). These controversial representations, though, are made all the more complex by the fact that they can be interpreted as criticism of the very social, historical, and cultural canons they appear to be based on. A particularly appropriate example can be Moore's latest, the debated and very divisive comic book *Neonomicon*, the four-issue mini-series drawn by Jacen Burrows and released by Avatar Press in 2010.

An evident tribute to H.P. Lovecraft, *Neonomicon* features much of Moore's usual rewriting techniques and attempts to elaborate on its source — in this particular case, the Cthulhu myth — by bringing its covert, repressed contents to the surface. The title of the comic is revealing, for the Greek root *nekros* (meaning "corpse") is removed from the Lovecraftian word *Necronomicon* to be replaced with *neo*. The *Book of the Dead* thus becomes the *Book of the New*, referring to multiple aspects of this work, both diegetic and extradiegetic: the new era heralded by the terrifying coming of Cthulhu, who will be given birth to by protagonist Merril Brears[1]; the new light shed on the hidden contents of Lovecraft's narrative; and a new look at the self-reflexiveness of the language of comics (which has already been hinted at in the introduction to this book). Of course, what we need to focus on here is the second aspect. In many ways, this comic is a similar exercise to the one Moore performed when writing *Lost Girls*, for much of the veiled content in Lovecraft's narrative — just like in Barrie, Carroll, and Baum's case — is of sexual nature. Here, too, Moore challenges the genre by working within its boundaries, but with a different outcome: while the narrative standards of porn allow him to build a story which, while mirroring the repetitive, mechanic quality of pornographic literature, ultimately depicts sex as a cathartic, beneficial force, the canons of horror require generating disgust and disruption. Moore attempts to take this notion to its extreme consequences. As he stated in a 2010 interview, "I thought, if I'm writing a horror story, let's make it horrible. Let's make it the kind of stuff that you don't see in horror stories." *Neonomicon* thus becomes "very ugly" and "dark as hell" (Gieben, "Alan Moore") and shows the harshest, bleakest sides of sex. Agent Brears' abduction and rape at the hands of a group of twisted Lovecraftian cultists and then of a scary fish-monster, pictured by Burrows' skilful hand with plenty of graphic detail, occupies considerable portions of issue 2 and 3 of the mini-series (Moore and Burrows 2, 21–5; 3, 4–13). A former nymphomaniac, once Brears is back in society after being impregnated by the beast, she declares that she feels "good about all this. For the first time ... I got no problems with my self-esteem" (4, 24). This statement, together with the significant length of the rape scene, has caused considerable debate on the internet. Besides being outraged by the general ferocity of the comic, many believe that Moore proves to be complacent in scripting so many pages of gratuitous sexual violence, and also to be deeply misogynist in "punishing" his character's sexual addiction with rape and to later have her proclaim that she even feels well (see for instance Basque's blog entry).

But some further consideration is required here: arbitrariness is hardly a feature of Moore's work, and *Neonomicon* is no exception to this. The series can prove a truly disturbing read, but nothing is shown for its own sake, or for the sake of mere provocation. As regards the extent of the rape scene, it complies with the above-mentioned determination to challenge common patterns of representation, and by prolonging the reader's exposure to the horrific details of the story, a critique of his/her own voyeurism is also elicited. This is something Moore already did in the past, in collaboration with Eddie Campbell, in the tenth chapter of *From Hell*, where Marie Kelly's dead body is ravaged by insane Doctor Gull for thirty-one pages (Moore and Campbell X, 1–31). As for Brears' self-esteem, her "feeling good" does not seem caused by the conviction of having somehow deserved the violence she suffered because of her past sexual addiction. Rather, she thinks that the whole human species — including herself — has justly earned the frightful coming of Cthulhu, which, unlike Promethea's apocalypse, is not heralded as a Revelation, but as a carnage: "They deserve his presence. I mean, look at this species. We're pretty much vermin. Never mind. He'll sort that out, once he arrives.... It's the end" (Moore and Burrows 4, 24).[2] *Neonomicon* thus appears as a sort of counterpart to the theses Moore exposed in *Promethea* and *Lost Girls*. Instead of a means to the materialization of a utopian future (*Promethea*) or to the discovery and liberation of one's real self (*Lost Girls*), sexual practice here is only the product of deranged minds (as in the case of the perverted Lovecraftian cultists) or the method to reach a tragic apocalypse where humankind will be annihilated (as in that of Brears' impregnation by the monster). Humanity and human deeds are thus here exposed at their worst. Declined in the horror genre, carnality ushers forth an appalling conclusion, where Brears is so alienated that the idea of the impending destruction of the world makes her feel "good."

In search for a clarification of this complex narrative and philosophical landscape, we can finally mention the venture Moore lately devoted a considerable part of his efforts to, i.e., the magazine *Dodgem Logic*, made in collaboration with several noteworthy contributors such as Josie Long, Kevin O'Neill, Savage Pencil, and Melinda Gebbie. The publication of *Dodgem Logic* started in late 2009 and was recently interrupted at Issue 8 (Spring 2011) due to a lack of funding. The final accomplishment of an ambitious project for a fanzine Moore had devised in 1975, when he "was young and feckless and didn't manage to put the whole thing together" ("Issue 1"), the magazine is an attempt to bring back the spirit and function of the underground magazines of the 1960s. With its irreverent attitude and outspoken political agenda, *Dodgem Logic* indeed brings to mind the mood of those years. And, just like the countercultural publications of the Sixties, it dedicates plenty of room to sex and its manifestations. A few fitting examples can be Melinda Gebbie's memoirs about the burlesque and bondage scene (see Gebbie and Jenkins, and Gebbie), Kevin O'Neill's surrealistic, mostly mute comics pages featuring openly sexual content, Dick Foreman's overview on the phenomenon of crossdressing (see Foreman), and much else. Moore's own contributions often touch upon the issue, displaying both a mischievously playful, provocative attitude and a more serious, committed tendency to theorize and instruct about sexual identity and diversity. The former can be epitomized by *Astounding Weird Penises*, a free insert included in the second issue of the magazine. Teasingly defined "the first and only comic book that Alan Moore has ever both written and drawn himself, for fairly obvious reasons" in the announcement beside the table of contents (*Dodgem Logic*, Feb.-Mar. 2010, 1), the booklet faithfully follows the style of EC science fiction comic books from the 1950s in format and layout. But the style it is drawn in is distinctively Moore's, in a more Crumbian, genuinely 1960s fashion. The legacy of underground comics is also mirrored by the story: the tale of Astro Dick, a clumsy little penis in a spacesuit who travels the galaxies in the awkward attempt to preserve order in outer space, is told with plenty of bawdy, hilarious detail and a considerable amount of crazy humor. When he moves away from pure iconoclastic *divertissement*, however, Moore takes on a more sober, committed tone, such as in the defense of counterculture — seen, among other things, as crucial in promoting sexual freedom and diversity — that he offers in "Going Underground," the opening article of the first issue of the magazine (see Moore, "Going"). It is in *Dodgem Logic*, then, that Moore's interests and commitment have recently found their clearest and most articulate exposition. It is here that the anarchic views embraced by the author since the early days of his career are most overtly spoken. Moore engages in anarchism in its purest sense, advocating a vision where the individual subject's freedom — which evolves into collective freedom, for each subject's self-determination is supposed to naturally incorporate respect for everyone else's liberty — is to be treasured as the highest value in existence: "This [...] is the face of politics in the twenty-first century. And the face of art, and probably of spirituality and everything: it is down to the individual" (Thill, "Alan Moore: Comics"). From this freedom logically stems individual engagement, which thus transforms into local action, resulting in collective, global benefit — hence the magazine's commitment to green politics and recycling, to minorities and to various social and political issues, especially the ones related to the author's own Northampton.[3]

In this broader view, sex once again becomes central. As the most personal, intimate human drive, sex can perhaps be seen as the triumph of the individual — but an individual incessantly reaching out toward sharing his/her experience with one or more others. The triumph of sex, then, is to become the triumph of anarchism, the full accomplishment of the self striving towards the fulfillment of an ideal collectivity. What is theorized in *Dodgem Logic* has found its utopian narrative realization in the finale of *Promethea*, or in the view of sex as a liberating force championed by *Lost Girls*. As K.A. Laity has appropriately reminded us of through Angela Carter, this is indeed "moral pornography." Nevertheless, Moore is perfectly aware of the possible downfalls of individual agency, of the risk of the rise of individualism in its dourest, most abject expression. Human society is often far from struggling toward the anarchist utopia of universal freedom and respect, hence the controversial depiction of this extreme perspective in *Neonomicon*. If the world, as, again, Angela Carter once wrote, is "a gigantic brothel" (21), Moore is incessant in his investigation of the lights and shadows of sex and of society, of their pleasures and pains, of their zeniths and nadirs. In this light, then, he and his writing could be epitomized by his own description of the figure (a Venus, or a goddess of pornography) etched by Felicien Rops in his *Pornokrates*, which Moore mentions in the conclusion to his *25,000 Years of Erotic Freedom* essay: "rightly unconcerned about the controversy [he's] causing, utterly unworried about the precipice [he] steps along [he] promenades along the moral tightrope of his path, [...] towards the hoped-for glow of an enlightened future" (89).

Notes

1. Moreover, it is Brears herself who, in her final dialogue with Aldo Sax, says she keeps thinking she has to find "a book of names ... a book of new names, y'know? Not dead ones" (Moore and Burrows #4, 24).

2. In Lovecraft's original tale "The Call of Cthulhu," its coming is described with these words: "The secret priests would take great Cthulhu from his tomb to revive His subjects and resume his rule of earth.... Then mankind would have become as the Great Old Ones; free and wild and beyond good and evil, with laws and morals thrown aside and all men shouting and killing and reveling in joy. Then the liberated Old Ones would teach them new ways to shout and kill and revel and enjoy themselves, and all the earth would flame with a holocaust of ecstasy and freedom" (141).

3. I am using the terms *local* and *global* even though Moore himself, as is characteristic of his tongue-in-cheek attitude, undercuts this line of reasoning by writing: "We are neither global nor local. We are lobal" (Moore, "Welcome" 1).

Selected Bibliography

Ali, Barish. "The Violence of Criticism: The Mutilation and Exhibition of History in *From Hell*." *The Journal of Popular Culture* 38.4 (2005): 605–631. Print.
Alice in Wonderland. Dirs. Clyde Geronimi, Wilfred Jackson and Hamilton Luske. Walt Disney Productions, 1951. Film.
Altevers, Nanette. "Gender Matters in *The Sadeian Woman*." *Review of Contemporary Fiction* 14.3 (Fall 1994): 18–23. Print.
Althusser, Louis. "Ideology and Ideological State Apparatuses (Notes Towards an Investigation)." *Mapping Ideology*. Ed. Slavoj Žižek. London: Verso, 1994. 100–140. Print.
Altman, Janet Gurkin. "Of Confidence and Confidants." *Epistolarity: Approaches to a Form*. Columbus: Ohio State University Press, 1982. 47–86. Print.
Amar, Akhil Reed. "Architexture." *Faculty Scholarship Series*. Paper 857 (2002). Web. 24 May 2011. <http://digitalcommons.law.yale.edu/fss_papers/857/>.
Atkinson, Doug. *The Annotated* Watchmen: *Your Complete Guide to the Classic Series*. n.p. 1995. Web. 28 November 2010. <http://files.spontaneousderivation.com/files/Annotated_Watchmen/Annotated_Watchmen.pdf >.
Babcock, Jay. "Magic Is Afoot." Interview with Alan Moore. *Arthur* 4 (May 2003). Web. 28 November 2010. <http://www.arthurmag.com/2007/05/10/1815/>.
Bachofen, J.J. *Myth, Religion and Mother Right: Selected Writings of J.J. Bachofen*. Trans. Ralph Manheim. Princeton: Princeton University Press, 1967. Print.
Barrett, Michèle. "Ideology, Politics, Hegemony: From Gramsci to Laclau and Mouffe." *Mapping Ideology*. Ed. Slavoj Žižek. New York: Verso, 1994. 235–264. Print.
Barrie, J.M. *Peter Pan, or The Boy Who Wouldn't Grow Up*. 1904. *Project Gutenberg Australia*. Feb. 2003. Web. 21 Mar. 2011. <http://gutenberg.net.au/ebooks03/0300081h.html>.
Barthes, Roland. *Mythologies*. Trans. Annette Lavers. New York: Hill and Wang, 1957/1972. Print.
Basque, Yan. "*Neonomicon* #4 — 'I feel good about it.'" *Irrelevant Comics*, 24 March 2011. Web. 17 April 2011. <http://irrelevantcomics.blogspot.com/2011/03/neonomicon-4-i-feel-good-about-it.html/>.
Bataille, Georges. *Erotism: Death & Sensuality*. Trans. Mary Dalwood. San Francisco: City Lights, 1986. Print.
Baum, L. Frank. *The Wonderful Wizard of Oz*. 1900. *Project Gutenberg*. 1 July 2008. Web. 21 Mar. 2011. <http://www.gutenberg.org/ebooks/55>.
Beggan, James K. "Reflexivity in the Pornographic Films of Candida Royalle." *Sexualities* 6 (3–4): 301–324. 2003. Print.
Benjamin, Jessica. *The Bonds of Love: Psychoanalysis, Feminism and the Problem of Domination*. New York: Pantheon Books, 1988. Print.
_____. *A Desire of One's Own: Psychoanalytic Feminism and Intersubjective Space*. Milwaukee: University of Wisconsin–Milwaukee Center for Twentieth Century Studies, 1985. Print.
_____. "Revisiting the Riddle of Sex: An Intersubjective View of Masculinity and Femininity."

Dialogues on Sexuality, Gender and Psychoanalysis. Ed. Iréne Matthis. London: Kamac. 145–172. Print.

Bentley, Jason. "Morning Becomes Eclectic." *KCRW* 7 January 2009. Web. 30 June 2011. <http://www.kcrw.com/music/programs/mb/mb090107hans_zimmer_and_jame>.

Bifo. "Alterity and Desire." *Deleuze, Guattari and the Production of the New*. Ed. Simon O'Sullivan and Stephen Zepke. New York: Continuum, 2008. 22–32. Print.

Blaine, Neil, and Hugh O'Donnell. *Media, Monarchy and Power*. Bristol: Intellect Books, 2003. Print.

Bogaert, Anthony. "Asexuality: Prevalence and Associated Factors in a National Probability Sample." *Journal of Sex Research* 41. 3 (2004): 279–88. Print.

Botting, Fred, and Scott Wilson. Introduction. *Bataille: A Critical Reader*. Ed. Fred Botting and Scott Wilson. Malden, MA: Blackwell, 1998. 1–23. Print.

Boyer, Paul. *When Time Shall Be No More: Prophecy Belief in Modern American Culture*. Cambridge: Harvard University Press, 1992. Print.

Brie, Steve. "Spandex Parables: Justice, Criminality and the Ethics of Vigilantism in Frank Miller's *Batman: The Dark Knight* and Alan Moore's *The Killing Joke*." *Literature and Ethics* (2010): 203–215. Print.

"Britain's Most Watched TV — the 1980s." Chart. *The BFI*. Broadcasters' Audience Research Board, British Film Institute, British Broadcasting Corporation and Audits of Great Britain. 29 October 2010. Web. 1 November 2010. <http://www.bfi.org.uk/features/mostwatched/1980s.html>.

Brody, Michael. "Batman: Psychic Trauma and Its Solution." *Journal of Popular Culture* 28 (1995): 171–178. Web. <http://onlinelibrary.wiley.com/doi/10.1111/j.0022-3840.1995.00171.x/abstract>.

Bronfen, Elisabeth. *Over Her Dead Body. Death, Femininity and the Aesthetic*. Manchester: Manchester University Press, 1992. Print.

Bukatman, Scott. *Matters of Gravity*. Durham: Duke University Press, 2003. Print.

Burrus, Virginia, and Catherine Keller, eds. *Toward a Theology of Eros: Transfiguring Passion at the Limits of Discipline*. New York: Fordham University Press, 2006.

Bushnell, Jack. "Transsexing Technological Man: (Re)Writing the Comic Book Male/Scientist in *Swamp Thing*." *Popular Culture Review* 11 (2000): 31–42. Print.

Butler, Judith. *Bodies That Matter: On the Discursive Limits of Sex*. London: Routledge, 1993. Print.

_____. "Critically Queer." *GLQ: A Journal of Lesbian and Gay Studies* 1.1 (1993): 17–32. Print.

Campbell, Eddie. "Interview with Eddie Campbell." By David Carroll. *Tabula Rasa* 4 (1994). Web. 30 November 2010. <http:/www.tabula-rasa.info/AusComics/EddieCampbell.html>.

Campbell, Joseph. Introduction. *Myth, Religion and Mother Right: Selected Writings of J.J. Bachofen*. By J.J. Bachofen. Trans. Ralph Manheim. Princeton: Princeton University Press, 1967. xxv–lvii. Print.

Campbell, SueEllen. "The Land and Language of Desire: Where Deep Ecology and Post-Structuralism Meet." *Ecocriticism Reader: Landmarks in Literary Ecology*. Ed. Cheryll Glotfelty and Harold Fromm. Athens: University Georgia Press, 1996. 124–36. Print.

Caputi, Jane. *The Age of Sex Crime*. Bowling Green: Bowling Green State University Press, 1987. Print.

Carney, Sean. "The Tides of History: Alan Moore's Historiographic Vision." *ImageText* 2.2 (2006). <http://www.english.ufl.edu/imagetext/archives/v2_2/carney/>.

Carroll, Lewis. *Alice's Adventures in Wonderland*. 1865. *Alice in Wonderland*. Ed. Donald J. Gray. New York: W.W. Norton, 1971. 1–99. Print.

_____. *Through the Looking-Glass and What Alice Found There*. 1871. *Alice in Wonderland*. Ed. Donald J. Gray. New York: W.W. Norton, 1971. 101–209. Print.

Carter, Angela. *The Sadeian Woman: An Exercise in Cultural History.* London: Virago, 1979. Print.
Cawelti, John G. *Mystery, Violence, and Popular Culture.* Madison: University of Wisconsin Press, 2004. Print.
Cooke, Jon B., and George Khoury. "Alan Moore Interview: The Magic of Comics." *Comic Book Artist* 1.25 (June 2003): 8–45. Print.
Crowley, Aleister, and Rose Edith Crowley. *The Book of the Law, Liber al Vel Legis.* Centennial ed. York Beach: Weiser Books, in association with Ordo Templi Orientis, 2004. Print.
Deleuze, Gilles, and Félix Guattari. *A Thousand Plateaus: Capitalism and Schizophrenia.* Trans. Brian Massumi. Minneapolis: University of Minnesota Press, 1987. Print.
Denton-Borhaug, Kelly. "A Theological Reflection of Torture and Democracy." *Dialog: A Journal of Theology* 47.3 (2008): 217–227. Print.
Derrida, Jacques. "Living on/Border Lines." *Deconstruction and Criticism.* Ed. Harold Bloom et al. New York: Continuum, 1992. 75–176. Print.
_____. "Structure, Sign and Play in the Discourse of the Human Sciences." *Writing and Difference.* Trans. Alan Bass. New York: Routledge Classics, 1978. 351–370. Print.
Despentes, Virginie. *King Kong Theory.* Trans. Stéphanie Benson. 2006. London: Serpent's Tail, 2009. Print.
Di Liddo, Annalisa. *Alan Moore: Comics as Performance, Fiction as Scalpel.* Jackson: University Mississippi Press, 2009. Print.
Doane, Mary Ann. *The Desire to Desire.* Bloomington: Indiana University Press, 1987. Print.
Dodgem Logic. Feb.–Mar. 2010. Print.
Doran, John. "Hipster Priest: A Quietus Interview with Alan Moore." *The Quietus.* 13 July 2010. Web. 29 April 2011. <http://thequietus.com/articles/04603-alan-moore-interview-unearthing-2>.
Dubose, Mike. "Holding Out for a Hero: Reaganism, Comic Book Vigilantes, and Captain America." *Journal of Popular Culture* 40 (2007): 915–935. Print.
Duenwald, Mary. "For Them, Just Saying No Is Easy." *New York Times.* Web. 9 June 2005. <http://www.nytimes.com/2005/06/09/fashion/thursdaystyles/09asexual.html>.
Earle, Rebecca. "Introduction: Letters, Writers and the Historian." *Epistolary Selves: Letters and Letter-Writers, 1600–1945.* Ed. Rebecca Earle. Brookfield, VT: Ashgate, 1999. 1–12. Print.
Ellison, Marvin M. *Erotic Justice: A Liberating Ethic of Sexuality.* Louisville: Westminster John Knox Press, 1996. Print.
Epstein, Daniel. "Heath Ledger Talks Joker." *Newsarama.* 7 November 2006. 20 June 2010. Web. <http://forum.newsarama.com/showthread.php?t=90305>.
Epstein, William H. "Fanny Hill." *John Cleland: Images of a Life.* New York: Columbia University Press, 1974. 84–107. Print.
Erhart, Julia. "Laura Mulvey Meets Catherine Tramell Meets the She-Man: Counter-History, Reclamation, and Incongruity in Lesbian, Gay and Queer Film and Media Criticism." *A Companion to Film Theory.* Ed. Toby Miller and Robert Stam. Malden, MA: Blackwell, 1999. 165–81. Print.
"Essentialism." *Key Concepts in Post-Colonial Studies.* New York: Routledge, 1998. Print.
Ferguson, Christine. "Victoria-Arcana and the Misogynistic Poetics of Resistance in Iain Sinclair's *White Chappell Scarlet Tracings* and Alan Moore's *From Hell.*" *Literature Interpretation Theory* 20 (2009): 45–64. Print.
Fisher, Mark. "Gothic Oedipus: Subjectivity and Capitalism in Christopher Nolan's *Batman Begins.*" *ImageTexT: Interdisciplinary Comics Studies* 2 (2006). Dept. of English, University of Florida. 20 June 2011. Web. <http://www.english.ufl.edu/imagetext/archives/v2_2/fisher/>.

Foreman, Dick. "Pretty As You Feel." *Dodgem Logic* Mar.–Apr. 2011: 2–7. Print.
Freud, Sigmund. *Three Essays on the Theory of Sexuality*. Trans. James Strachey. New York: Basic Books, 1962. Print.
Gaiman, Neil. "*Lost Girls* Redux." *Neil Gaiman's Journal*. 19 June 2006. Web. Accessed 10 January 2008. < http://journal.neilgaiman.com/2006/06/lost-girls-redux.html>.
Gare, Arran. "The Postmodernism of Deep Ecology, the Deep Ecology of Postmodernism, and Grand Narratives." *Beneath the Surface: Critical Essays in the Philosophy of Deep Ecology*. Ed. Eric Katz, Andrew Light, and David Rothenberg. Cambridge: MIT Press, 2000. 195–214. Print.
Gebbie, Melinda. "Oh Bondage Up Yours!" *Dodgem Logic* Oct.–Nov. 2010: 18–21. Print.
_____, and Mitch Jenkins (photographs). "Kitten, Goddess, Bitch." *Dodgem Logic* Feb.–Mar. 2010: 17–24. Print.
Gibson, Ian. "Halo Jones." *Ian Gibson*. 12 March 2009. Web. 27 October 2010. <http://ian-gibson.com/Pages/Halo.htm>.
Gieben, Bram A. "Alan Moore: Unearthed and Uncut." *Weaponizer.com*. 30 June 2011 Web. 10 April 2011. <http://www.weaponizer.co.uk/onearticle.php?category=nonfic&articleid=181javascript:void(printSpecial())>.
Gilman, Sander L. "'Who Kills Whores?' 'I Do,' Says Jack: Race and Gender in Victorian London." *Death and Representation*. Ed. Sarah Webster Goodwin and Elisabeth Bronfen. Baltimore: Johns Hopkins University Press, 1993. 263–284. Print.
Goatly, Andrew. *Washing the Brain: Metaphor and Hidden Ideology*. Philadelphia: John Benjamins, 2007. Print.
Goldman, Jonathan E. "Extraordinary People: The Superhero Genre and Celebrity Culture in *The League of Extraordinary Gentlemen*." *The Rise and Reason of Comics and Graphic Literature*. Ed. Joyce Goggin and Dan Hassler-Forest. Jefferson, NC: McFarland, 2010. 142–153. Print.
Gopalan, Nisha. "Alan Moore Still Knows the Score!" *EW.com*. Entertainment Weekly 16 July 2008. Web. 24 November 2010. <http://www.ew.com/ew/article/0,,20213004,00.html>.
Groensteen, Thierry. *The System of Comics*. 1999. Trans. Bart Beaty and Nick Nguyen. Jackson: University of Mississippi, 2007. Print.
Gubar, Susan. "Representing Pornography: Feminism, Criticism, and Depictions of Female Violation." *Critical Inquiry* 13 (Summer 1987): 712–741. Print.
Halberstam, Judith. *Skin Shows. Gothic Horror and the Technology of Monsters*. London: Duke University Press, 1995. Print.
_____. *In a Queer Time and Place: Transgender Body, Subcultural Lives*. New York: New York University Press, 2005. Print.
Hamilton, Robert. "When the Seas Are Empty, so Are the Words: Representations of the Task Force." *Framing the Falklands War: Nationhood, Culture and Identity*. Ed. James Aulich. Buckingham: Open University Press, 1992. 129–139. Print.
Haraway, Donna. *The Companion Species Manifesto: Dogs, People and Significant Otherness*. Chicago: Prickly Paradigm Press, 2003. Print.
Harvey, David. *A Brief History of Neoliberalism*. New York: Oxford University Press, 2005. Print.
Hassler-Forrest, Dan. "From Trauma Victim to Terrorist: Redefining Superheroes in Post-9/11 Hollywood." *Comics as a Nexus of Cultures*. Ed. Mark Berninger et al. Jefferson, NC: McFarland, 2010. 33–44. Print.
Hatfield, Charles. "ImageSexT: a Roundtable on *Lost Girls* (A Review and a Response)." *ImageTexT* 3.3 (2007). <http://www.english.ufl.edu/imagetext/archives/v3_3/lost_girls/hatfield.shtml>.
Heyward, Carter. *Touching Our Strength: The Erotic as Power and the Love of God*. San Francisco: Harper & Row, 1989. Print.

Ho, Elizabeth. "Postimperial Landscapes: 'Psychogeography' and Englishness in Alan Moore's Graphic Novel *From Hell: A Melodrama in Sixteen Parts*." *Cultural Critique* 63 (2006): 99–121. Print.
Holland, Eugene W. *Deleuze and Guattari's* Anti-Oedipus: *Introduction to Schizoanalysis*. New York: Routledge, 1999. Print.
Holquist, Michael. "What Is a Boojum? Nonsense and Modernism." *Alice in Wonderland*. Ed. Donald J. Gray. New York: W.W. Norton, 1971. 402–418. Print.
Horowitz, Josh. "*Dark Knight* Opening Scenes Reveal 'Radical' New Joker." *MTVNews* 3 Dec 2007. Web. 20 June 20011. <http://www.mtv.com/news/articles/1575671/dark-knight-opening-scenes-reveal-radical-new-joker.jhtml>.
How, James. "*2000 AD* and Hollywood: The Special Relationship Between a British Comic and American Film." *Comics and Culture: Analytical and Theoretical Approaches to Comics*. Ed. Anne Magnussen and Hans-Christian Christiansen. Copenhagen: Museum Tusculanum Press, 2000. 225–42. Print.
Hurley, Kelly. *The Gothic Body. Sexuality, Materialism and Degeneration at the Fin de Siècle*. New York: Cambridge University Press, 1996. Print.
Hutcheon, Linda. *A Poetics of Postmodernism: History, Theory, Fiction*. New York, NY, USA: Routledge, 1988. Print.
_____. *The Politics of Postmodernism*. New York: Routledge, 1989. Print.
_____. *A Theory of Adaptation*. New York: Routledge, 2006. Print.
Hutton, Ronald. *The Triumph of the Moon: A History of Modern Pagan Witchcraft*. Oxford: Oxford University Press, 1999. Print.
"Issue 1." Dodgem Logic Video Archive. *Dodgemlogic.com*, 2009. Web. 11 April 2011. <http://www.dodgemlogic.com/videoarchive>.
Itzin, Catherine. *Asexuality Visibility and Education Network*. 2005. Web. <http://www.asexuality.org/home/overview.html. Accessed 28 August 2010.>
_____. "Stages for Revolution." *The Guardian*. 31 July 1981: 10. *The Guardian and Observer Digital Archive*. Web. 27 October 2010.
Johnson, Freya. "Holy Homosexuality Batman! Camp and Corporate Capitalism In *Batman Forever*." *Bad Subjects* 23 (1995). Web. <http://www.development.umd.edu/Diversity/Specific/Sexual_Orientation/Reading/Essays/camp-batman>.
Jones, Matthew T. "Reflexivity in Comic Art." *International Journal of Comic Art* 7 (2005 Spring/Summer): 270–286. Print.
Jung, C.G. *Collected Works v. 10. Civilization in Transition*. 2d ed. New York: Bollingen, 1970. Print.
Katz, Eric, Andrew Light, and David Rothenberg. "Introduction." *Beneath the Surface: Critical Essays in the Philosophy of Deep Ecology*. Ed. Eric Katz, Andrew Light, and David Rothenberg. Cambridge: MIT Press, 2000. ix–xxiv. Print.
Keller, James R. *V for Vendetta as Cultural Pastiche*. Jefferson, NC: McFarland, 2008. Print.
Khoury, George. *The Extraordinary Works of Alan Moore*. Raleigh: TwoMorrows, 2003. Print.
_____. *The Extraordinary Works of Alan Moore: Indispensible Edition*. Raleigh: TwoMorrows, 2008. Print.
Kidner, David W. *Nature and Psyche: Radical Environmentalism and the Politics of Subjectivity*. Albany: SUNY Press, 2001. Print.
Kincaid, James R. *Child-Loving: The Erotic Child and Victorian Culture*. New York: Routledge, 1992. Print.
_____. "Producing Erotic Children." *Curiouser: On the Queerness of Children*. Ed. Bruhm, Steven and Natasha Hurley. Minneapolis: University of Minnesota Press, 2004. Print.
Klock, Geoff. *How to Read Superhero Comics and Why*. New York: Continuum, 2002. Print.
Kowalik, Jessica. "Miller Misunderstood: Rethinking the Politics of *The Dark Knight*." *International Journal of Comic Art* 12 (2010): 388–400. Print.

Kraemer, Christine Hoff, and J. Lawton Winslade. "The Magic Circus of the Mind: Alan Moore's *Promethea* and the Transformation of Consciousness through Comics." *Graven Images: Religion in Comic Books and Graphic Novels*. Ed. A. David Lewis and Christine Hoff Kraemer. New York: Continuum, 2010. 274–91. Print.

Kress, Gunther R., and Theo Leeuwen. *Reading Images: The Grammar of Visual Design*. 1996. New York: Routledge, 2006. Print.

Kristeva, Julia. "Bataille, Experience and Practice." *On Bataille: Critical Essays*. Ed. Leslie Anne Boldt-Irons. Albany: SUNY Press, 1995. 237–64. Print.

Krueger, Rex, and Katherine Shaeffer. "Introduction: Alan Moore and Adaptation." *ImageTexT: Interdisciplinary Comics Studies* 5 (2011). Dept. of English, University of Florida. 20 June 2011. Web. <http://www.english.ufl.edu/imagetext/archives/v5_4/introduction.shtml/>.

Kukkonen, Karin. "Beyond Language: Metaphor and Metonymy in Comics Storytelling." *English Language Notes* 46 (2008): 89–98. Print.

Kushner, Tony. *Angels in America: Perestroika*. New York: Theater Commissions, 1993. Print.

Lakoff, George, and Mark Johnson. *Metaphors We Live By*. Chicago: University of Chicago Press, 1980. Print.

Landry, Donna. "Love Me, Love My Turkey Book: Letters and Turkish Travelogues in Early Modern England." *Epistolary Histories: Letters, Fiction, Culture*. Ed. Amanda Gilroy and W.M. Verhoeven. Charlottesville: University Press of Virginia, 2000. 51–73. Print.

Legler, Gretchen. "Toward a Postmodern Pastoral: The Erotic Landscape in the Work of Gretel Ehrlich." *The Isle Reader: Ecocriticism, 1993–2003*. Ed. Michael P. Branch and Scott Slovic. Athens: University Georgia Press, 2003. 22–32. Print.

Leitch, Thomas. "Adaptation Studies at a Crossroads." *Adaptation* 1.1 (2008): 63–77. Web. 18 March 2009. <http://daptation.oxfordjournals.org/content/1/1/63.full>.

Lewis, Charles. "Indifferent and Proud: Asexuality Is Emerging as a Fourth Orientation." *National Post* 9 February 2008. Print.

Lewis, James R. "The Pagan Explosion: An Overview of Select Census and Survey Data." *The New Generation Witches*. Ed. Hannah E. Johnston and Peg Aloi. Aldershot: Ashgate, 2007. 13–24. Print.

Lioi, Anthony. "The Radiant City: New York as Ecotopia in *Promethea*, Book V." *Comics and the City: Urban Space in Print, Picture and Sequence*. Ed. Jörn Ahrens and Arno Meteling. New York: Continuum, 2010. 150–62. Print.

Lorde, Audre. "Uses of the Erotic: The Erotic as Power." *Sister Outsider: Essays and Speeches by Audre Lorde*. Trumansburg, NY: Crossing Press, 1984. 53–9. Print.

Lovecraft, H.P. "The Call of Cthulhu." *The Dunwich Horror and Others*. 1963. Sauk City, WI: Arkham House, 1984. 125–154. Print.

Marchetti, Gina. *Romance and the "Yellow Peril": Race, Sex, and Discursive Strategies in Hollywood Fiction*. Berkeley: University of California Press, 1993. Print.

McCloud, Scott. *Understanding Comics: The Invisible Art*. New York: HarperPerennial, 1994. Print.

McGowan, Todd. "The Exceptional Darkness of *The Dark Knight*." *JumpCut* 51 (2009). Web. <http://www.ejumpcut.org/archive/jc51.2009/darkKnightKant/text.html>.

Mitchell, David, and Sharon Snyder. "Narrative Prosthesis and the Materiality of Metaphor." *The Disability Studies Reader*. Ed. Lennard J. Davis. New York: Routledge, 2006. 205–216. Print.

Modleski, Tania. *Loving with a Vengeance: Mass-Produced Fantasies for Women*. 1982. New York: Routledge, 2008. Print.

Moore, Alan. *Alan Moore's Awesome Universe Handbook*. Fullerton, CA: Awesome Entertainment, April 1999. Print.

———. "The Ballad of Halo Jones." Art by Ian Gibson. *2000 AD* 376–385 (1984); 405–415 (1985); 451–466 (1986). London: IPC Magazines. N.pag. Print.

Selected Bibliography

_____. *DC Universe: The Stories of Alan Moore*. New York: DC Comics, 2006. Print.
_____. *From Hell: Being a Melodrama in Sixteen Parts*. Art by Eddie Campbell. Additional art by Pete Mullins. Marietta, GA: Top Shelf Productions, 1989/2009. Print.
_____. *Glory*, #0–2. Fullerton, CA: Awesome Entertainment, December 2001–January 2002. Print.
_____. "Going Underground." *Dodgem Logic* Nov. 2009: 2–7. Print.
_____. Interview with Barry Kavenaugh. "The Alan Moore Interview." *Blather.net*. 14 April 2008. Web. 17 October 2000.
_____. Interview by K. A. Laity. 19 March 2009. Telephone via Skype.
_____. Interview by Stewart Lee. *Chain Reaction*. BBC Radio 4. Jonah Weiland, ed. "Alan Moore 'Chain Reaction' Interview Transcript." *Comic Book Resources*. N.p., 27 January 2005. Web. 24 November 2010. <http://www.comicbookresources.com/?page=article&id=4533>.
_____. Interview with DeZ Vylenz. *The Mindscape of Alan Moore*. Shadowsnake Films, 2003. Film.
_____. Introduction. *Saga of the Swamp Thing*. New York: DC Comics, 1987. v–xi. Print.
_____. *The League of Extraordinary Gentlemen: Black Dossier*. Art by Kevin O'Neil. New York: America's Best Comics, September 2002–November 2003. Print.
_____. *The League of Extraordinary Gentlemen Century: 1910*. Art by Kevin O'Neill. Marietta, GA: Top Shelf Productions, 2009. Print.
_____. *League of Extraordinary Gentlemen 1 & 2*. Art by Kevin O'Neill. La Jolla, CA: America's Best Comics, 2003. Print.
_____. *Lost Girls*. Art by Melinda Gebbie. Letters by Todd Klein. Marietta, GA: Top Shelf Productions: 2009 (2006). Print.
Moore, Alan, writer. *The Mirror of Love*. Art by José Villarrubia. Atlanta: Top Shelf Productions, 2004.
_____. *Neonomicon*. Art by Jacen Burrows Rantoul, IL: Avatar Comics, 2011. Print.
_____. *Promethea*. Art by J.H. Williams. v. 1. Reprints issues #1–6. La Jolla, CA: America's Best Comics, 2000. Print.
_____. *Promethea* v. 2. Reprints issues #7–12. La Jolla, CA: America's Best Comics, 2001. Print.
_____. *Promethea* v. 3. Reprints issues #13–18. La Jolla, CA: America's Best Comics, 2002. Print.
_____. *Promethea* v. 4. Reprints issues #19–25. La Jolla, CA: America's Best Comics, 2003. Print.
_____. *Promethea* v. 5. Reprints issues #26–32. La Jolla, CA: America's Best Comics, 2005. Print.
_____. *Saga of the Swamp Thing: Book One*. Art by Stephen Bissette, John Totleben, Dan Day, and Rick Veitch. Color by Tatjana Wood. Letters by John Costanza and Todd Klein. Vol. 1. New York: Vertigo-DC Comics, 2009. Print.
_____. *Swamp Thing: The Curse*. Art by Stephen Bissette, John Totleben, Rick Veitch, Alfredo Alcala, and Stan Woch. Color by Tatjana Wood. Letters by John Costanza. Vol. 3. New York: Vertigo-DC Comics, 2000. Print.
_____. *Swamp Thing: Earth to Earth*. Art by Rick Veitch, John Totleben, and Alfredo Alcala. Color by Tatjana Wood. Letters by John Costanza. Vol. 5. New York: Vertigo-DC Comics, 2002. Print.
_____. *Swamp Thing: Love and Death*. Art by Stephen Bissette, John Totleben, Shawn McManus, Rick Veitch, Alfredo Alcala, and Ron Randall. Color by Tatjana Wood. Letters by John Costanza. Vol. 2. New York: Vertigo-DC Comics, 1990. Print.
_____. *Swamp Thing: A Murder of Crows*. Art by Stephen Bissette, John Totleben, Rick Veitch, Alfredo Alcala, Ron Randall, and Stan Woch. Color by Tatjana Wood. Letters by John Costanza. Vol. 4. New York: Vertigo-DC Comics, 2001. Print.

_____. *Swamp Thing: Reunion.* Art by Rick Veitch, John Totleben, Alfredo Alcala, Stephen Bissette, and Tom Yeates. Color by Tatjana Wood. Letters by John Costanza. Vol. 6. New York: Vertigo-DC Comics, 2003. Print.
_____. "Tharg the Mighty." Art and letters by Ian Gibson. *2000 AD* 500 (1986). London: IPC Magazines. N.pag. Print.
_____. *Top Ten.* Art by Gene Ha. La Jolla, CA: America's Best Comics, 2003. Print.
_____. *25,000 Years of Erotic Freedom.* New York: Abrams, 2009. Print.
_____. *Unearthing.* Photographs by Mitch Jenkins. Perf. Crook & Flail: Adam Drucker, Andrew Broder. London: Lex, 2010. LP/CD.
_____. *V for Vendetta.* Art by David Lloyd. New York: Vertigo-DC Comics, 1990. Print.
_____. *Watchmen.* Illustrated by Dave Gibbons. New York: DC Comics, 1986. Print.
_____. "Welcome to Dodgem Logic." *Dodgem Logic* Nov. 2009: 1. Print.
Moore, Alan, and Brian Bolland. *The Killing Joke: The Deluxe Edition.* New York: DC Comics, 2008. Print.
Moore, Alan, and Ian Gibson. *The Ballad of Halo Jones: Book 1.* London: Titan, 1986. Print.
Morag, Raya. *Defeated Masculinity: Post-Traumatic Cinema in the Aftermath of War.* New York: P.I.E. Peter Lang, 2009. Print.
Murray, Noel. "Lost Girls." *AV Club.* 20 September 2006. Web. 20 June 2011. <http://www.avclub.com/articles/alan-moore-melinda-gebbie-lost-girls,3792>.
Naess, Arne. *Ecology, Community, and Lifestyle.* Trans. David Rothenberg. Cambridge: Cambridge University Press, 1989. Print.
Nancy, Jean-Luc. *The Birth to Presence.* Trans. Brian Holmes. Stanford: Stanford University Press, 1993. Print.
_____. *The Inoperative Community.* Ed. Peter Connor. Trans. Peter Connor. Minneapolis: University of Minnesota Press, 1991. Print.
_____. "Love and Community: A Round-Table Discussion with Jean-Luc Nancy, Avital Ronell and Wolfgang Schirmacher." Interview. *Jean-Luc Nancy-Biography.* The European Graduate School, Aug. 2001. Web. 25 May 2011. <http://www.egs.edu/faculty/jean-luc-nancy/articles/love-and-community/>.
Noble, David. *Death of a Nation: American Culture and the End of Exceptionalism.* Minneapolis: University of Minnesota Press, 2002. Print.
Nolan, Christopher, dir. *Batman Begins.* Warner Bros., 2005. Film.
_____, dir. *The Dark Knight.* Warner Bros., 2008. Film.
Olechnowicz, Andrzej. *The Monarchy and the British Nation 1780 to the Present.* Cambridge: Cambridge University Press, 2007. Print.
Paik, Peter Y. *From Utopia to Apocalypse: Science Fiction and the Politics of Catastrophe.* London: University of Minnesota Press, 2010. Print.
Parkin, Lance. *Alan Moore.* Harpenden: Pocket Essentials, 2009. Print.
Peters, Jeffries. "Alan Moore." *British Science Fiction and Fantasy Writers Since 1960 (Dictionary of Literary Biography, Volume 261).* Detroit: Gale, 2002. Print.
Pitzl-Waters, Jason. "The Importance of Alan Moore." *The Wild Hunt* 1 March 2009. Web. 28 November 2010. <http://wildhunt.org/blog/2009/03/the-importance-of-alan-moore.html>.
_____. "Parsing the Pew Numbers." *The Wild Hunt* 26 February 2008. Web. 28 November 2010. <http://wildhunt.org/blog/2008/02/parsing-pew-numbers.html>.
Prause, Nicole, and Cynthia Graham. "Asexuality: Classification and Characterization." *Archives of Sexual Behavior* 36, 3 (2007): 341–356. Print.
Priest, Stephen. *Merleau-Ponty.* New York: Psychology Press, 1998. Print.
Pugh, David. Cover Image. *2000 AD* 461 (1986). London: IPC Magazines. N.pag. Print.
Pynchon, Thomas. *Gravity's Rainbow.* New York: Viking, 1973. Print.
Quiring, Björn. "'A Fiction That We Must Inhabit'—Sense Production in Urban Spaces according to Alan Moore and Eddie Campbell's *From Hell.*" *Comics and the City: Urban*

Space in Print, Picture and Sequence. Ed. Jörn Ahrens and Arno Meteling. New York: Continuum, 2010. 199–213. Print.
Recchia, Edward. "Through a Shower Curtain Darkly: Reflexivity as a Dramatic Component of *Psycho*." *Literature Film Quarterly* 19.4 (1991): 258–266. Print.
Regis, Pamela. *A Natural History of the Romance Novel*. Philadelphia: University of Pennsylvania Press, 2007. Print.
Reynolds, James. "'Kill Me Sentiment': *V for Vendetta* and Comic-to-Film Adaptation." *Journal of Adaptation and Film Performance* 2 (2009): 121–136. Print.
Ricoeur, Paul. *The Rule of Metaphor: Multi-Disciplinary Studies of the Creation of Meaning in Language*. Trans. Robert Czerny. Toronto: University of Toronto Press, 1975. Print.
Robinson, Tasha. "Alan Moore." *AV Club: The Onion* 24 October 2001. Web. 28 November 2010. <http://www.avclub.com/articles/alan-moore,13740/>.
Rodowick, D.N. *The Difficulty of Difference*. New York: Routledge, 1991. Print.
Rose, Steve. "An Extraordinary Gentleman." *Guardian* 16 March 2009. Web. Accessed 16 March 2009. <http://www.guardian.co.uk/books/2009/mar/16/alan-moore-watchmen-lost-girls>.
Rosen, Elizabeth. "Sentient Vegetable Claims End Is Near: The Graphic Novels of Alan Moore." *Apocalyptic Transformation: Apocalypse and the Postmodern Imagination*. Lanham, MD: Lexington, 2008. 1–44. Print.
Russ, Joanna. *Magic Mommas, Trembling Sisters, Puritans & Perverts: Feminist Essays*. Trumansburg NY: Crossing Press, 1985. Print.
Sabor, Peter. "Introduction." *Memoirs of a Woman of Pleasure: Unexpurgated Text* by John Cleland. Ed. Peter Sabor. New York: Oxford University Press, 2008. vii–xxvi. Print.
Sarchett, Barry. "The Joke(r) Is on Us: The End of Popular Cultural Studies." *Arizona Quarterly* 52 (1996): 71–97. Print.
Sartre, Jean-Paul. "Consciousness and the Other." *The Philosophy of Jean-Paul Sartre*. Ed. Robert Denoon Cumming. New York: Random House, 1965. Print.
Saussure, Ferdinand de. "Nature of the Linguistic Sign." *The Critical Tradition: Classic Texts and Contemporary Trends*. Ed. David H. Richter. Boston: Bedford Books, 1998. 832–835. Print.
Schechner, Richard. *The Future of Ritual: Writings on Culture and Performance*. 1993. London: Routledge, 1995. Print.
Scherrer, Kristin. "Coming to an Asexual Identity: Negotiating Identity, Negotiating Desire." *Sexualities* 11 (2008): 621–642. Print.
Schrag, Calvin O. "The Grammar of Transcendence." *Philosophy of Religion For a New Century: Essays in Honor of Eugene Thomas Long*. Ed. Jeremiah Hackett and Jerald Wallulis. Dordrecht, Netherlands: Klewer Academic, 2004. 25–36. Print.
Serith, Ceisiwr. "The Sources of the Charge of the Goddess." 2003. Web. 28 November 2010. <http://www.ceisiwrserith.com/wicca/charge.htm>.
Simone, Gail. *Women in Refrigerators*. Web. 23 Nov. 2010. <http://www.unheardtaunts.com/wir/index.html>.
Sinclair, Iain, ed. *London: City of Disappearances. Myths and Memories Retrieved*. London: Penguin, 2006. Print.
Singer, Marc. "Unwrapping the Birth Caul." *Alan Moore: Portrait of an Extraordinary Gentleman*. Leigh-on-sea: Abiogenesis Press, 2003. 41–46. Print.
Sontag, Susan. *Styles of Radical Will*. 1969. New York: Anchor Books, 1991.
Stam, Robert. "Beyond Fidelity: The Dialogics of Adaptation." *Film Adaptation*. Ed. James Naremore. New Brunswick, NJ: Rutgers University Press, 2000. 54–76. Print.
_____. *Reflexivity in Film and Literature: From Don Quixote to Jean-Luc Godard*. Ann Arbor: UMI Research Press, 1985. Print.
Starhawk. *The Spiral Dance: A Rebirth of the Ancient Religion of the Great Goddess*. 20th Anniversary Edition, Revised and Updated. New York: HarperCollins, 1999. Print.

Stone, Brad. "Alan Moore Interview." *Comic Book Resources* 22 October 2001. Web. 30 June 2011. <http://www.comicbookresources.com/?page=article&id=511>.

Strmiska, Michael F., ed. Introduction. *Modern Paganism in World Cultures: Comparative Perspectives*. Santa Barbara, CA: ABC-CLIO, 2005. 1–53. Print.

Suleiman, Susan Rubin. "Transgression and the Avant-Garde: Bataille's *Histoire de l'oeil*." *On Bataille: Critical Essays*. Ed. Leslie Anne Boldt-Irons. Albany: SUNY Press, 1995. 313–333. Print.

Theweleit, Klaus. *Male Fantasies. Volume 1. Women, Floods, Bodies, History*. Foreword by Barbara Ehrenreich. Minneapolis: University of Minnesota Press, 1987. Print.

Thill, Scott. "Alan Moore: Comics Won't Save You, But *Dodgem Logic* Might." *Wired.com*. 31 Dec. 2009. Web. 16 April 2010. <http://www.wired.com/underwire/2009/12/alan-moore-dodgem-logic/all/1>.

———. "Alan Moore Gets Psychogeographical with *Unearthing*." *Wired.com*, 9 Aug. 2010. Web. 25 August 2010. <http://www.wired.com/underwire/2010/08/alan-moore/all/1>

Tonnac, Jean-François de. *La Révolution asexuelle*. Paris: Albin Michel, 2006. Print.

Turner, Victor. *From Ritual to Theatre: The Human Seriousness of Play*. New York: PAJ Publications, 1982. Print.

Tyree, J. M. "On Frivolity and Horror in 2008's Summer Superhero Movies: *The Dark Knight, The Incredible Hulk*, and *Iron Man*." *Film Quarterly* 62 (2009): 28–34. Print.

Urban, Hugh B. *Magia Sexualis: Sex, Magic, and Liberation in Modern Western Esotericism*. Berkeley: University of California Press, 2006. Print.

Uriccho, William. "The Batman's Gotham City: Story, Ideology, Performance in Comics and the City." *Comics and the City*. Ed. Jorn Ahrens et al. New York: Continuum. 119–132. Print.

Valiente, Doreen. *Charge of the Goddess: The Mother of Modern Witchcraft*. Brighton: Hexagon Hoopix, 2000. Print.

———. *The Rebirth of Witchcraft*. Custer, WA: Phoenix, 1989. Print.

Van Ness, Sara J. Watchmen *as Literature*. Jefferson, NC: McFarland, 2010. Print.

V for Vendetta. Dir. James McTeigue. Perf. Natalie Portman and Hugo Weaving. Warner Bros., 2006. Film.

Waddell, James. *Erotic Perception: Philosophical Portraits*. Lanham, MD: University Press of America, 1997. Print.

Walkowitz, Judith. "Narratives of Sexual Danger." *Jack the Ripper. Media, Culture, History*. Ed. Alexandra Warwick and Martin Willis. Manchester: Manchester University Press, 2007. 179–196. Print.

Waugh, Patricia. *Metafiction: The Theory and Practice of Self-Conscious Fiction*. New York: Methuen, 1984. Print.

Wegner, Phillip. "Alan Moore, 'Secondary Literacy,' and the Modernism of the Graphic Novel." *ImageTexT: Interdisciplinary Comics Studies* 5 (2010). Dept. of English, University of Florida. 20 Jun 2011. Web. <http://www.english.ufl.edu/imagetext/archives/v5_3/wegner/>.

White, Michael. "Batman Score. *Frost/ Nixon*, Concert Tour Keep Hans Zimmer Busy." *Bloomberg* 31 March 2008. Web. 20 June 2011. <http://www.bloomberg.com/apps/news?pid=newsarchive&sid=awU13G3Od_0c>.

Williams, Linda. *The Erotic Thriller in Contemporary Cinema*. Bloomington: Indiana University Press, 2005. Print.

Wolk, Douglas. *Reading Comics*. Cambridge: Da Capo Press, 2007. Print.

About the Contributors

Zoë **Brigley-Thompson** is a poet and lecturer in English literature and creative writing at the University of Northampton in England. Her research interests include preventing violence against women and analyzing contemporary literature. She edited with Sorcha Gunne the volume *Feminism Literature and Rape Narratives* (2010).

Matthew **Candelaria** (Ph.D., University of Kansas) is a writer for a search engine optimization company, writing blogs, pages, and articles on medical and legal topics. His scholarly interests include biopoetics (evolutionary aesthetics), vermin, and science fiction. He has over a dozen scholarly publications, including *Reading Science Fiction* (2009), coedited with James Gunn and Marleen Barr.

Todd A. **Comer** (Ph.D., Michigan State University) is an associate professor of English at Defiance College. He has published essays on Joel and Ethan Coen, Samuel R. Delany and Flann O'Brien in such journals as *SubStance*, the *Journal of Narrative Theory*, and the *Journal of Modern Literature*. He contributed a recent chapter to *Ruminations, Peregrinations, and Regenerations: A Critical Approach to Doctor Who*, and is writing *Mourning, and the Day After: Contemporary Fiction and Film*.

Nico **Dicecco** is a Ph.D. candidate in the English program at Simon Fraser University. He earned his M.A. degree from McMaster University's Critical Theory and Cultural Studies program with a project that examined the convergence of adaptation theory and the figure of the queer child. His research interests include play theory, adaptation studies, and performativity.

Annalisa **Di Liddo** (Ph.D., *Università degli Studi di Milano*) is an English-to-Italian literary translator (among her translations are books by Angela Carter, Arthur Machen, and Doris Lessing). She published essays on Angela Carter (*Cityscapes: Islands of the Self*, 2007), Art Spiegelman (*Rappresentare la Shoah*, 2005), and Alan Moore (*Londra tra memoria letteraria e modernità*, 2006, and *A Comics Studies Reader*, 2008) and is the author of *Alan Moore: Comics as Performance, Fiction as Scalpel* (2009).

Kate **Flynn** is a Ph.D. candidate in literary studies at the University of Worcester with research interests in children's literature and media, comics for girls, and intersectional feminism. Her dissertation focuses on changing constructions of the fat child in *Jackie* magazine and British juvenile fiction between 1960 and 2010.

Brian **Johnson** is an associate professor at Carleton University where he teaches courses in literary and cultural theory. Recent publications include essays on ecology and literature, northern gothic nationalism, Canadian detective fiction, and Mordecai Richler's James Bond parody, *Cocksure*. He is working on a book-length study of libidinal economy in the work of Robertson Davies.

About the Contributors

Orion Ussner **Kidder** (Ph.D., University of Alberta) has pursued research in comics as both imagetext and objects of popular culture. His areas of interest include science fiction and posthumanism, film and film theory, and drama. He has published in *The Journal of the Fantastic in the Arts* and *The International Journal of Comics Art*.

Christine Hoff **Kraemer** (Ph.D., Boston University) is chair of the Nature, Deity, and Inspiration department at Cherry Hill Seminary and coeditor of the collection *Graven Images: Religion in Comic Books and Graphic Novels* (Continuum, 2010) with A. David Lewis. Her research interests include contemporary Paganism, sexuality, literature and popular culture.

K. A. **Laity** (Ph.D.., University of Connecticut) is an associate professor of English and coordinator of the Women's and Gender Studies Program at the College of Saint Rose as well as a fiction writer and weekly columnist for BitchBuzz.com, the global women's lifestyle network. She has delivered papers and published essays on comics and Alan Moore, medieval literature, film, creative writing, gender studies, and horror.

Karl **Martin** (Ph.D., University of Minnesota) has taught at Northwest Nazarene University, Arizona State University West, and Point Loma Nazarene University. His teaching and research interests include 20th century American literature, American exceptionalism, American religious narratives, American evangelicalism, and popular culture.

Mervi **Miettinen** is a Ph.D. candidate at the University of Tampere in Finland. Her dissertation focuses on superhero comics and their political and ideological dimensions, especially in connection to American geopolitical identity. She spent a year as a Fulbright scholar in the U.S., and is currently finishing her licentiate thesis in Tampere.

Paul **Petrovic** is a Ph.D. candidate in American film and literature at Northern Illinois University. His work is published or forthcoming in *Studies in American Naturalism, Extrapolation, Black Ball: A Negro Leagues Journal*, and *ImageText: Interdisciplinary Comics Studies*. Other interests include the representation of gender and sexuality in film and graphic narratives, as well as the intersections between capitalism and national trauma in American literature and contemporary Asian cinema.

Joseph Michael **Sommers** (Ph.D., University of Kansas) is an assistant professor of English at Central Michigan University, where he teaches courses in children's and young adult literature as well as modern and contemporary literature, visual narratives, and critical theory. He has written essays on topics including the culture of children in 19th century lady's books, the maturation of Marvel Comics' characters post–9/11, and *Twilight*.

Evan **Torner** is a Ph.D. candidate in German studies and film studies at the University of Massachusetts, Amherst. His dissertation is titled *The Race-Time Continuum: Race Projection in DEFA Genre Cinema*. His recent publications include "Civilization's Endless Shadow: Time of the Wolf" in *A Companion to Michael Haneke* and "Transnational System Schlock: The Case of Uwe Boll" published online at *kunsttexte.de*.

Lloyd Isaac **Vayo** (Ph.D., Bowling Green State University) is an instructor of arts and humanities at Defiance College. His research focuses on sound studies and 9/11, including attention to the use of voice recordings of the hijackers in popular media, as well as the ways in which such usage endows those voices with a presence-in-absence.

Index

Abby Arcane Cable (character) 17–18, 21, 23–25, 27–28, 30–39
abstinence 114
Adam Strange (character) 37–38
Adam Susan (character) 102–104
Adrian Veidt *see* Ozymandias (character)
agency 19, 35, 56, 78, 100–101, 104–107, 109–110, 116, 118, 122, 181, 205
A.I.D.S. 119, 123
Alan Moore: Storyteller 3
Allan Quatermain (character) 112–113, 118, 186, 191
Aldo Sax (character) 116, 206
Alec Holland (character) 16, 19, 24–25, 29; *see also* Swamp Thing (character); *Swamp Thing*
Alfred Pennyworth (character) 47, 50
Alice (character) 6, 78, 130, 132–134; *see also* Carroll, Lewis
Alice Fairchild (character) 78, 84–86, 100, 125–134, 141–147, 186, 200; *see also Lost Girls*; Moore, Alan
Alice's Adventures in Wonderland (film) 127
Alice's Adventures in Wonderland (novel) 2, 125–127, 132, 135, 200; *see also* Carroll, Lewis
alienation 26–27, 104–105
Allana (character) 37–38
Althaus-Reid, Marcella 154; *The Queer God* 154; *Toward a Theology of Eros* 154
Altman, Janet Gurkin 194, 199; *Epistolarity: Approaches to a Form* 194
America's Best Comics 184
Anderson, Benedict 66
Angel Passage 152
Angels in America 175
Anna (character) 180–182
Annie Chapman (character) 79, 88, 95, 99
Annie Crook (character) 79, 85, 88
anti-authoritarian 104
Antoine Arcane (character) 23, 31–34
Armageddon (film) 117
Aronofsky, Darren 117; *Black Swan* 117
asexuality 10, 111–112, 114–123

Astounding Weird Penises 204
Astro Dick (character) 205
Austria 83

Bachofen, Johann Jakob 77, 79–82
Bakhtin, Mikhail Mikhailovich 51
The Ballad of Halo Jones 9, 52–64
Balthasar (character) 119
Barbara Shelley (character) 159–161, 172, 180–182, 186
Barnes, Barry 50; *see also* dualism
Barrett, Michèle 89
Barrie, J.M. 6, 125, 200, 203
Barthes, Roland 89, 91, 98
Bataille, Georges 17–18, 22–25
Batman (character) 7, 40–45, 47–50, 115, 184; *see also* Miller, Frank; Moore, Alan; Nolan, Christopher
Batman (comic) 7, 48; Gotham City 25–26, 35–36, 38, 40, 43–44, 47, 49
Batman (film) 50
Batman Begins 41, 44, 46–48, 50; *see also* Nolan, Christopher
Batman: The Dark Knight Returns 1, 50; *see also* Miller, Frank
Batwoman (comic) 164
Baum, Lyman Frank 125, 200
Bay, Michael 117; *Armageddon* (film) 117
Beardsley 141
Beauvoir, Simone de 141
Being 150, 153–154, 156–157, 159–161
Benjamin, Jessica 76–80, 83–87
Bill Woolcott (character) 155, 164–173, 175, 182–187
bisexuality 111, 115–116, 118–119, 121, 123, 154, 165, 174, 186–187
Bissette, Stephen 21, 141; *Taboo* 141
Bifo 112
"The Birth Caul" 79
The Bitter Tea of General Yen 62
Black Freighter (comic) 72
Black Swan 117
Blaine, Neil 61
Blake, William 81–82, 152, 162; *Ghost of a*

219

Flea 82; *The Marriage of Heaven and Hell* 152
Blank (character) 120
Bloor, David 50; *see also* dualism
Bluestone, George 124; *Novels into Film* 124
Bogaert, Anthony 208
Bolland, Brian 45, 47, 51; *see also The Killing Joke*
Boudicca (character) 81
bourgeois 66–67, 73–74
Boys Don't Cry (film) 185
Bradbury, Ray 60; *Fahrenheit 451* 60
Brady, Ian 82
Brie, Steve 43
Brinna (character) 53–54, 59–60
British Task Force 61
Buddhism 151, 157
Bunny (character) 85
Burrows, Jacen 202
Burrus, Virginia 155–156
Burton, Tim 50
Bush, George W. 168
Butler, Judith 167, 170–171
Byrne, John 7

"The Call of Cthulhu" 206
Campbell, Eddie 79–82, 88, 91–92, 95, 191, 203; *see also From Hell*; Moore, Alan
Campbell, Joseph 77
capitalism 19, 65–66, 70, 72–73, 77
Capra, Frank 62; *The Bitter Tea of General Yen* 62
Captain Clegg 195, 197–198, 200
Captain Metropolis (character) 68
Captain Nemo (character) 118, 121, 191
Caputi, Jane 90, 93–94
Carl (character) 157, 174–175
Carroll, Lewis 85, 125, 127, 130, 132–134, 200; *Alice's Adventures in Wonderland* (novel) 2, 125–127, 132, 135, 200; *Through the Looking-Glass* 125–126, 129, 132–135
Carter, Angela 27, 138–143, 146, 149, 205; *The Sadeian Woman* 138
Cartesian: humanism 17, 22; objectivity 20; philosophy 20; post–Cartesian 17, 23
Casablanca 58
Catholicism 114, 174
celibacy 114–115, 119, 121
Cervantes 181; *Don Quixote* 181
Charge of the Goddess 153
Charles, Prince of Wales 61
Charlton Sennet (character) 180–182; *Faerie Romance* 180
Chaucer, Geoffrey 1, 6

Chokhmah 160
chronotope 51
Cixous, Hélène 20; *see also* feminism; French
Clara Pandy 58, 60
Clarke, Arthur C. 5, 8
class 53, 59–61, 67–68, 89, 138, 149; capitalist 66, 73; middle 55, 142, 144; upper 92; working 63, 80, 144
Cleland, John 11, 189, 191–193, 195–199
the Cold War 73
The Comedian (character) 65, 68–71, 73–74
Comic-Con 111
Constantine (film) 118–119, 121; *see also* Lawrence, Francis
Cooper, James Fenimore 200; *Leatherstocking Tales* 200
Coronation Street 60
Cowardly Lion (character) 84–85
Crook, Alice (character) 85
Crowley, Aleister 152, 154, 156, 160, 162; (character) 152
The Crying Game (film) 182–185
Cthulhu 11, 202, 204, 206
Cultural Pastiche: A Critical Study of the Graphic Novel and Film see Keller, James
cynicism 65, 69, 71

Dallas 60
Dallas, Texas 73
Dante 181; *Divine Comedy* 181
The Dark Knight 40–41, 44–51; *see also* Nolan, Christopher
DC Comics 28, 39, 50, 120, 166
DC Universe 122–123
Death of a Nation: American Culture and the End of Exceptionalism 65, 74; *see also* Noble, David
Death: The High Cost of Living 1
deconstruction 18–20, 50, 89, 99, 115, 163, 166, 174
Defoe, Daniel 192; *Moll Flanders* 192
Deleuze, Gilles 23
denaturalization 89, 103, 165, 167–169, 171
Dennis Drucker (character) 165–173, 175, 184–187
Depp, Johnny 117, 123
Derrida, Jacques 107, 179
Despentes, Virginie 148; *King Kong Theory* 148
Diana, Princess of Wales 58, 61
Dick Tracy (film) 120
didacticism 150, 158
Di Liddo, Annalisa 2, 3, 11, 16, 93, 115, 121, 164, 191, 197, 201

Disney 127–128
Divine Comedy 181
Doane, Mary Ann 115
Dr. Jekyll (character) 82, 191
Doctor Manhattan (character) 8, 12, 65, 68, 69, 72–74, 78; *see also* Moore, Alan; *Watchmen*
Doctor Syn 200
Dodgem Logic 11, 204–205
Dolmance (character) 138
domination 20, 77–78, 85; male 77, 98; patriarchal 77, 113; violent 83–84
Don Quixote 181
Donne, John 154
Dorian Gray (character) 118
Dorothy Gale: *Lost Girls* 78, 84–86, 116, 125, 141–146; *The Wonderful Wizard of Oz* 6, 200; *see also* Baum, Lyman Frank; Gebbie, Melinda; Moore, Alan
Dracula 191
dualism 41, 43, 50, 156, 162
Ducard cum Ra's al Ghoul (character) 41, 46–47
dystopia 52, 119

Earle, Rebecca 193; *Epistolary Selves: Letters and Letter-Writers, 1600–1945* 193
ecofeminism 17, 20–22, 26, 153; ecofeminist 17, 21, 25
ecology 16–17, 20–21, 23, 25–27; deep ecology 17, 20–22, 25–27; libidinal ecology 18, 24–27
ecophilosophy 17
Écriture Féminine 10, 109, 137
Edward Blake (character) 65–67; *see also* The Comedian
Ehrlich, Gretel 21; *see also* ecofeminist
Eisner award 164
Elizabeth Stride (character) 79–81, 88
Ellison, Marvin 135–154; *Erotic Justice* 154
England 5, 117, 154, 189, 193
Environmentalism 16, 25–27
epistolamory 189–190, 192–195, 198–199
Epistolarity: Approaches to a Form 194
Epistolary Selves: Letters and Letter-Writers, 1600–1945 193
Epstein, William H. 44, 192, 198
Erl-Kings (characters) 34–35, 38
Erotic Justice 154
Eroticism 16–17, 21–23, 25–27, 108, 146, 153–155, 157, 161; homunculi 31–32
escapism 59–60
Escher, M.C. 159
Essentialism 105–106, 165, 167
Europa 5

Evey Hammond (character) 78, 101, 103–110, 119–120
The Extraordinary Works of Alan Moore: Indispensable Edition 192

Faerie Romance 180
Fahrenheit 451 60
Fanny Hill (character) 28, 189–192, 195–200
the Fantastic Four 169
fascist 84, 90, 100–101, 103–109, 112, 123, 184
Fate 101–104
Faulkner, William 1; *The Sound and the Fury* 1
femininity 31, 58, 60, 63, 80, 160, 165, 187, 196
feminism 17–18, 76, 177, 180, 182, 186–187, 202; French 20
Ferguson, Christine 91, 97–98
Feuer, Jane 54
Finch (character) 101, 103, 105, 107–110, 120–123
the Five Swell Guys (characters) 166, 169
Flemyng, Jason 117
Foreman, Dick 204
Freud, Sigmund 6, 22, 94, 112, 122
From Hell 9–10, 28, 76–86, 88–96, 98–100, 111–112, 116–117, 119, 121, 191, 203
The Future of Ritual 145

Gabriel (character) 118–119, 121
Gaiman, Neil 7, 118, 146–147; *Death: The High Cost of Living* 1; *The Sandman* 1, 118; *Stardust* 1
Gambol (character) 46
Gardner, Gerald 152
Gebbie, Melinda 2, 78, 83–85, 138–139, 141–142, 144, 146, 147–149, 204; *see also Lost Girls*; Moore, Alan
gender 53, 55–56, 74, 76–77, 85, 90, 113–114, 118, 120, 140, 147, 163, 165–168, 183, 186, 188, 194, 196–197, 199; identity 119, 165, 183, 196–198; norm 57, 171–172; role 55–56, 63, 139, 149, 166; theory 171; transgender 154, 165, 177, 182–183, 185, 187
Germany 74, 84, 90, 100
Ghost of a Flea 82
Gibbons, Dave 12, 65, 120, 164, 191; *see also* Moore, Alan; *Watchmen*
Gibson, Ian 57–58, 63
Gilliam, Terry 42
Glycon 152
the Glyph (character) 55–57, 59

Goatly, Andrew 63
God 25, 38, 68–69, 96–97, 151–152, 154–157, 159, 161
Goldman, Emma 139
Gothic 16, 23, 43, 52, 88
Goyer, David 40; see also The Dark Knight; Nolan, Christopher
Graham, Heather 117
Gravity's Rainbow 108
Great Rite 152; see also Wicca
the Great Whore 157, 160
"The Great Work Begins" 175
the green 19, 21, 24, 25, 29–30, 32, 34–36, 38; love 29, 32–33, 38; politics 17–18; superhero 16
Green Lantern (character) 116
Green Lantern (comic) 7
Griffin, Susan 20
Groensteen, Thierry 163, 167, 171
Grossman, Lev 1
Guattari, Félix 23
Guy Fawkes 104, 119

Ha, Gene 164
Haggard, H. Rider 191; *King Solomon's Mines* 191
Halberstam, Judith 90, 183–185, 187
Haley, Jackie Earle 120
Halo Jones (character) 52–64
Hamilton, Robert 61
Haraway, Donna 55
Harvey, David 66; see also neoliberalism
Harvey Bullock (character) 36
Harvey Dent (character) 40–41, 46
Hawley Griffin (character) 113, 118, 191
hegemony 44, 89–90, 92
Hellblazer 118, 123
hetaerism 77, 80, 86
heteronormative 57, 117, 163–164, 168, 170–171, 173–175, 185, 187
heterosexuality 57–59, 103, 111–112, 114–115, 117–119, 121, 123, 152163, 165–167, 170, 185–187, 190, 196
Heyward, Carter 153; *Touching Our Strength* 153
hierosgamos 21
Hit Girl (character) 122
Hollis Mason (character) 67–68, 74; *Under the Hood* 67–68
holo-soap 53–56, 59–60
homophobia 84, 123, 164–168, 171, 175, 177, 182, 186
homosexuality 50, 110–112, 114, 116, 119, 121, 123, 152, 154, 164, 165, 182, 185, 188
Hooded Justice (character) 74

Hook (character) 84–85, 141, 144, 147
the Hoop 53–54, 57, 59–60, 63
the Hotel Himmelgarten 83–84
How, James 53
Howard, Newton 50
Hughes, Albert 117
Hughes, Allen 117
Hughes, Jamie 45
humanist 22, 24
Hutcheon, Linda 124–125, 135, 179–180, 182

idealism 114, 126, 135
idealization 17, 57, 78, 129, 177, 187
ideologem 51
immanence 102–103, 105
Immateria 167, 170–172, 174
impotence 114–115
In the Shadow of No Towers 1
Inanna 158
individuality 23, 78, 95, 99, 102, 108, 205
injustice 154
Inspector Abberline (character) 79, 82, 117, 119, 123
instrumentalism 77
internationalism 66–67, 71–72; marketplace 66–67, 73–74
The Invisible Man 191
Iran-Contra 72
Ireland 83, 86
Irigaray, Luce 20, 112, 122; *possession* model 113, 122
Irwin, William 3
Islam 183

Jack Faust (character) 152, 1557, 161, 174
Jack Phantom 116
Jack the Ripper 77, 79, 81–82, 88, 90–93, 97–99, 114, 117
James Gordon (character) 36, 40, 48–50
Jason Woodrue (character) 19–20, 26, 30, 35–36, 39
Jay, David 114
Jeff Smax (character) 116
Jenkins, Mitch 201
Jerry Maguire 40
Jersey Shore 5
Jesus Christ 154, 159
Job 43
Joe Pi (character) 116
John Constantine (character) 118–119
Johnson, Freya 184
Johnson, Mark 127
The Joker (character): *The Dark Knight* 40–41, 44–51; *The Killing Joke* 9, 40–41, 43–45, 47, 49–51

Index

Jones, Matthew T. 178–179, 181–182
Juan (character) 160
Judge Dredd 52
Jung, C. J. 153
justice 43, 61, 79; social 61, 154
the Justice League 117

Kabbalah 152, 159
Kant 121
Karen Breughel (character) 162, 170,
Kate Eddowes (character) 88, 94, 97, 99
Keena Roo (character) 37–38
the Keene Act 74
Keller, James 3
Kennedy, John F. 73
kenosis 29
Kensington Gardens 142
Khoury, George 38, 192, 197; *The Extraordinary Works of Alan Moore: Indispensable Edition* 192
Kick-Ass (film) 122
Kierkegaardian philosophy 175
The Killing Joke 2, 9, 40–41, 43–45, 47, 49–50
Kincaid, James R. 135
King Kong Theory 148
King Solomon's Mines 191
Klein, Todd 169
Klock, Geoff 28–29, 39
Kraemer, Christine Hoff 150, 152, 168,
Kress, Gunther 64
Kristeva, Julia 18, 23
Krueger, Rex 42
Kukkonen, Karin 45
Kushner, Tony 175; *Angels in America* 175

Lacayo, Richard 1
Lakoff, George 127
Landry, Donna 194
Larkhill Resettlement Camp 104, 108–109
Laurie Juspeczyk 78
Lawrence, D.H. 6
Lawrence, Francis 118–119,
The League of Extraordinary Gentlemen 100, 111–113, 117, 121, 123, 177, 186
The League of Extraordinary Gentlemen: Black Dossier 11, 28, 38, 186–187, 189
League of Extraordinary Gentlemen Century: 1910 122
Leatherstocking Tales 200
Ledger, Heath 44
Legler, Gretchen 20
Leland, Charles 162
Lemuel Gulliver (character) 191, 196–198, 200

Levinas, Emmanuel 112–113, 122; Infinite 113; *simultaneity* model 113, 122
LGBT 165
Lloyd, David 100–102, 106, 109, 164, 191; see also Moore, Alan; *V for Vendetta*
Loeb, Jeph 40; *The Long Halloween* 40
London 8, 77, 80–81, 83, 86, 88, 89, 91–93, 95, 99, 101, 123, 201
London: City of Disappearances 201
Long, Josie 204
The Long Halloween 40
Lorde, Audre 153
Lost Girls 2–3, 5–7, 9–10, 12, 78, 84–86, 116, 125, 141–147
Lovecraft, H.P. 8, 11, 202–204, 206; "The Call of Cthulhu" 206
L.S.D. 108
Luiz Cannibal (character) 55, 58–59, 61–63
Lux Roth Chop (character) 60–61

"Madman of Charenton" see de Sade, Marquis
Madonna 92
Marchetti, Gina 62–63
Margaret (character) 155, 162, 187
Marie Kelly (character) 80–83, 88, 93, 95, 97–99, 203
The Marriage of Heaven and Hell 152
Marston, William Moulton 183–184, 186
Martians 113
masculinity 17, 52, 77–78, 80–82, 89–90, 92–93, 95, 97, 99, 108, 113, 121, 183
Masons 88, 94
matriarchy 77, 81
Matt Cable 30–32, 37, 39
Maus 1
Mayor Uvula Cascade (character) 202
McClintock, Anne 79
McCloud, Scott 109, 131; *Understanding Comics* 130
McGowan, Todd 44, 46, 50
McTeigue, James 109;
melodrama 52, 54, 62
Memoirs of a Woman of Pleasure 189–190, 192–193, 195–199; see also Cleland, John
Merleau-Ponty, Maurice 112–113, 117, 122; *vision* model 113, 122
Merrill Brears (character) 116, 202–204, 206
metacomics 109, 178–180, 182
metafiction 179–180, 182
metamorphosis 89, 94, 97–98
metonymy 45–47
A Midsummer Night's Dream 180

Milledge, Gary Spencer 2; *Alan Moore: Storyteller* 3
Miller, Frank: 1, 7, 50; *Batman: The Dark Knight Returns* 1, 50; *Sin City* 1; *300* 1
Mina Harker (character) 112–113, 118, 123, 186, 191
The Mindscape of Alan Moore 3; see also Moore, Alan; Vylenz, DeZ
minimalism 50
Minutemen 67–68
The Mirror of Love 154, 186
misogyny 78, 81, 84, 86, 91, 95, 98–99, 206
Mr. Hyde (character) 82, 118, 191
Mitchell, David 107
Mix Ninegold (character) 55, 58
modality 57, 64
Modleski, Tania 52, 54–55, 60, 62
Moll Flanders 192
Moll Flanders (character) 196, 198
Moloch (character) 69–70, 120
monarchy 61, 88
monotheism 183
Monsieur Rougeur (character) 86, 129, 148, 186
Montag, Mildred 59
Moore, Alan: on basic rights 39; *The Ballad of Halo Jones* 9, 52–64; "The Birth Caul" 79; on cinema 116; on comics as magic 151; *Dodgem Logic* 11, 204–205; as a feminist 76; on film adaptations 124; *From Hell* 9–10, 28, 76–86, 88–96, 98–100, 191, 203; *Hellblazer* 118, 123; *The Killing Joke* 2, 9, 40–41, 43–45, 47, 49–50; *The League of Extraordinary Gentlemen* 100, 112–113, 123, 177, 186; *The League of Extraordinary Gentlemen: Black Dossier* 11, 28, 38, 186–187, 189; *League of Extraordinary Gentlemen Century: 1910* 122; *Lost Girls* 2–3, 5–7, 9–10, 12; as magician 152; *The Mirror of Love* 154, 186; *Neonomicon* 8, 116, 202–205; as performer 79, 152; on pornography 140; *Promethea* 11, 150–152, 154–169, 171–172, 174–177, 179–188, 202, 204–205; on superheroes 7; *Superman: Whatever Happened to the Man of Tomorrow?* 2; *Supreme* 2; *Swamp Thing* 1–2, 9, 16–18, 22, 26–30, 35–36, 38–38, 42, 118; *Tom Strong* 1/4, 1//, 184; *Top Ten: Season One* 116, 164; *25,000 Years of Erotic Freedom* 25–27, 79, 84, 87, 154, 162, 206; *2000 AD* 9, 52–53, 57–58, 61, 63; *Unearthing* 11, 201–202; *V for Vendetta* 3, 8, 10, 39, 78, 100–101, 108, 110, 123, 164, 186, 191;

Watchmen 1–3, 7–9, 12, 28–29, 39, 42, 65–67, 69–70, 72–74, 78, 164, 177, 184, 191; on the Willendorf Venus 79
Moore, Allan Oswald see Moore, Alan
Moore, Steve 201–202
morality 6, 35, 50, 52, 62, 68, 109, 117–118, 139–140, 142–143, 154, 157, 187, 206; amoral 71; immoral 88, 139, 142; integrity 62
Moretz, Chloe 122
Moriarty (character) 100
Mulvey, Laura 178, 181, 186; "Visual Pleasure in Narrative Cinema" 178
Murray, Noel 122
mythicization 89, 92, 94–95, 97–99

Naess, Arne 18
Nancy, Jean-Luc 102–103, 107–109
nationalism 66–67, 73–74
Native American 85
Natty Bumppo (character) 200
neoliberalism 66, 70–73, 123
Neonomicon 8, 116, 202–205
Netley (character) 81, 96, 99, 117, 121
Neverland 144; see also Peter Pan
The Next Men 7; see also Byrne, John
Nietzsche 17, 22–23
nihilism 69
1984 see Orwell, George
Nite Owl II 12, 68, 71, 113, 121; see also Moore, Alan; *Watchmen*
Nixon, Richard 69, 73
Noble, David 65
Nolan, Christopher 9, 51; *Batman Begins* 41, 44, 46–48, 50; *The Dark Knight* 40, 41, 44–47, 49–50
Norsefire 101–102, 104, 107
Novels into Film 124

Occident 79
O'Donnell, Hugh 61
O'Neill, Kevin 189, 191, 196–200, 204
ordinary 17, 52, 53, 57–63, 86, 91, 140, 150, 153, 155, 157
Orlando (character) 187–188, 196
Orwell, George 1
Other 90, 113, 122, 156
Ozymandias (character) 12, 65–67, 69–74; see also Moore, Alan; *Watchmen*

Pagels, Elaine 162
Paleolithic Age 5
pansexuality 201–202
Parliament 103
Parliament of Trees 34

patriarchal domination 77
Pencil, Savage 204
Peter Pan 2, 6, 125, 200; *see also* Barrie, J.M.
Petrarchan 25
phallus 58, 78, 91–94, 103, 118, 158; antiphallus 79, 83, 85; language 20; non-phallic 17, 21
philosophy 18, 20, 26, 27, 35, 37, 77–78, 81–82, 87, 112, 114–115, 141, 150, 204
The Philosophy in the Boudoir 138
Phoebe (character) 31
Plato 105, 129; *Phaedo* 105; platonic 29, 32, 114–115, 118, 120–121
Polly Nicholls (character) 79–81, 88, 95–96, 99
popular romance 52, 53, 55–57, 59–63
pornography 1–2, 5–6, 10, 17, 20, 26–27, 37, 79, 115–116, 123–125, 130, 138–141, 146–149, 178, 180, 197, 199, 203, 206; child 120; immoral 139, 142; internet 5; mainstream 141; moral 139–140, 146, 205; novel 125, 130–132, 189; star 202; tentacle 5
Pornokrates 206
Portman, Natalie 119
posthumanism 17–18, 21, 23–24
postnationalism 66–67, 71, 73
Post-Traumatic Stress Disorder 43
Prince Albert Victor (character) 79, 85
Promethea 11, 150–152, 154–169, 171–172, 174–177, 179–188, 202, 204–205
Promethea (character) 152, 155–158, 161–162, 165–175, 180–187, 204; Christian 168, 173, 175, 182; Muslim 168, 173, 175, 182
prostitution 77, 79–83, 86, 88–89, 92–93, 101, 103, 117, 120–121, 148, 160, 192, 198
Prothero (character) 104
Pynchon, Thomas 108; *Gravity's Rainbow* 108

Quality Comics 63
Queen Venus (character) 198
Queen Victoria (character) 79, 85
The Queer God 154
The Question (character) 120
Quiring, Björn 168

race 53, 79, 104, 175
Rachel Dawes (character) 41, 46
Rann (location) 37–38
rape 17, 23, 68, 74, 76, 81, 84–85, 119–121, 144, 148, 161, 175, 203; child 115
rationalism 77

Raw 1
Rea, Stephen 120, 123
Reagan, Ronald 8, 72, 100
realism 44, 91, 104; social 60
the red 19, 29–34, 36, 38; sex 29–33, 37–38; supervillain 36
"Red Emma" *see* Goldman, Emma
Red Hood (character) 40, 48, 51
the Red King (character) 133; *see also* Carroll, Lewis
the Red Queen (character) 85, 134; *see also* Carroll, Lewis
Reeves, Keanu 118–119
reflexivity 125, 135, 177–179, 202
Regis, Pamela 63
regularity 55–57; *see also* popular romance
reification 53–55, 58, 63
repression 77, 100, 112–115, 117, 144–145, 165, 192, 202
Reynolds, James 50
Richardson, Samuel 194
Ricoeur, Paul 126–128, 134–135; *The Rule of Metaphor* 126
The Rite of Spring 141–142, 145
Rodice (character) 53
Rodowick, David 122
Rolf Bauer (character) 143
Rolf Müller 74
Rops, Felicien 206; *Pornokrates* 206
Rorschach (character) 68–71, 73, 111, 120–121
Rosa Coote (character) 113
Rosetta Stone 2
The Rule of Metaphor 126
Rumi 153
Russ, Joanna 148–149
Ruth (character) 106

Sabor, Peter 192, 197–198
Sade, Marquis de 23, 27, 138–139, 142–143, 145–146; *The Philosophy in the Boudoir* 138
The Sadeian Woman 138
Sally Jupiter (character) 68, 74; *see also* Silk Spectre I (character)
Sam Slade (character) 63
The Sandman 1, 118
Sartre, Jean-Paul 112–113, 117, 120, 122; choice model 113, 122; Will 113
satire 179; social 52; political 52
Saussure, Ferdinand de 104
The Scarecrow (character) 50
Schechner, Richard 145; *The Future of Ritual* 145
Schiller, Dorman 6

Schrag, Calvin O. 175
scopophilia 132, 178, 181, 186–187
secular philosophy 151
Selene (character) 201–202
Self 156
semiotics 45
separatism 169, 174
sex 6, 17, 21, 25–34, 37–38, 57, 61–62, 76, 79–80, 83–87, 90–95, 97, 103–108, 110, 112–113, 115–122, 125, 128–130, 140–145, 148–155, 157–158, 160–165, 170, 178, 180–182, 184, 186; appeal 58; desire 83, 111–116, 119, 131, 152, 165, 173–174, 186–187, 189, 191, 194, 196, 198–199, 201–206; domination 76–77, 79, 82, 84, 86; drive 26; expression 6, 25–26; freedom 86, 90, 138–139, 175, 205; God sex 160; identity 59, 118, 165, 204; orientation 53, 186; persuasion 22; politics 104, 115–116, 142, 177; predator 79; relationship 25, 74; violence 54, 76, 86, 89–90, 94, 98, 203
sexism 57, 63, 180
sexuality 6–8, 10, 22, 26, 37–39, 53, 59, 79, 83, 85–86, 88–89, 99, 105–106, 110–111, 114–119, 121–122, 125, 135, 138, 142, 144–145, 148, 153–155, 160–162, 164–166, 177–178, 184, 186–188, 196, 202
Shaeffer, Katherine 42
Shah, Naseeruddin 118
Shakespeare, William 6; *A Midsummer Night's Dream* 180
The Silhouette (character) 120
Silk Spectre I (character) 67, 78
Silk Spectre II (character) 113, 184
Simone, Gail 76; *Women in Refrigerators* 76
Sin City 1
Sinclair, Iain 201; *London: City of Disappearances* 201
Singer, Marc 79
Sláine 58
Snyder, Sharon 106
Snyder, Zack 111
Sonny Baskerville (character) 202
Sontag, Susan 140–141, 147
Sophie Bangs (character) 152, 155–161, 164–175, 182, 186
The Sound and the Fury 1
South Africa 84
Spiegelman, Art: *In the Shadow of No Towers* 1; *Maus* 1; *Raw* 1
Stacia (character) 158, 165–166, 170, 172–174, 182–183, 187
Stam, Robert 124, 128, 178
Stardust 1
Starhawk 153

Sterne, Laurence 198
Steve Shelly (character) 180–183
Stevenson, Robert Louis 191; *The Strange Case of Dr. Jekyll and Mr. Hyde* 191
Stoker, Bram 191, 200; *Dracula* 191
Stoller, Robert 147
The Strange Case of Dr. Jekyll and Mr. Hyde 191
Stravinsky 39, 141–142, 145; *The Rite of Spring* 141–142, 145
subversion 27, 56, 59–62, 79, 130, 138–139, 141, 146, 163, 166
Sunderland (character) 19, 30
superhero 7, 16, 23, 25, 28, 36, 45, 100, 110, 115–116, 120–122, 140, 155, 163, 177, 181, 184
superheroine 181, 183–184, 187
Superman (character) 7, 8, 100, 174
Superman (comic) 7, 42; *see also* Byrne, John; Miller, Frank; Moore, Alan
Superman: Whatever Happened to the Man of Tomorrow? 2
Supreme 2
Sutcliffe, Peter 82
Swamp Thing 1–2, 9, 16–18, 22, 26–30, 35–36, 38–38, 42, 118
Swamp Thing (character) 16–21, 23–26, 28–30, 32–39, 100, 115
Swinton, Tilda 118

Taboo 141
Tharg (character) 63
Thatcher, Margaret 8, 61, 100, 186
theology 150–155, 157, 162; Christian 89, 123, 150–154, 156, 160–162, 174, 182; Judaism 150; Judeo-Christian 38; Pagan 150–154, 161–162, post–Christian 152, 154; Wicca 152–153
Theweleit, Klaus 89–90, 92, 94–98
Thorndike, Russell 200; *Doctor Syn* 200
"Thousand Year Reich" 106
300 1
Through the Looking-Glass 125–126, 129, 132–135
Toby (character) 53–58, 62
Tom Carnacki (character) 122
Tom Sawyer (character) 118
Tom Strong 174, 177, 184
Top Ten: Season One 116, 164
totalitarianism 100, 106
Toto (character) 116
Touching Our Strength 153
Toward a Theology of Eros 154
Townsend, Stuart 118
Toy Molto (character) 54, 56–61

Toybox (character) 116
transgression 17, 22, 23, 132, 149
trauma 40, 43, 46–48, 60, 81, 86, 115, 117, 126, 140–143, 145, 147, 169, 185–186; childhood 43–44, 125, 142, 147; incestual 143; physical 78; psychological 46, 78, 126, 133; sexual 142
Tree of Life 157, 159, 181
trope 52; asexual 120; film 111; romantic 53, 61–62; "Splitting the male" 55; superhero film 121
Turner, Viktor 145
25,000 Years of Erotic Freedom 25–27, 79, 84, 87, 154, 162, 206
Twenty Thousand Leagues Under the Sea 191
2000 AD 9, 52–53, 57–58, 61, 63
Tyree, J.M. 44, 49

The Uncanny X-Men see Byrne, John
Under the Hood 67–68
Understanding Comics 130
Unearthing 11, 201–202
Uriccho, William 43
utopia 18, 21, 25, 28, 38, 115, 156, 204–205

V (character) 78, 100, 101, 104–110, 119–120
V for Vendetta 3, 8, 10, 39, 78, 100–101, 108, 110–112, 119–123, 164, 186, 191
V for Vendetta as Cultural Pastiche: A Critical Study of the Graphic Novel and Film see Keller, James
vagina dentata 84
Valerie (character) 101, 106–109
Valiente, Doreen 152–154, 162; *Charge of the Goddess* 153
Van Gogh, Vincent 159
Van Leeuwen, Theo 64
Verne, Jules 191, 200; *Twenty Thousand Leagues Under the Sea* 191
Vess, Charles 176
Victorian (style) 1–2, 6, 77, 79, 89, 92–93, 117, 135, 142–143, 177, 191–192
Vietnam 69
Vietnam War 69, 74
Villarrubia, José 154, 164, 167, 170–171; see also *The Mirror of Love*; Moore, Alan

"Visual Pleasure in Narrative Cinema" 178
Voice of Fate (character) 101–102, 104
von Bayros, Baron 141, 148
Vylenz, DeZ 3

Waddell, James 113, 122
Walter, Prior 175; "The Great Work Begins" 175
Warner Brothers 11
Watchmen 1–3, 7–9, 12, 28–29, 39, 42, 65–67, 69–70, 72–74, 78, 111, 113, 115, 119–121, 164, 177, 184, 191
Watchmen and Philosophy: A Rorschach Test see Irwin, William
Waugh, Patricia 180
Weaving, Hugo 119
Weisz, Rachel 118–119
Wells, H.G. 191, 200; *The Invisible Man* 191
Wendy Potter: *Lost Girls* 78, 84–86, 125, 141–142, 144–147; *Peter Pan* 6, 125, 200
West, Shane 118
Western (doctrine) 20, 62, 77, 79, 86, 150, 154; esotericism 150, 152; occultism 152; religion 160
the White Rabbit (character) 127, 132
Whitechapel 42, 88–93, 95
Wicker (character) 35
Willendorf Venus 23, 79, 83–85, 87
William Gull (character) 77–86, 88–89, 91–100, 203
Williams, J.H., III 150; see also Moore, Alan; *Promethea*
Williams, Michelle 119
Wilson, Patrick 121
Winslade, J. Lawton 150, 152, 168
Wolk, Douglas 41, 43, 121
Women in Refrigerators 76
Wonder Woman (character) 183–184
Wonder Woman (comic) 184
The Wonderful Wizard of Oz 2, 6, 125, 200; see also Baum, Lyman Frank
Woolf, Virginia 196
World Trade Center 169
World War One 83

Zimmer, Hans 50
Žižek, Slavoj 109, 112